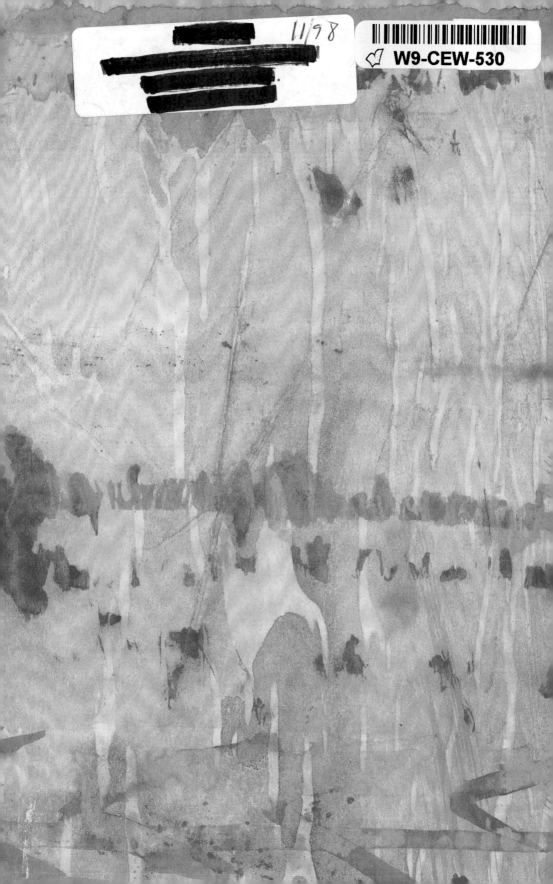

crossing borders

crossing borders

rigoberta menchú

TRANSLATED AND EDITED BY
ANN WRIGHT

VERSO
London • New York

First published by Verso 1998
This edition © Verso 1998
Translation © Ann Wright 1998
Worldwide rights © Giunti Gruppo Editoriale S.p.A.

Verso
UK: 6 Meard Street, London W1V 3HR
USA: 180 Varick Street, New York NY 10014–4606

Verso is the imprint of New Left Books

ISBN 1–85984–893–1

British Library Cataloguing in Publication Data
A catalogue record for this book is available from the British Library

Library of Congress Cataloging-in-Publication Data
A catalog record for this book is available from the Library of Congress

Jacket and text illustrations by Sophie Herxheimer
Typeset by M Rules
Printed by RR Donnelley & Sons in the USA

CONTENTS

It is fifteen years since I translated Doña Rigoberta's first book *I, Rigoberta Menchú*. It had a tremendous impact. Although it is terrible that she 'had to have a tragic life and relate it in a book for people to become aware of the plight of indigenous people in Guatemala', her powerful message did much to raise awareness both of human-rights abuses and indigenous rights. The years that she and her colleagues have spent lobbying the UN and speaking on countless platforms round the world since then have given these two issues an even higher profile.

One mark of their success is that in this translation I have felt able to leave the names of ethnic groups, their languages, and various other words, in her original K'iche' rather than use the Spanish equivalents. The exception is the case of place names, like El Quiché, which are widely known as such. Greater awareness has also meant that the adjective 'indigenous' has commonly replaced 'Indian' over the years. Doña Rigoberta's first narrative was coloured by the influence of the linguistic constructions and expressions of her native K'iche' on her newly learned Spanish. The same influence is felt in the parts of this second book where she talks about her family, the

natural world, and Mayan customs and traditions. Here again, by following some of the repetitions of the syntax and phrasing I have tried to keep the flavour of her speech and preserve its poetry and passion. (I hope, by the way, that Doña Rigoberta's description of the Mayan cosmovision will one day be translated straight from K'iche' to English. Given that the imagery and references of K'iche' are all connected to the natural world it must surely be a more graphic version.) The parts of the book, however, that deal with the more abstract concepts at the UN, and the wider social and political struggle, reflect the many years Doña Rigoberta has now worked in Spanish. Here, I have tried to make the translation much more compact and concise. These different approaches explain some of the unevenness in the translated text, wavering as it does between the quite literal and a freer form.

Readers of the first book will be familiar with many of the Spanish words, like *compañero*, *ladino*, *compadre*, again left in the original because there is no precise equivalent in English and explained in the Glossary. Many more words have been left in K'iche' and explanations incorporated into the text. Doña Rigoberta explains that *haciendo corridores* at the UN does not literally mean 'working the corridors', although that was often what she did, but that she lobbied, networked, hustled and even harassed people so that they took notice of her. What she calls *la unidad nacional* refers to a nation-state confronting ethnic, linguistic or territorial groups pressing for greater autonomy from central government not only in the case of Guatemala, but also of Canada and Quebec, Spain and Euskadi, the United Kingdom and Scotland. America naturally refers to the continent of The Americas, not to the United States. The specific use of some of Doña Rigoberta's Spanish words is not entirely clear and I have chosen the ones that seem the most appropriate in the context. For example, *abuelos* may alternatively mean grandparents or forefathers, or more generally village elders. *Pueblo* may be people in general, a people as in an indigenous nation, or the people as in the masses. *Civil* can be civil or specifically civilian as in non-military. *Humanidad* can be alternatively humanity, humankind, people, the world. I hope Doña Rigoberta will forgive me if I have not always chosen the right one. Also for any mistakes in the way I have inserted linking text or reorganised the taped testimony where I felt clarification was needed for English-speaking readers.

Just as I was moved by Doña Rigoberta's courage and wisdom in her first book, her second narrative amazed me by the sheer guts and determination with which she has taken on 'the great monsters of political intrigue' as she set forth quite unprepared into the world political arena. It is an enormous achievement and related with her unique frankness and forthrightness. The Nobel Prize is a just reward for a truly extraordinary woman. My thanks to Isabel Varea, Mandy Macdonald, Margarita Michel and the Rigoberta Menchú Foundation for their help and advice.

Ann Wright
April 1998

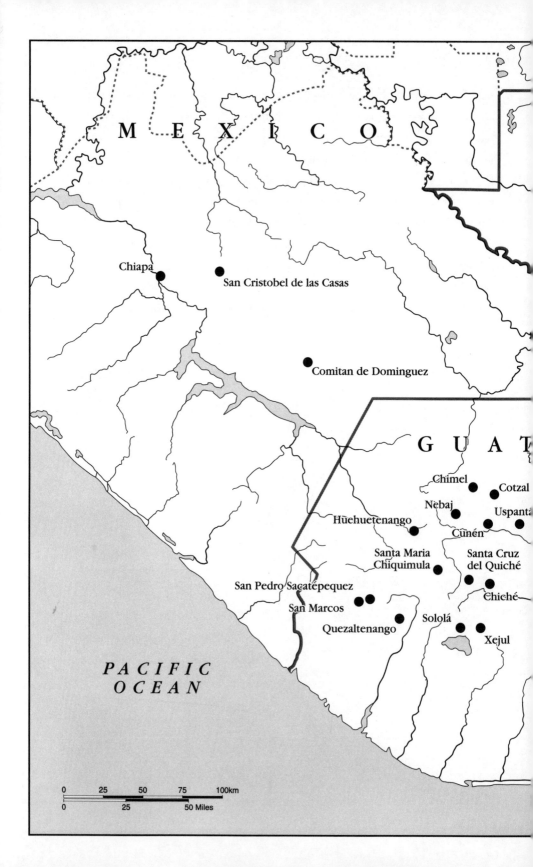

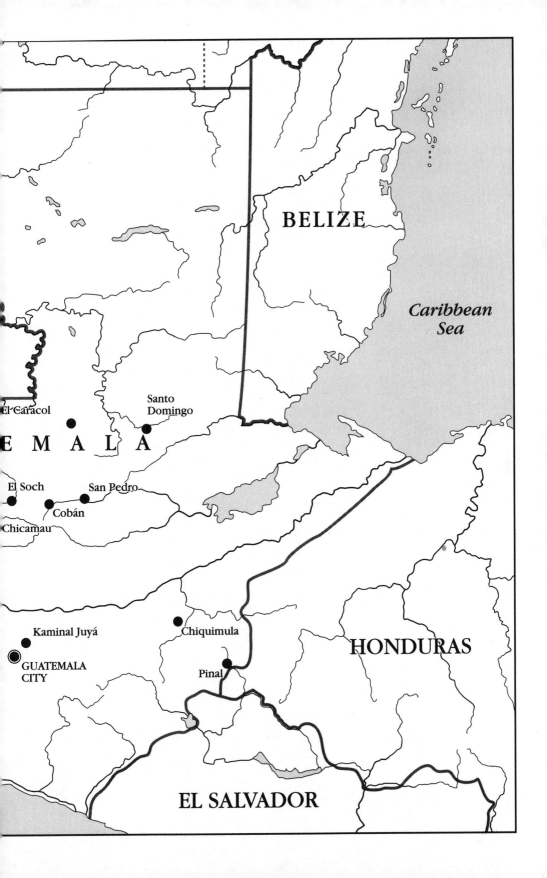

INTRODUCTION:

THE NOBEL PEACE PRIZE,

OCTOBER 1992

Many things have changed for me since I won the Nobel Peace Prize in October 1992. Let's hope it was for the best. Let's hope it will further the cause of humanity or help to save the planet. Let's hope I was awarded it out of affection or because they had finally accepted me as part of their community. Let's hope it was not just because – and I know this is how things often are – you have to have some honour or diploma to be important on this earth.

I will never forget that I have a commitment to my humble home, to my own poor people, women with calloused hands and shy uncertain smiles, a people with a profound sense of dignity. My debt to this people is not easily repaid. My commitment to them is not just from the past, it is in the present and the future. I know that millions of people would like to speak the words I speak, but they do not have the chance. They know their own reality, and I know the things I have related. I stand as a witness and, if I do not speak out, I would be a party to great injustices.

The biggest change in my life since receiving the Nobel Prize is that I can no longer devote the time to my work at the United Nations that I used to. Now I have many more tasks. I dash in and out of the UN buildings, and I no longer pass unnoticed. Yet in the days when I was a nobody, I learned a lot.

Several groups had wanted to put me forward as a candidate for the Nobel Peace Prize as long ago as 1989, but I never really thought it would happen. Many people said I could be elected, and it made me laugh. 'Only important people win the Nobel Prize,' I said. The solidarity organisations put forward lots of reasons. There was a lot of support in Italy. There were friends of Guatemala and of indigenous peoples in other European countries, and in Australia. There was support from individuals connected to Amnesty International and other similar organisations. People in Europe kept saying I was a candidate, and I kept denying it. I thought it was impossible, a pipe dream.

In 1991, during the second continental conference on 'Five Hundred Years of Indigenous, Black and Popular Resistance', held in Quetzeltenango, in Guatemala, there was a resolution proposing that I should be put forward as a candidate for the Nobel Prize. The proposal proved very controversial. Many indigenous brothers and sisters did not agree with my candidacy. They said, 'Who does she represent? Who made her a leader? Who elected her?' The proposers of the resolution had to admit that this was a true criticism. Nobody had elected me. Fate had just put me where I was. I might have been representing my own experience, but nobody had given me a mandate to do so.

It's sometimes a hard thing to acknowledge, but relations with our indigenous brothers on the continent are not always easy. There are personality clashes, leadership battles and petty jealousies. Attitudes reminiscent of the Cold War still abound. Who is aligned and who isn't? It's not all our fault. We have to be cautious – even in our own backyard – if we are to survive as politicians, as leaders and as a people, especially an indigenous people.

Other indigenous brothers and sisters, who understood that the Nobel Prize was a significant symbol, insisted that it would be an important historic moment in the fight for justice. So some groups were for, some were against, and others just sat on the fence. The atmosphere during the conference was quite tense. Even the Guatemalans were divided. Some were worried about what I would do with the Prize money. They thought only of the money, not of the cause. Thank the Gods, thank my Creator, I lost my voice for a whole week. I couldn't speak or take part in the conference in any way. I felt ashamed and sad. It tore me apart. This often happens to oppressed peoples when they make a little space for themselves. Everybody wants to occupy it, though they do not always succeed.

Amid all this controversy and complex debate, the proposers of the resolution stood firm. In the end, a vote was taken, and the motion was carried, although not everyone agreed. Afterwards, naturally, everyone said they had been in favour. This happens in indigenous circles as it does anywhere else.

It was of course of critical importance that a resolution proposing Rigoberta Menchú as a candidate for the Nobel Prize should come out of the conference in Quetzaltenango. I was delighted that the brothers hotly debated the issue for so long, though that wasn't the end of it. There were still formal procedures for the candidates to go through.

Adolfo Pérez Esquivel had won the Peace Prize in 1980, and at the end of 1991 he formally presented my candidacy to the Nobel Institute in Norway. Pérez Esquivel has been a tireless fighter for human rights in Argentina, America and every corner of the world. His proposal received the wholehearted support of Bishop Desmond Tutu. The Norwegian parliament, a group of Italian academics and celebrities, and a group of British citizens also proposed me. I was a candidate with a lot of different backers: religious orders, Catholics and Evangelicals, rich people, poor people, diplomats, intellectuals, scientists, academics. All these were involved, as well as many ordinary uneducated people.

The important part of the final process began for me at the beginning of

October 1992, when I left my home in Mexico to attend the third continental conference on the Quincentenary of Resistance, held that year in
Nicaragua. I tried to imagine two scenarios. One: if they awarded me the
Nobel Peace Prize, what options would I have? What would be the best way
of paying tribute to the dignity of my people? Two: how would I face the
difficult situation that awaited me if I didn't get it? There were long hard
hours of reflection.

Before leaving for Nicaragua, I had talked to the organisers of the
Guatemalan National Revolutionary Union, the URNG, in Mexico. I was
worried about their reaction. I first talked to my friend Miguel Angel
Sandoval who was a member of the URNG's political committee. I had
known Miguel for quite a while, from the numerous occasions we had discussed the issue of the political participation of indigenous peoples in the
organisation. He was always open to my criticisms and opinions. He recommended that I should talk to Comandante Rolando Morán. I didn't
meet with much enthusiasm there, but the important thing for me was to
initiate an institutional relationship that we would need later on.

On the way to Nicaragua, I stopped in Costa Rica to consult my friend
Arturo Taracena. I arrived at about ten at night and I talked to Arturo
until three in the morning. Dr Taracena was the person who persuaded
me to write my first book, *I, Rigoberta Menchú*. He knew all the details
of the massacre in the Spanish embassy in Guatemala in 1980, when my
father had been killed. He is a man who, throughout his time in exile, has
always supported the Guatemalan cause. He is a historian with a deep
love of his profession, his country and his people. He also knows the history of the popular movements, the social movements, and has made a
special study of the indigenous issue. He is one of the few Guatemalans
to devote time to studying their demands. A *ladino* from a well-off family,
he is even a relative of the General Taracena who took part in the recent
peace negotiations, yet like many other Guatemalans, he had to go into
exile.

That night, talking until three in the morning, Arturo gave me various ideas. If I was awarded the Nobel Prize, it was important that I should set up an independent foundation. The people who had won the Prize previously had had strong institutions behind them through which they had been able to campaign for peace.

I saw the establishment of the Rigoberta Menchú Foundation as a chance both to support a new peace mission, and to challenge the orthodox ideas about development. Development projects have always been conceived on the desks of experts or specialists who study indigenous people and then try to take a 'development' message to them. Yet twenty years after these experts first went round giving hand-outs in our villages, things are not any better. Our people have been left with a yearning for better conditions, and nothing to show for it.

In addition, I wanted to honour the memory of my father and of our people, reviving indigenous memory and honouring the struggle for our land. I hoped that we could return to the idea of co-operativism as an expression of social organisation. I didn't just want to honour my father. I wanted to honour the spirit of his entire struggle.

Arturo Taracena suggested that our proposed Foundation should combine our own native wisdom and experience with present-day technology. It should set an example. People have rather lost their faith in institutions, for institutions are only useful if and when they fulfil people's expectations.

Dr Taracena was subsequently an enormous help in establishing the philosophical framework of our Foundation. He told me I should not forget the wider nation. The Nobel Prize did not only honour indigenous peoples. It honoured all Guatemalans, and the whole of our continent. We had to see the Prize as belonging to everybody, and perceive it as an exhortation to everyone to work for a lasting peace.

That night, Dr Taracena reminded me of Miguel Angel Asturias, the Guatemalan writer who had won the Nobel Prize for Literature in 1967. Asturias had later died in obscurity, in exile. He was only appreciated in Guatemala after his death. How wonderful it would be if, twenty-five years after Miguel Angel's death, the Nobel Prize were to come back to

Guatemala. A *ladino* man and an indigenous woman, united by our way of thinking.

There was so much to talk about! Dr Taracena also reminded me that Don Miguel Angel's Prize was not for having written a lot of books. It was awarded for his creation of an image of the Guatemalan people, both in memory and in real life. For my part, I had lived through experiences that, in a few short years, had come to symbolise the cause not just of poor and indigenous people in Guatemala but of poor people throughout the world. Dr Taracena thought that the door to understanding cultural diversity, pluralism and peaceful coexistence was beginning to open just a little.

This was not the first time we had discussed these issues. In fact, I did not really go to ask his opinion. I just felt I needed a friend with whom I could talk frankly about what I was feeling, a friend to share my fears about the difficulties that might arise.

We talked for most of the night, and at five in the morning I went to the airport to catch the plane for Nicaragua where I was to attend the third conference of the Quincentenary of Resistance. Accompanying me was Hugo Benítez, a young *compañero* from Mexico who had been working in my team for about a year. He was one of those people you really get to know, because he has been there in good times and in bad.

We arrived at Nicaragua airport at eight in the morning. There was an escort from the Nicaraguan government waiting to accompany us, despite the fact that the President, Violeta Chamorro, had refused to receive me. I had asked for a meeting with her, but she said she didn't have time. I talked to Daniel Ortega, and many other friends in the government. It was the first time in my life I had had an official escort. I never imagined that this was just the beginning.

I arrived at the conference and met Mirna Cunningham, my friend and sister. She is a courageous Miskito woman for whom I have special affection. She warned me that it would be difficult for me to attend. Many journalists had asked if I was coming. My contribution to the conference would be different from that of previous years because the word was out that I might win the Nobel Prize. I was sad not to be able to enjoy the conference in peace as in other years, but I hoped things would soon get back to normal.

It certainly was a strange moment. My little office in Mexico City, in Patricio Sanz Street, had been inundated with phone calls. Countless numbers of people had called to express their friendship before the Prize was even awarded. They said they didn't want to congratulate me afterwards because they loved me just as I was, as a person. Those friends have a special place in my heart. I started getting very emotional. Everything suddenly seemed unreal. I was not used to receiving so much attention, affection and appreciation.

Mirna advised me to prepare a message for the conference because we did not know if I would be able to stay till the end. 'If you come,' she said, 'people are going to be congratulating you, or wanting photos and autographs. You being here could distract from the main business of the meeting. We have important issues to discuss and take decisions on, and we have to draw up programmes for future work. If you prepare a speech, we can read it even if you're not here.' Yet I could not just leave. I did not want to say goodbye to Mirián Miranda, Anaí Llao Llao, Juana Vásquez and all my other *compañeros* in the 'Five Hundred Years of Resistance' campaign.

I had been staying at the house of Tomás Borge, because staying at a hotel was very difficult. Tomás said he wanted to write an article about me. We set off for the conference. I didn't know whether to stay or not. There were so many journalists that it was nearly impossible. I did the interview with Tomás, though I don't remember what paper it came out in.

In the end, I just stayed for the inauguration of the conference. With me were Adolfo Pérez Esquivel and lots of my indigenous brothers and sisters from all over the continent. Adolfo was very happy. He knew that if I were awarded the Prize, we would make a good team. And we do. He and I always have a common cause. Adolfo Pérez Esquivel and Rigoberta Menchú, winners of the Nobel Peace Prize, will work together all our lives.

I stayed in Nicaragua for three days, and followed the conference without being directly involved in it. I had meetings with several of the leaders. Courageous people like Anaí Llao Llao, Luís Macas from Ecuador, Mirna Cunningham, our friends from Canada, Ted Monser, Rosalina Tuyuc from Guatemala, Nestor Babo and many others. It gave us the chance to meet again and to learn more about each other. It showed us the diversity of indigenous peoples, each with their own distinct problems, their own histories and their own hopes for the future.

A few days before I returned to Guatemala, the Central American University (UCA) in Nicaragua awarded me an honorary doctorate in humanities. The platform was decorated with corn, fruit and plants. It was all very beautiful. There were so many people that the microphone and television lights failed. Loads of people who wanted to attend the ceremony were left protesting outside. There was such a crush that I barely made my way to the platform. It was the same for everyone, including the rector, Javier Gorostiaga. The ceremony gave me some idea of what was in store for me if I won the Nobel Prize. It confirmed my worst fears. Javier Gorostiaga and all my wonderful friends at the UCA were very moved to be sharing this historic moment with me.

When I arrived at Guatemala City at ten in the morning on 9 October, there was a huge crowd at the airport to welcome me. I had never seen so many people. The only thing I could think of to do was to recite 'My Country', one of my poems. I couldn't find words to give thanks for what was happening to me. These are times when your thoughts disappear and your most heartfelt words won't come out.

How life comes full circle! Not all that many years ago, at that same airport, a whole load of policemen had been waiting to arrest me, and ordinary people had been afraid to come near me. Now it was all so different. There were indigenous people, *ladinos*, foreigners, journalists, everybody. And I was lost for words. The things happening to me made me feel awkward and small.

When I began reciting, my emotions got the better of me. I didn't think of myself as a poet, I never have. I had written a poem to express my feelings, not because of any poetic vocation. It is one thing to devote your life to choosing wonderful words, and quite another simply to express important feelings.

I went to the headquarters of CONAVIGUA, the National Coordinating Committee of Guatemalan Widows. I had never seen such a full programme as the one they had planned for me. I think they had nine activities every day. For those tireless women, this was a normal working day. We began working with Rosalina Tuyuc and Vitalino Similox. Rosalina and Vitalino are both Kaqchikels. Coincidentally, so are the majority of the others. Juana Tipaz and María Tuj are K'iche's, however. And our distinguished compatriots Arlena and Rolando Cabrera are *ladinos*. They are both professionals, and had been with us since June that year when the team to promote a Nobel Prize candidate in Guatemala was formed.

The team was headed by Doña Luz Méndez de la Vega, a brilliant journalist and writer, Rosalina Tuyuc, the CONAVIGUA president, and union leader Byron Morales. They had defied everybody. They were courageous. It wasn't an easy role in those days. They were waiting for me with the programme of activities, most of which meant travelling to the interior. It is quite unusual to promote a Nobel Prize candidate like they did, or like the other thousands of citizens round the world did. The campaign simply became a standard-bearer for our struggle.

The French ambassador Paul Tudap, a great friend of Guatemala, was also at the airport to offer me his help and support if I needed it. We started thinking about security. We didn't rule out the possibility that, at that particularly crucial moment, somebody could create havoc or even make an attempt on my life. For the first time we accepted an official escort, a bullet-proof car and armed guards. I insisted the guards wore uniforms because in those days it was plain-clothes police who were doing all the killing. We ran the risk that they would be detained or disarmed in one of the war zones, as often happened, although I was confident that the guerrillas would respect us. I had had talks with the URNG in Mexico before returning to Guatemala.

The next day we left for the interior. The most important demonstration was held in Sololá on 12 October, the anniversary of the day Columbus landed on American soil. That wasn't a cause for celebration for us, of course, but we used it to raise our profile. Everybody was there; the local authorities, the *cofradías*, indigenous leaders, *ladino* leaders. The whole of Sololá was there. The demonstration was so beautiful, so huge, and the people so diverse, that I was truly moved. It wasn't always that way in a country like ours. The army had asked the Civil Defence Patrols not to come but they disobeyed the order, so everybody – civil patrols, Catholics, Evangelicals, Mayans – congregated in Sololá. The only problem was that twenty thousand people were waiting for our team in Santa Cruz del Quiché. They wanted us to go there too, but we couldn't do two things at the same time. We had to send our apologies.

The next day, 13 October, we went to Escuintla. We knew that 14 October would be the most complicated day, for on that day they would announce the winner of the Nobel Peace Prize.

In Escuintla, everybody – labourers, peasants, volunteers, peons, workers on the sugar-cane, coffee and banana plantations – came to the huge demonstration that had been organised. The local governor refused to give us microphones or to lend us a public hall. Some said he was just rude and ill-mannered, others said he was a racist of the first order. I never met him. I prefer not even to know the names of people like that in case my soul is contaminated.

The demonstration was huge. They touched my hair and arms in gestures of affection, for when our people want to show their feelings from the depths of their hearts, they do it by passing their hand over your head and back.

At three in the afternoon, we left for San Marcos, the main town in the province of the same name. It lies in the west of the country, bordering on Mexico. We arrived at seven. The people's slogan was 'We love you, Rigoberta, with or without the Prize.' That's what they shouted. 'We love you, Mayan daughter, with or without.' A lot of hate and racism had been poured out on me, and my people saw it as an attack on their own integrity.

Not all the media supported me. Some prestigious newspapers attacked me. They questioned the right of an Indian to aspire to an international prize. Articles were written saying I didn't deserve it, because there were other figures outside Guatemala who were better qualified to receive such a distinction. The President of the Republic, Serrano Elías, had promoted a candidate of his own, a *ladino* lady, a Señora Elisa Molina de Stahl. She was never officially proposed to the Nobel Institute, she was just fêted in Guatemala. They gave her the Order of the *Quetzal* and put her on the front page of all the papers.

I think they used her. I don't know if she knew about it and consented to it all. I think the press knew it was a farce but went along with the game. I didn't like them doing this to her, because she represents a charity and had founded the Institute for the Blind and Deaf and Dumb. This sector suffered from repression too. A lot of handicapped people had to leave the country. Even blind and deaf and dumb people were persecuted. I'm thinking of the writer Mario René Matute, for instance. He is blind and had to go into exile in Mexico. They persecuted him for joining a union and demanding more humane conditions. In Guatemala, the blind and deaf and dumb people's movement has continually lost its leaders. They have been persecuted. Some died, others had to go into exile.

Her work was not the reason why Señora de Stahl was proposed. They just wanted to put someone up against Rigoberta Menchú as a candidate for the Prize. A *ladina* against an indigenous person. It was a very racist attitude by President Serrano Elías, as if he were saying an Indian can't win the Nobel Prize, *ladinos* deserve it more. It was an attempt to divide indigenous people and *ladinos*.

I had never met Doña Elisa, but I would like to pay her a tribute. This unfortunate situation was probably not her fault. The problem isn't whether she was born a *ladina*, or what charity she works with. It is more complex than that. It is a political problem.

The word went round that the winner of the Nobel Prize was about to be announced. On 12 October, we planned our activities. We decided that if I was awarded the Prize there would be celebrations in all corners of Guatemala. I said, 'Let there be lots of parties, let the Evangelicals light their fireworks and the Catholics ring their church bells. Let the wait for the Nobel Prize be a vigil for the peace everybody in Guatemala craves. Let it be a joyous occasion for everybody.' What I said came out in the press and on radio and television, so that on the night of 13 October people had already rung their bells and lit their fireworks before the Prize had actually been announced.

In San Marcos, we discovered that the boarding house we were going to stay at had received threats. So we set off on a pilgrimage in search of hospitality. In the end our saviour was the Catholic Church. They lent us their diocese headquarters for the night. Bishop Ramazzini was in Santo Domingo for the Quincentenary celebrations, and we had to phone him there. The monsignor is well known for his social work and his unconditional support for civil society, so we did not doubt he would help us at such an important time. He gave us the use of his office, and we installed ourselves there at ten at night. Then we rushed out to hear a tribute from the people of San Marcos in a big hall. That is when they presented me with the *huipil* I wore the day the winner of the Peace Prize was announced. It was too small for me, so that night my *compañeras* began unsewing and sewing.

On the way to San Marcos it had suddenly occurred to me, 'What am I going to wear if they give me the Prize?' Rosalina said, 'Your *huipils* are so well known, you can tell the day of the week by them. They've been all round the world. There are enough stereotypes about indigenous people without you adding to them. They'll think we never change our clothes. You have to wear something different on the day.'

So I needed to change my *huipil*. Buying a nice one was for tourists not for me. The best *huipils* are made not bought, and that takes time. It would be better to borrow one. María Toj, a dear friend of mine from the CUC, went off, up and down the Panamerican highway, looking for *huipils* to borrow.

She brought back a suitcase full of clothes from which to choose. The women were very happy, it was an honour to lend their best *huipils* for the day. There were ceremonial *huipils*, wedding *huipils*, *huipils* for all big occasions.

The San Marcos *huipil* was very beautiful. It was perfect. We got back to the diocese office at half past eleven. We put our heads together – Vitalino, Rosalina, Juana Tipaz, María Toj, Hugo Benítez, Byron Morales and I – to decide what we were going to do if I won the Prize. We realised we had to go back to the capital. Yet how could we get there from San Marcos in three hours? It usually takes four hours by road. At about midnight, we thought of hiring a helicopter. Rosalina went out to find a friend who worked in a helicopter company. She asked if they could send a helicopter to San Marcos at five in the morning, guarantee that we would be in Guatemala City at eight, and back in San Marcos a couple of hours later.

I will never forget my seven journalist friends who accompanied us day and night during the tour. All of them had been with me on many other occasions. When they heard we were leaving, a big battle commenced, as always happens with journalists. They said, 'How can you suddenly go to the capital when we've come all the way here with you?' They wanted the news first, of course. We came to an agreement whereby they would get their scoop. At five in the morning, if I won the Prize, I would say a few words. Then I would go to the capital and come back to San Marcos for the proper press conference. The journalists with us were Hugo Gordillo, Rony Iván Véliz Samayoa from AP, photographers Carlos López and Daniel Hernández, and cameraman Felix Zurita. I had known Rony Véliz since 1988 when I was arrested. All of them had been with me on many other occasions. They had always supported us by spreading the message of the underprivileged.

The telephone service in San Marcos was pretty limited. The diocese had two lines but they only worked for a few minutes at a time. The calls had to stop while the connection was re-established. At one in the morning, Rosalina rang to say that we had a helicopter and would be leaving at five. Meanwhile, another *compañera* was altering my dresses. Everything was going well. There was just one worry. If we didn't win the Prize, who would pay for the helicopter?

I slept peacefully for a couple of hours, and was woken by the telephone. My *compañeros* had been up all night, drinking coffee. The journalists, shivering with cold, were waiting outside in their cars. I got up and went to answer. It was the Norwegian ambassador in Mexico.

'In nine minutes,' he said, 'it will be announced that you have won the Nobel Peace Prize. Let me be the first to congratulate you. You have nine minutes to prepare yourself, after that the news will be out.'

I still felt I had to ask if the news was official. He laughed. 'I am the Norwegian ambassador in Mexico,' he said. 'It is my job to give you the news.'

I still couldn't believe it. I didn't know whether to laugh or cry. I didn't know what to do. I just froze. I hung up and everyone asked, 'What happened?'

I replied 'Well! We've got the Nobel Prize.'

My *compañeros* cried and cried. We were all lost for words. The priest at the church thought of lighting fireworks, and that set off fireworks all over the town. It was like torrential rain falling. They rang the bells.

A terrible thought suddenly occurred to me. My parents were not here with me. I would have loved to see my father and my mother. My brother Nicolás and his wife had come to San Marcos to be with me, but I missed my parents and my little brothers and sisters. I missed a normal life. Nicolás just hugged me. He didn't speak. He just wanted to show he loved me. He is a man of few words. He didn't hide his joy and his pain.

At midnight, I had received my first Nobel Prize present. Don Angel, the mayor of Olera, a town in Spain, was travelling with us. He said, 'Before leaving Olera I had this present made. It is for you, whether you get the Prize or not.' It was a jar with a plaque on it saying 'Nobel Peace Prize. Rigoberta Menchú Tum.'

I went into Bishop Ramazzini's office. I didn't know what to say. I had to say a few words to the press. All I could think of was, 'How I would love to have all my family alive and here with me! Because life is peace. I desire life and peace.' Then words failed me. I left, and the helicopter came.

We flew to Guatemala City. At the airport I was met by my friend and sister, Helen Mack, the sister of Myrna Mack. Myrna had been given the alternative Nobel Prize in Sweden. We hugged each other and cried. The editor of *Prensa Libre*, a Guatemalan newspaper that had not treated me very well at the beginning, was also at the airport. It was a sign of reconciliation and I was very pleased. *Prensa Libre* was the only paper to get the news in its headlines that day. The editor had stopped the presses at dawn and waited. He had taken a risk and I took it as a vote of confidence in me. The attorney-general of Guatemala, Señor Acisclo Valladares Molina, was also at the airport.

From the airport we went to CONAVIGUA, the Guatemalan widows' association. It was full of my friends, delegations from the countryside, the press. The first thing I did was to congratulate the widows, and my *compañeras* Arlena Cabrera and Luz Méndez de la Vega, who had given such unconditional support by fighting disinformation in the press. The two of them, together with Rosalina, Vitalino, Byron and Rolando, comprised the team that promoted my candidacy in Guatemala in the period after June 1992. The award is as much theirs as mine. It was a day of celebration at CONAVIGUA, a day for celebrating dignity, the dignity of a whole people, the dignity of a continent. It was a day for honouring my humble home, poor women with calloused hands, the cause of the poor.

I phoned my office in Mexico and Dora Mirón answered. She and I have worked together for at least fifteen years. How much Dora has done for us! She dealt with all the difficult work for 1992, voluntarily, and with very few resources. I called Dora and couldn't hold back my tears. The eyes of the press were on me but I forgot them all. 'We've won the Nobel Prize! We have been awarded the Nobel Prize!' Dora was crying too. She couldn't help it. The first thing she said was, 'Wretched woman, how you have made us suffer. At least now we can pay for the helicopter.'

'This time the pain was worth it,' I said, 'after all we have suffered.' If we hadn't won the Prize, she would have had to go round trying to get money to pay the costs we had incurred.

I congratulated all my team in Mexico, and told them to go out and drink themselves silly on *tequila* in my honour. They said they couldn't do that because the phone never stopped ringing. They were amazed at all the work in store for them. I insisted. There was plenty of time for that later. Today was a day to celebrate. I cried the whole time I was talking. I felt a great lump in my throat, I felt as if my heart would stop.

Suddenly I came to my senses. I only had an hour and a half in the capital, and there was much to organise. I called the reception committee and asked for their advice. I wanted a reception that night for all the different political and social sectors in the country. This posed countless problems. Not only was the guest list getting longer and longer, but many of the politicians would not want to sit with each other. The President would not want to sit with the representatives of the popular movements.

The list of guests was drawn up as if by magic. Then the idea of inviting the army came up. The tone of the discussion in the committee went up a level. If we invited the army, we would have to invite the URNG, since we were in the middle of a civil war. Peace depended on both sides. The party should be a symbol of dialogue.

I rang the French embassy and asked if they could, in the course of the day, get hold of a representative of the URNG. Only then would I invite the army. Nobody at the embassy could take responsibility for a request of that kind. So there was no guarantee. I realised it was too short a time to get the URNG, the army, the government and civil society all together in one room. It was an impossible dream.

I decided just to invite the Head of State. This presented a difficulty too. The President had made no statement and it was already nine-thirty. He hadn't shown whether he was angry or pleased about the Nobel Prize. I rang Señor Valladares, the attorney-general, and asked him to get in touch with the President and discover whether he had heard the news, and whether we could expect him to attend. I wanted the reception to reflect national unity between indigenous peoples and *ladinos*, between the popular movements and all opposition groups. This wasn't a time for confrontation.

The attorney-general phoned the President with the utmost discretion. Ironically, one of the widows showed me a cartoon that had appeared in a newspaper that morning. The cartoonist was a good friend, Juan Manuel Chacón, known by his countless admirers as 'Filóchofo'. He is very famous in Guatemala. The cartoon symbolises President Serrano's deafness to the Nobel Prize. Juan Manuel drew me as a dove of peace. The caption said 'The President can't hear, he has an infection in his left ear.' Just then the attorney-general phoned to say the President had asked him to say he had an ear infection and could not come to the reception. It seemed like a joke. Juan Manuel Chacón's crystal ball had predicted the President's infection. I would have liked the President to come to the reception. The President said his wife would represent him. My hopes of having the URNG and the army at the same reception had been dashed, and now the President had said no. This didn't preclude the possibility, however, of having a historic reception at a big hotel, as smart famous people in this city tend to do.

When we had finished planning the reception, we returned to San Marcos in the helicopter, arriving at eleven-thirty. The town was filled to overflowing. Thousands of people were waiting for me to arrive. People had come from all the surrounding provinces. The *huipils* worn by the women from different ethnic groups made the streets look like multicoloured gardens. When we got in the car – it was a bullet-proof Ministry of Works vehicle – the crowd almost lifted it off the ground. They wanted me to get out, and I had to get out and greet them all.

We then went to San Pedro Sacatépequez, in the province of San Marcos. Something rather strange happened there in the last century. On 13 October 1876, President Justo Rufino Barrios signed Decree No. 165, a law that took away the legal identity of the indigenous people there and turned them all into *ladinos*. Yet over a hundred years later, they are still Mayan, the same colourful people that they always were.

We took the road to Xela, passing through many towns and villages where the people were waiting for us. Some carried flowers, some carried fruit, everyone was celebrating. We arrived eventually at Quetzaltenango. Its

17

ancient name, *Xe' Lajuj Noj'*, means 'under ten great principles or wisdoms'. Here the great Mayan chief Tucum Umam died. His name means 'built or made by his forefathers'. He fought the Spaniards on the plains of Urbina.

Quetzaltenango is a town with a lot of character and a long historical memory. It was important for me to pay tribute there. The ten wisdoms are the ten principles that rule the life of the Mayans. It represents the cosmovision of our ancestors. This is where the story of the *quetzal* was born. The *quetzal* is our national symbol and the spirit of the Mayan people. It represents the spirit of Tucum Umam, it was his *nawaal*. When Tucum Umam died, the *quetzal* flew over the earth and into the memory of the Mayans. The *quetzal* cannot bear to live in a cage or to be domesticated. The spirit of Tucum Umam can never be captured or imprisoned.

This is why Quetzaltenango was chosen as the site of the largest and most historic commemoration ceremony our people has ever known. Thousands and thousands of indigenous people gathered for the continental Quincentenary Conference held there in 1991. Mayan priests often come to pray to life and to the earth on the hills around. Since that time, it has again become an area that honours light. As dawn breaks, so our way is illuminated, so darkness ends, so rain falls, and in this way earth and the seeds will flourish.

The park that day in 1992 in Quetzaltenango was packed. For security reasons, I could only stay for a short while. Already the day was being stretched like elastic, and I wanted to hold on to every second of it. Yet the crowd was nearly crushing me. It was a difficult situation. We had to take refuge in the town hall. We could not stay any longer.

Eventually, at half past five, we set off on the road back to Guatemala City. The drivers flew along to get us back by eight. The journey usually takes a little over three hours. There are a lot of bends, and often there is mist, especially at night. We hoped to get to the capital in time, for the reception had to be a big success. We arrived at ten to eight. I had to go just as I was.

At the hotel I was delighted to see that everybody had turned up, including the diplomatic corps. Everybody, that is, except the President and his wife. She arrived eventually when we had already had the toast. She said,

'I'm sorry I'm late, there was so much traffic.' I didn't really believe her, since a first lady can fly across town much quicker than I came from San Marcos. She had twenty or thirty policemen cutting through the traffic for her. I thought I would keep those details to myself for another occasion.

I read a poem, and my speech was very short. I said that we all had a commitment to peace in Guatemala. After the toast, I talked to a lot of people and I noticed there was deep feeling. For the first time, I felt Guatemalans were warm towards me. For the first time, I felt *ladinos* were sincere. For the first time, activists from the popular movement and their leaders were present together with industrialists and political leaders, with media chiefs and celebrities, with academics and journalists. For the first time, I was with Rosalina Tuyuc and Luz Méndez, and with my great friend Byron Morales and other *ladino compañeros*, at an event where we were celebrating a symbol of great hope.

There are moments when we should celebrate our nation, our country, and our life, and celebrate it together, especially if we can celebrate something that, in my lifetime, has been no more than an illusion. Peace, to live in peace, no more war. It strengthened my belief in a multi-ethnic, multi-lingual, pluri-cultural society, where indigenous people and *ladinos* can celebrate the nation's triumphs together.

After the cocktail party, I went back to my house to continue the celebration with lots of friends who couldn't go to the official event. The phone kept ringing at home, too. There were endless requests for interviews. I was still on the phone when I realised that it was three in the morning. At nine I was supposed to be leading a huge demonstration in the capital. It was to be the most important demonstration we had organised in recent times.

Thousands and thousands of people were expected. It had been planned before they gave me the Nobel Prize, and its organisation was a huge achievement on the part of the union movement, the popular movement, the co-operative movements, the indigenous movement and the different religious groups. We had spread the word that, Nobel Prize or not, we would expect people in Kaminal Juyú to celebrate. Kaminal Juyú is an important ceremonial and political centre for the ancient Mayans. It is the only reminder of the Mayan civilisation left in the city centre. We chose it because we wanted to symbolise national unity: a great city built by both *ladinos* and indigenous people, and a monument to the Mayans in the heart of the city.

A great multitude came. We didn't count heads, but I know that almost everyone in the capital was out on the streets that day. There were also a lot of people from the interior, indigenous people from all parts of the country. We rode to Kaminal Juyú in a lovely carriage. My dream is that one day this place will be declared a Centre of National Unity and Peace in Guatemala. One day they should build a great temple to the memory of our ancestors and the heroes of this century, a national centre demonstrating a deep belief in Guatemala's rich culture. We are all *chapínes,* whether we are *ladino chapínes* or indigenous *chapínes.* May we some day live together and have a place where all Guatemalans can come without feeling superior or inferior, without feeling a foreigner in their own country. May it be a focal point. These great dreams and projects were already whirling round in my head.

Six months before the Nobel Prize was awarded, wonderful things appeared in the papers every day. People wrote letters and poems; the Prize occupied an important space in the media. Afterwards, however, the 'auto-coup' by President Serrano Elías in May 1993 changed the whole atmosphere. The fact that I and hundreds of other Guatemalans went out onto the streets to repudiate the coup was instrumental in thwarting it. Some of the media barons were angry at the part I played, and they began using the press against me again. A Nobel Prize winner, they argued, should not take part in street protests. Such actions discredited the honour of receiving the Prize. They did not understand that the Nobel Prize was not awarded to Rigoberta Menchú. It was given in recognition of a people's wisdom and of the reality of their lives. I carry that like a precious burden.

I will not be like those other leaders who pretend to lead our nation. I am well aware that my role will always be controversial, but I will try to be discreet. I will try not to be self-important. In the end, I am just a humble member of society.

There is something quite important that people don't know. I always travel like any other citizen of the world, squat and dark-skinned as I have always been. I will always have the face of a poor woman, my Mayan face, my indigenous face. At official ceremonies, when I am received by a king or a head of state, I am the winner of the Nobel Peace Prize. When there is a *coup d'état* or some other conflict, and my presence is requested, I am the winner of the Nobel Peace Prize. Yet when I cross borders, it's another story. Customs and immigration officials act impatiently. They take my things out one by one, even my underclothes. They are often very offensive and racist.

After they have finished going through my things, taking out my *huipils*, and making me pack my case again, I always try to teach them a little awareness. You need humanity wherever you are. 'The world should be a fairer place,' I tell them, 'it should be more humane, less aggressive and less racist.' I start to give them a talk.

When my case is finally packed again, I take out my identity papers and say, 'Look, I'm a humble winner of the Nobel Peace Prize, and the humble president of a Foundation devoted to peace studies, civic responsibility and teaching the world about the profound value of ancient indigenous cultures.'

They are of course very surprised. I know they will never forget me. They will probably be among the most avid readers of this book. So everything serves some purpose. I believe that the dignity of the people in Guatemala, their strength, their struggles and their creativity, are part of life. No one can dislodge us from here, not by violence, war or hatred. Let us hope this will always be so. I dream of living in a Guatemala at peace. Some day.

My youth in Guatemala was cut short, and my youth and old age were combined. I have lived such an accelerated life that I often feel I have been an adult for a very long time. I would like to be able to remember my childhood but there are many things that I do not recall. My youth passed me by. How I would love to relive that time calmly! Then I think that for a woman who is still young and has been so fortunate, with so much to thank life for, asking for more would be asking too much. I could not be happier. Many people fight to get to the top, they strive for diplomas and degrees, they always have to get top marks, they sacrifice everything for their careers, they chase bits of paper and have no time to serve others. They pay a high price to get where they want to be.

I am one of those who never had the chance to get top marks. Those people's memories were never considered important, and nor were mine.

Yet even so, I remember the magic in Chimel, the village where I was born. It is a region of so much mystery and so many myths. My elders, my grandfather and my grandmother, my father and my mother, they have always lived there, and in my mind they still do. Chimel is a place where the clouds float lazily over the humid mountains. The colour of the mountains is dark blue, but when the sky clears, limpid and stark, it is as if the world is born anew. The colours shine, the faces of the people glow, the air is crystal clear.

All these things together are a sign of time. I am a product of a sign of time and, according to the ancient Mayans, it is not chosen, it just happens. It happens as one walks through time. I may die tomorrow, or the day after. I will not be here forever, like the eternal things on earth, but I will always be a sign of time that will remain in our Mayan memory. I am very conscious of this. A lot of people will remember me when I am dead. They'll remember the good things and the mistakes I have made, for that is how the history of humankind is made up. The attacks made on me now will be compensated for in the future.

All this is a sign of the balance that exists in the Mayan memory. It is harmony. Mayans understand well that you cannot have a world that is totally good without having a bad side to it. Negative aspects are offset by good ones. Neither the Nobel Prize, nor any other award or distinction, nor even the sacrifice of my own life, will change the problems that face humankind. What we are is just a drop of hope for those who are in need of it.

While I live my Nobel Prize will have meaning. The physical medal may be kept in the Great Temple in Mexico, in a Temple of Cultures in Guatemala, in a special fortress of its own, but the most important thing is its essence, what it stands for. While I live, I will fight for peace, life and dialogue. When I die, our children will fight for the same cause.

The medal will remain as a symbol, in a world that is made up of myths and symbols. Of the place where I was born, I have only symbols, memories and dreams. I always carry with me my coral necklace and my medallion of our Father Sun. I may change my clothes and my hair ribbons, but my necklace and my medallion are always inseparable from me.

My other mementoes are photographs of my parents and of my brother Patrocinio. The photos of my father and brother were given to me by the village priest. My father's photo is quite blurred, but at least I have his face with me. I also have a photo of my mother, sent to me years ago by some American health workers in Uspantán. She looks quite thin and drawn, and I think it must have been taken when she was breast-feeding. When she died she was much fatter. She was quite fat and very jolly. She seemed rejuvenated when she was no longer bringing up children.

In my garden, too, I have a little piece of earth from Chimel.

1

TROUBLE IN THE FAMILY:
THE ENEMY WITHIN, NOVEMBER 1995

We indigenous families would be most unhappy living without people and children around us. We couldn't exist without this sense of family. Our families have always been large and my own household is no exception. Six children live here and sometimes in the holidays, on ceremonial days and on special family occasions, others come too. Our house in Guatemala City is like a nursery school. Edy often comes, he's the son of my husband's sister María. So do my sister Lucía's children, Juanita and Chente. They're big now. Chente is about to turn twelve and Juanita seven. They have gone to live with their mother now – it's the first time they've had a home of their own – but for several years they lived with me. Through the hardships of exile and war, I watched them grow as if they were my own, and I'll always miss them. They taught me to love so many of the children of my *compañeros*, children who grew up without parents.

A sister and brother of Angel, my husband, also live with us. He had fifteen brothers and sisters. Two were killed by the army, and another died

when she was a baby. They can drop round any time. We get a party going, play games and dance. Chico, Chente, Angel and Manuel are coming next week. We miss these four lads when they're not here, they're part of the fun. The house has become a small village, a copy of our old life in the country at Laj Chimel. We had to start rebuilding our family, having something of our own again, after all the years spent moving from house to house in Mexico, often living in the poorest areas. In exile, I never bothered much about having a house, or anything of my own. I only carried with me my keepsakes – and the ideals of my people of creating a just and decent country. I know I have left bags and books and memories in countless corners of Mexico, where there was always a poor family to take me in and adopt me like a long-lost daughter.

Building my family and rebuilding it – finding my brother Nicolás, my sisters Anita and Lucía, my sister-in-law and her children – these have been momentous events in my life. They all survived in different places, with their own particular experiences of the war. They escaped death and destruction so many times. Yet wherever we were, we always had common premonitions, a spiritual bond, shared memories and similar dreams. It is something inexplicable, as if there were a continual link between us. On the few occasions we managed to meet, that sense of family was rekindled. It is what we call our umbilical cord, it binds us together.

Of course as kids we used to fight. Yet even that is part of the deep imprint left on us by our little hut, our village of Laj Chimel, the land where we were born. My brother Nicolás takes after my father. He loves the earth and the fields, the maize and the mountains. He too fights for his community. Burned by the sun like my father, he works and works, and life's scars are plain to see. He and my sister Marta are older than I am. We respect each other very much.

The story I'm going to tell happened at a very special time: the wedding of my niece Regina Menchú Tomás. She is the daughter of my brother Víctor who was shot in 1983. Regina, his eldest child, survived. Hearing that Víctor's children had been left at the army barracks, my half-sister

Rosa had plucked up her courage and gone to get them. Neighbours told her there were three children, a girl and two boys. They were very ill, bloated from malnutrition. Rosa was so poor she could not feed all three, so she passed Regina on to another family. The two little boys died. From 1983 onwards, Regina went from house to house seeking shelter. She had no fixed home.

I had had no news of her until I finally met Nicolás again in 1992, and he told me about her. I felt terribly sad and was filled with a need to find her. She was already a young woman when I met her. She was very shy and found it very difficult at first. She was an orphan, she had been rejected so often, and she had suffered so much, all alone. Her father had been shot and dumped in a communal grave in Uspantán. Her mother, María, had been kidnapped and butchered, and had her throat cut. It happened in Chimel in 1980. Her body was found, just like that.

When my sister Anita and I finally met Regina, we asked her to come and live with us. She said yes, and at the end of 1992 she lived with us for a while in Mexico. Then she came back to Guatemala where she decided to get married. I was sad to see her go for she was one of our household by then, and we all loved her because she was the child of Víctor and María.

When Regina told us she was getting married, I said, 'I'll give you a beautiful *despedida*, child.' Her new family belongs to the Evangelical church, so we thought it best to have a civil wedding to avoid any arguments over beliefs. We would let them decide the religious question for themselves.

About six weeks before the wedding we started organising the *despedida*. We wanted to do things properly, although we could never bring back the wonderful days when our brothers and sisters were married in Chimel. They were happy, they had beautiful ceremonies just like our forefathers. But times had changed.

The wedding had been agreed in June 1995, and it was to take place on Saturday, 4 November. On the morning of the day before, the whole family started arriving – my sisters and my brother, with nephews and nieces, cousins and grandchildren, and loads of other children.

The last to arrive was my niece Cristina, the mother of three-year-old Kalito. She already had another baby on her back. 'How old is he?' I asked. 'Three months,' she replied. I put my hand on the baby's head according to K'iche' custom, to bless him, to wish him a long life, and to welcome him to our family and our home.

Little Kalito then came in and started playing with my computer. He began pulling the cables out and I chased him round the house. 'What about your husband?' I asked his mother. 'Where is he?'

'He's in Playa Grande, auntie, in Cantabal,' she replied. 'He has gone to sell flowers.'

I was a little surprised and said, 'Flowers in El Ixcán, how come? There are so many wonderful flowers there, why are they selling flowers?' Then she explained. 'The flowers they sell are made of plastic, auntie.' I thought to myself, 'Some people obviously like synthetic things, something plastic instead of a natural flower.'

I left it at that, saying 'Isn't he coming to the wedding?'

'No,' she replied, 'he doesn't know I've come to the wedding. I'm worried what will happen when he gets home and finds I'm not there. I didn't have time to tell him.' It was very late in the day and she wanted to chat, but I said, 'Let's leave it for tomorrow, child. We're busy getting ready for the ceremony.'

In Mayan culture, on the day before the wedding, we bring the couple together and give them advice about life, and encourage them. We remind the bride that she must not forget her nest – her first family, her old home. We tell them to always listen to their elders. The bridegroom's family does the same. If there is any problem, we want them to confide in us, so that they don't feel isolated. The idea is to set them up in life, united and strengthened. We remind them of the collective sense of the family.

Other people, meanwhile, are cooking and making *pul-ik*. This is a dish made with lots of different seeds – sesame, pumpkin, coriander and cumin – and flavoured with many kinds of condiments. It is a ritual dish that needs patience. The seeds are ground up, and then baked for a long time. It has chili too, three kinds of chili, and three kinds of tomato, and garlic, and a bit of *achiote*. You prepare it quite a long time beforehand.

We had decided to make chicken *pul-ik* this time, though not with factory chickens which are pure chemicals. We had gone round the markets to get fresh chickens, and then we had to kill them, pluck them and prepare them.

Regina's new family, her in-laws, had decided that they would make turkey for us, in a spicy white sauce. The turkeys are cooked whole, in big earthenware pots, and the sauce is made separately. They gave us the cooked turkeys to eat on the day after the wedding.

When we met, we exchanged gifts. The bride's family always gives the bride clothes: her *huipils*, her *cortes*, her *perrajes* and other little things.

The wedding was to be held in the Instituto Santiago, some fifteen kilometres from the centre of Guatemala City so everyone had to leave early. When I went downstairs at about half past eight, I saw that my niece Cristina was still there. 'Haven't you left yet?' I said. 'Didn't you go with the others?'

She answered, 'No, Kalito wants to go with you.' I laughed, and said, 'Don't be silly, he can't even talk yet. Never mind, you can come in my car.' She put her little boy in my car, I took my son, and off we all went.

Before we left, she said, 'Auntie, you'll have to excuse me, but I can't stay at the wedding for long.'

'Why not?' I asked.

'Because I have to go to 18th Street to buy some clocks to sell in the market in Cobán. Lots of people have asked me for wall clocks. I have to reserve some to take back with me on Monday.'

'Don't worry, child,' I said, 'come for a little while. Then my car will take you to 18th Street.' So off we went.

We had decorated the altar with flowers, put the candles in the four corners and prepared the *pom*. Then we had gone through the ceremony, exchanged the gifts and given the couple our advice. That took quite a time. When all that was over, they had to go to the civil ceremony.

My husband and I gave the bride away. It should have been her parents, of course, but as she didn't have any we became her elders. We gave away the bride, and the bridegroom's parents gave him to us. All this is part of the ceremony, and part of our culture. When it was all over, we served up the meal and attended to the guests. All our *compañeros* from the Rigoberta Menchú Foundation came, and the meal went on till two in the afternoon. Then the dancing started. Dr Eduardo Salerno, our adviser in the case of the Xamán massacre, was there. So too was Dorita, and the Foundation's lawyer, María Estela López.

Everyone was milling around when a nephew arrived, a boy who had stayed behind to look after the house. He was crying.

'Somebody's been kidnapped,' he said.

All I heard was that there had been a kidnapping, and that it was near our house. Clearly it was someone from our family or my nephew wouldn't have been so upset. So I stopped everything and asked, 'What happened?'

Kalito, Cristina's small boy, had been kidnapped by two men in a white car. There was another man in the car, the driver. It had happened just fifty metres from our front door. They had hit Kalito's mother.

As soon as I heard the word 'kidnapped' I thought of my own mother. It brought home to me the enormous risks we run every day. This had been my constant fear ever since I came back from exile.

I don't know what time it was when my brother, my sister and I, and a handful of others, made our way back to the house. We didn't say goodbye to anybody. Everyone was in a state of shock. When we arrived home, Cristina was standing in the hallway, pale, frightened and crying. I remember saying, 'Cristina, tell me what happened? What have they done to your son?' Still crying, she told the story of the kidnapping.

'What do you want me to do, Cristina?' I asked, and she said, 'Bring my son back alive.'

'Should we tell the police,' I asked, 'or the press? What should we do?' She was the boy's mother, after all.

'Do whatever you want,' she begged, 'but do it quickly.' There was no time to waste. The kidnappers could easily be taking the boy across a frontier, the border with El Salvador was the nearest. I wondered if he was nearby or had already been taken far away. Kidnapping had now become big business in Guatemala; kidnapping children, businessmen, celebrities. It happened all the time.

We were terribly scared. I was trembling with fright. So many things had happened all at once. It was 4 November, barely a month after the dreadful massacre of the returning refugees at Xamán in Alta Verapaz. I remembered, by coincidence, that my niece Cristina had a stall in the market in Cobán, which was also in Alta Verapaz. Why did it have to be my niece from Alta Verapaz? Why did it have to be the daughter of my elder brother? Not only was the little boy the first grandchild, he was also the son of my eldest brother's eldest daughter. All these things are very important in our family, because the eldest son's first child is very significant, very respected.

I started thinking that this message must be directed at me. It was an attack on me, an attack on the heart of the family. It had happened on a most solemn occasion, when I was saying farewell to the daughter of my brother who had been shot and my sister-in-law who had been butchered. I was also terrified at the thought that they had got mixed up and had thought Kalito was my son. Kalito and my son look very much alike. If my son Mash Nawalja' had already been walking, they would have been identical. He wasn't walking; that was the only difference.

I also started thinking about army harassment. Some sectors of the army in Alta Verapaz, in Playa Grande, had harassed me all through October and November, accusing me of demanding the death penalty for all soldiers. This wasn't true. I had merely asked for the maximum prison sentence – thirty years – for those involved in the massacre at Xamán. The army, however, had said that I wanted the death penalty for soldiers committing crimes in the future. Certain elements within the army considered me a dangerous enemy. They even whipped up hostility among relatives of soldiers in the armed forces. Reactionaries jumped at the chance to write newspaper articles accusing me of demanding the death penalty, and saying that I should have won the Nobel Prize for war instead of for peace. All this had happened in October.

I was under a lot of pressure. In these situations, the more you explain, the worse things get. I know when to keep silent. If something happens which I know will generate racism, intrigue, hate, confrontation, I say nothing. Even if it means being vilified for a few days, I deliberately say nothing.

'This is a political act,' I realised, 'it isn't just coincidence.' I talked it over with my *compañeros* in the Foundation, with Dorita, Dr Salerno and Helen Mack. 'What should I do?' I asked. They also thought it was a political act, an attack on me and my family. It was a way of blackening the Menchú family name.

I called the chief commissioner of police, the chief inspector of the CID, the ministry of the interior, even the army. The press turned up in the person of a great friend, Don Eduardo Mendoza, who has a radio programme called *Radio Sonora*. He was very indignant and also quite worried. Indeed everyone who came to the house was worried, for it was only a month before the general election.

The Foundation had taken a big risk in sponsoring a voter-registration drive – the National Campaign for Citizens' Participation – and encouraging people to vote. This horrible kidnapping, a month before the election, dampened the whole atmosphere. Other events during the electoral campaign had already helped to create a climate of violence. There was the Xamán massacre, but there had also been other kidnappings and assassinations, with an average of eight to eleven corpses a day throughout the country, especially in urban areas. Violence permeated everything. The violence in Guatemala causes chaos, uncertainty and intimidation. It is psychological warfare to frighten people.

Kalito's kidnapping was part of this warfare, and not just for me. I experienced yet again what people feel when a loved one is kidnapped. My house was inundated with friends and strangers. I called the police, and Cristina answered all their questions.

I summoned the press and said, 'I want to make it clear that I will not rest until I find who is responsible. If it is the army, I want them punished. If it isn't, let them prove the contrary by a thorough and exhaustive investigation. Not a half-hearted investigation. I want those who gave the orders and those who carried them out to be punished. Kidnapping doesn't just happen out of the blue. I can only believe in justice if it is rigorously applied.'

While I was saying this, I heard Cristina cry, 'Why didn't I go with Miguel? He told me to protect our son. He wanted me to go back to Cobán with him.' I heard her say this from across the room, it seemed just a small detail.

Afterwards, I asked, 'Cristina, when did you see Miguel?' 'Today,' she said, 'today in 18th Street.'

'But didn't you tell me he was in Playa Grande and selling flowers in Cantabal? How did he get here? When did he come?'

'Ah . . . no,' she said, 'the thing is, he went to our house in Cobán last night, and when I wasn't there he came to the capital, and I bumped into him.'

I said, 'But why didn't he come to our house, Cristina?' and she replied, 'He . . . he . . . he didn't come because he imagined I'd be at the wedding, and he didn't know where the wedding was.'

'So where did you see him?' I asked. 'Near the market,' she replied. 'Where exactly?' 'In the Almacén Imperial,' she said, almost crying.

I didn't know what sort of place that was, a boarding house or a shop, perhaps. I didn't insist, but I felt slightly uneasy, slightly on edge. I can't say it made me suspicious because it was too small a thing.

Kidnapping is horrible. There were times when I thought – these may be cruel inhuman thoughts, I know – that if the little boy had died, it would of course have been a huge tragedy to lose a beautiful life like Kalito's, but we would have mourned him and performed our rituals for him. It would have affected us in a different way. But when a child is kidnapped, all you can think of is whether he'll come back alive or dead, and what they're doing to him . . .

A person who kidnaps a child is someone wholly without scruple. I kept thinking about what they would do to the child, what would happen to him. It is so cruel. I started seeing the little boy at home, hearing him. I'd wake up in the night and open the window, and look out in the garden for him. The child's image was so clear. Even the way he behaved. He pierced my heart and mind, day and night. I didn't even know him that well. I'd only spent a short time with him.

I talked again to Cristina and asked if she had spoken to her husband. She said he had phoned at seven in the morning just to say he wanted his son back safe and sound. He had told her, 'This is your fault, because you went to your aunt's house. You know your aunt gets herself into lots of trouble. If my son dies, it's your fault, your fault and your aunt's. I want my son back.' Then he hung up.

She started crying. She said, 'It's true, it's my fault, it's my fault.'

This made me very sad. I said, 'How can it be your fault, child? It's the kidnappers' fault, not yours.' I was afraid she would spend her life feeling guilty about the loss of her son. I was also afraid for myself. I couldn't stop thinking that one day everyone would say it was my fault their son had died, and that my son is alive because they had mistaken hers for mine. All this was very painful.

On Sunday at one o'clock, her husband arrived. He came in, cried and accused me. 'You want to kill my son. You have put my son in danger. If they've killed him, you're responsible. Why did you have to involve the authorities? Why did you go to the press? What did you tell them? Why didn't you wait for me? You want them to kill my son. If he dies I'll avenge him, and you'll never be happy. You'll have your family and a part of mine will be gone.' Just like that.

For a time it made me sad and very frightened. Then I pulled myself together and said, 'Miguel, first of all, look how late you turned up! Then you start accusing me, saying I'm responsible for your son's kidnapping. What have you done for him? Show me that you've done any better! What plans do you have for getting your son back? Besides, I won't allow you to come to my house and start shouting. So, get to work. Stay by the phone.'

I got a chair and said, 'If the kidnappers phone, tell them you'll negoti- ate. You're the one who should talk to the kidnappers.'

He was taken aback. He changed colour and said, 'No. I don't want to, I'm not getting involved. It's your problem.'

This made me very suspicious. A desperate father would have done what my husband and I had done, sit by the phone continuously, day and night. We kept checking to see if the phone was ringing properly, or if it was off the hook. Every time it rang, our hopes rose.

'Look, Miguel,' I replied, 'if you don't want to get involved, that's all right. But have the goodness to leave us alone. Stay out of it, it's my busi- ness now.'

I made him go to another room, and I asked my husband to keep man- ning the phone. I went out, and when I came back I could see that Miguel was uneasy. He was pacing up and down.

'Sister,' said Anita, 'they look less worried than you. You must eat some- thing, and rest a little. They look resigned to me. They seem to have accepted the situation, and you must too, you can't go on like this.'

So I told my sister, 'I know what I'm doing. I'm going to do some inves- tigating. I have to.'

I went to the embassies and the human rights groups for help in trying to figure out what it all meant. It is always best to listen to other people's opin- ions if you have a problem like this, rather than to die waiting for a phone call. What would I do if they asked for money? I never believed they were after money.

A few months earlier I had discussed with my family what would happen if thugs kidnapped me for ransom. What would the Foundation do? What would my family do? I had told them 'Look, if you offer one, ten or a mil- lion *quetzales* or dollars to free me, you'll offend me for ever, because my dignity has no price.' I said the same thing in radio interviews.

A person's dignity has no price. Poor or rich, famous or unknown, a person is worth far more than any sum of money. Their value is spiritual, for dignity is what life is all about. Let me warn anyone who might try kidnapping me that I would consider it an insult if they put a monetary value on me. If anyone tries it, I hope they'll respect my life and set me free. If not, they'll have to kill me. I prefer to die with dignity.

That's my position, and my family knows that's how I think. That goes for my son, too. If they kidnap my son, he'll live because they have spared his life, or he'll die because life cannot be bought or sold. You cannot put a price on life, man is not a chattel. My family knows this, my brother knows I wouldn't give a cent for my life or for any of theirs.

At about four in the afternoon, I could see that Miguel was very agitated. I felt in my bones that all was not right. I was getting some weird and extraordinary messages that made me increasingly suspicious. Not because I thought he was involved, but several other possibilities remained.

'They may be in debt,' I thought to myself, 'and are being blackmailed. They may be connected to paramilitary groups, or even to the regular army. Maybe they're mixed up with the Mafia, or with weird groups. They may have information, or at least suspect who is behind all this.'

I got a book and started reading. I couldn't stand the strain. I went upstairs and called my brother Nicolás and his wife Juana. She was frightened because her nerves were very bad. They had lived with the Communities of the Population in Resistance (CPRs) in the mountains in the 1980s.

My brother Nicolás is lucky to be alive. He was taken to the barracks in Santa Cruz del Quiché. He saw many people tortured to death, and he was brutally tortured himself for six months. When he got back, his children were suffering from malnutrition and neglect. A tunnel had been dug under the Catholic church in Uspantán, and Juana and her six children had been held there for six months. All this had had a profound effect on her.

I called Miguel and sat him down in front of them. 'Look, Miguel,' I said, 'you're hiding something. What is it? What's going on? If you don't want to tell me, at least tell your elders, your father-in-law, your mother-in-law, they are both your elders. Tell them in private. You don't have to tell me. I'm sure you're keeping something important in your heart.'

He kept denying everything, but I persevered. 'I know you're hiding something,' I said. 'If you lie to your elders, your lie will be your shame all your life, and it will curse you.'

In the end, he admitted he had been hiding something. 'I was selling pirated cassettes,' he said. I felt as if I had had a cold drink or taken a good swig of *cuxa*.

'Pirated cassettes!' I exclaimed. 'How can anyone do business selling pirate cassettes in Cobán? You'd only sell one a week. The people are poor, they don't have cassette players. Only people in the towns have them, not in the country.'

'Miguel,' I went on, 'how could you think a few cassettes are worth the same as your son? What is more important, the kidnapping of a son, or being caught pirating a few cassettes? Why are you so afraid of the authorities?'

'It's your fault the police are at my house,' he said. 'They're checking on me. You're making things difficult for me.'

'If you're afraid they'll find a couple of cassettes,' I said, 'then tell me. It's best to get guilt out in the open, recognise it, deal with it.'

Miguel acted strangely that night. When the kidnappers did finally ring, they said, 'We have the boy nearby, but the police are snooping around. Call the police off or you'll never see the boy again.' They didn't mention money. Money, it seemed, wasn't the object. The purpose was political.

This was on the Sunday night, and we asked the police to withdraw. Miguel didn't want the police called off, because he was afraid the kidnappers would throw a grenade, or a bomb, or that they would machine-gun the house.

We discussed Miguel's behaviour with our good Argentine friend Dr Salerno. We concluded that Miguel probably knew exactly what was going on. How did he know they had grenades? How did he know they used bombs or could machine-gun the house? Why did he think the kidnappers were violent? What mess had he got himself into?

We looked for a pretext to confront him. He said he would be leaving at two in the morning for Cobán. 'You can't leave here at two in the morning,' I said. He insisted, sounding increasingly desperate. I said, 'Go and sleep somewhere else, then you can leave when you like. It's for your own safety. If the kidnappers are still around here, they'll see you leave. They could take you too, and kill you.'

I wanted to see his reaction. 'If anything happens to you, it'll create more problems for us. This is a delicate situation, you must do as we say.'

Miguel left, finally, and at nine o'clock that Sunday night we took him by car to Avenida Elena, a street near our house. The house there belongs to our Foundation. We didn't give him the key. If he went out and shut the door, he would have to stay outside.

At half past eleven, I asked Dr Salerno and Helen Mack to go and ask Miguel more questions: about the cassettes, if people were trying to get information from him, if he was an accomplice, if he was covering for anyone. If he wasn't, they had to convince him he had nothing to fear and make him talk.

Imagine their surprise when they got to Avenida Elena and found that he wasn't there. The idiot had left the house. They searched every corner and found no one.

They were most worried, and came back to tell me. My reaction was frank: 'He has to talk, and so must Cristina. She must know, or at least suspect something.'

I wanted to believe that our umbilical cord, our common blood, could never betray us. Sometimes we confuse our hearts, our feelings and tenderness, with our reason. I thought this was probably one of her husband's messes, because he didn't have a good reputation. I had quizzed him once and he admitted to having been in prison and getting drunk and other vices. Sometimes he beat his wife, too.

When I found out about his behaviour, I kept away from him after my niece married him in 1992. I told him he couldn't come to my house. I was living then at the CONIVAGUA headquarters (the National Association of Guatemalan Widows) with Rosalina Tuyuc. A man like that might be susceptible to blackmail and pressure, but I didn't think his wife could be too.

So now I talked to her, but she said nothing but good things about him; he was good, he was responsible, he never did bad things. She didn't mention the cassettes or anything like that. It was a waste of time. This was at about two in the morning on Monday, 6 November.

Miguel appeared again at six that afternoon. He had apparently come from Cobán. 'How did it go, Miguel?' I asked.

'Very well,' he replied. 'Did you get to Cobán in time?'

'Yes,' he said, 'I hid the cassettes we had in the house. I left Avenida Elena at six in the morning.'

'So where did you sleep, Miguel?' I asked.

'I slept at Avenida Elena.'

'No, you didn't,' I said. 'Where did you sleep? Where were you?'

In the end, he said, 'Look, if you doubt my word, show me the newspaper. I can tell you what the morning's headlines were because they had already pushed today's newspaper under the door when I left the house and I took it. Besides, I can tell you exactly where I left the TV remote control when I went to sleep.'

This wasn't a normal explanation. Somebody had taught him. It sounded like a plan, blackmail.

So I said, 'That's not true.' Then, in front of his father-in-law, his mother-in-law and his wife, he asked, 'Whom do you believe, your family or her colleagues? They are deceiving you, they want to create divisions and mistrust. Who do you believe, family or strangers?'

Then we started arguing again. This was Monday already. I didn't know what to do. I wasn't at all sure whether to keep this information and my doubts to myself, or to tell the police. Telling the police was risky. They might not investigate or they might misrepresent the facts. Another long anxious night awaited me.

I finally decided to talk to the police. At nine on the Tuesday morning, several officers arrived. I told them I was worried, but I didn't tell them everything. How could I when next day's newspaper headlines would attribute the kidnapping to my own family?

What I feared actually happened anyway. We gave them a few quite discreet details. The rest, they knew. I kept on investigating and a curious situation then arose. The police only came to find out what I knew. They never reported what they had done. They just questioned me every day.

On Monday night, I was afraid Miguel would stay at my house and I was worried for my own son. So we started taking precautions, although they were not too serious. By Tuesday, I had decided the fellow was a threat, a threat to the children. They are not used to being suspicious of visitors, and always run outside when someone opens the door.

While I was worrying about my son's safety, I had completely forgotten about feeding him or changing his nappy until I heard crying from the patio. He had fallen and was dripping blood, I thought he had broken his first two teeth. I picked him up and felt very impotent. I could forget many things but how could I have forgotten that?

Then it occurred to me that the fellow was probably armed. On Tuesday I took him upstairs and asked, 'Miguel, have you got a gun?' And he replied with a smile, 'I'm not an arms dealer, auntie.'

I said, 'I didn't ask if you sold arms, I asked if you had a gun.'

'No,' he said, 'No, I haven't.' He denied it and denied it, and each time he laughed at me. Finally, I said, 'Look, Miguel, don't think I'm an idiot. You can't fool me that easily. I know you have a gun, and I'm asking where you have left it.'

When he saw that I was serious, he said, 'Yes, I admit I have a gun, but it's legal, I have papers for it. Don't accuse me of carrying an illegal weapon because it won't work, I have the proper documents.'

I probed further. 'So, you have a gun, and you've got papers for it. Congratulations! As if a registered gun isn't just as bad. What I want to know is where you've left it.'

'I don't have money on me,' he said, 'so why would I carry a gun? I only carry it when I've got money. Why would I have a gun and no money?'

He left it at that, the cynic, but I kept repeating, 'Where's the gun?'

He was increasingly aggressive. I realised the gun could be in my house. He could have hidden it there, so it was risky for us, a real threat, a violation of our house. The idea that the enemy could be in your own home is a terrible torture.

At that stage, I gave the information to the police. Dr Salerno called them and said we suspected that the little boy's father had something to do with the kidnapping. We asked for him to be put under police surveillance immediately and be refused access to my house. The police suggested putting two policemen in my house to protect my family. I protested. 'No,' I said, 'I'm not asking for police in my house. I'm saying this man may harm us and shouldn't be allowed near here.'

The police said they would take the appropriate measures. I understood that from five o'clock on Tuesday afternoon they would be watching Miguel and we would be safe.

On Tuesday night I came home late. I found Miguel asleep in the house. I realised the authorities were not on my side and I felt very frustrated. We had to change my son's room. We had to leave. I had not slept on Saturday night, nor on Sunday or Monday. This was my fourth night without sleep. I was even able to admire the way I was coping. I was absolutely calm, not at all sleepy. Sleep had been scared off for good. So I took my son downstairs.

I was afraid, very afraid, of kidnapping. I wondered who the kidnappers were, what the thugs were like – would they be armed? On top of that, I had let the authorities into my house even though I was afraid of them, and after so many years of not trusting the police or the judicial system. Everyone seemed to expect something more from me, but I didn't know what was going on either. It was a terrible situation. Like a nightmare. You can't imagine it unless you have experienced it.

Dawn was breaking. At about three on Wednesday morning, I woke my brother Nicolás and told him my suspicions. I told him everything, from the story of Miguel selling flowers in El Ixcán where the army's most notorious barracks is located. He was very surprised. I couldn't bring myself to tell my sister-in-law. It would have destroyed her. She was the little boy's grandmother and, being Cristina's mother, she might not have believed me. She might wonder what my brother and I were plotting.

Nicolás now co-operated by watching what was going on. My husband and I didn't even tell my sister Anita, in case it complicated the situation more, and destroyed our valued family ties and trust.

By Wednesday I could see the situation had got worse. I told my brother Nicolás that they should go home. Not Cristina, though. She had to stay here until the little boy was found. My sister-in-law said, 'No, she must come with us, she'll die of grief here. Her other baby never stops crying.'

Cristina was frightened. I think that when they saw their plan wasn't working it affected them. They were living with their own shame. It was Wednesday, and by now Miguel was under police surveillance.

I had hoped to be very active in the week running up to the presidential elections. I had planned to organise observers at the polling stations, and to insist that the Electoral Monitoring Board provide translators for the different indigenous groups. I had hoped to participate fully in guaranteeing fair elections.

Kalito's kidnapping badly affected my contribution to the National Campaign for Citizens' Participation, and to the elections in general. By Wednesday I wasn't feeling well. I felt persecuted and listless. Above all, I was not well spiritually.

I summoned my whole family, including Cristina. Together with Gustavo Meoño, the Foundation's director, Dorita, my secretary, and everyone close to me, we went to Paraxchaj, some forty kilometres from the capital. We spent a while in the countryside, breathing fresh air and talking. I felt revitalised when I came back. I told my brother and sister-in-law that we would not rest until we found the boy. We went home and I finally got to sleep at three in the morning.

I have never been an emotional or nervous person. My problem is that I feel pain more deeply inside than outside. Everyone looks at me and thinks I'm all right. Yet I hadn't eaten or slept for nights on end. I was just wracking my brains for a solution. When terrible events are over, that's when I become unbearable because I want to sleep, I want to forget the whole thing. But until then I maintain a stable rhythm.

My husband Angel said, 'Go and sleep, I'll stay up.' He was manning the telephone. We had been taking it in turns. I went to bed, and at six in the morning my brother and sister-in-law left. Cristina left with them.

When I got up and asked, 'Where's Cristina?' I was told she had left. 'What? She's gone?' 'She went to El Quiché, to her home, to her parents' home.'

I was very angry. 'First, we're taking this case to court. She can't be so irresponsible. Secondly, how can a mother go calmly off with the case of her kidnapped son unsolved?' My sister Anita said, 'Leave them alone. Perhaps she is already resigned to the fact. Perhaps it is causing her so much pain that if she stays she'll go mad. Remember, she's still feeding her other baby, and he's crying a lot. Maybe she's resigned. Leave them alone.'

'All right,' I said. 'Maybe that's it. Life goes on, doesn't it?'

The kidnappers phoned on Tuesday night. They demanded money, but didn't say much else. 'Half a million dollars for the boy. Think it over and we'll call you back.' And they hung up.

After that, nothing. They just sent word telling us to stop the investigation straight away. They said nothing about how to pay the money. They only mentioned money once. So I was suspicious. I had never doubted it was politically motivated. But what was it they wanted? What harm could they do that they hadn't already done?

We waited for news until Friday when my brother Nicolás suddenly phoned to say the little boy was with them; he had come to their house with his mother. I said, 'But I thought Cristina had gone back with you yesterday?'

'No,' he said, 'she stayed in El Quiché. She said she had to visit her in-laws and, to her surprise, she found the child at their house. The grandmother had found the child in the park in Santa Cruz del Quiché near the monument to Tucum Umam.'

According to her version of events, the kid was wearing the same clothes and nappy as on the day of the kidnapping. I wasn't convinced. I thought it was very strange. I imagined the child would be ill and thin.

When I heard the little boy was well, I was very happy, I felt as if I'd been born again. I wanted to hold him in my arms. I wanted to bury all my doubts. After talking to my brother, I phoned the Foundation's director, Gustavo Meoño, I phoned Dora, I phoned my friends Helen Mack and Eduardo Salerno.

It was about ten at night, and I had just put down the phone when the kidnappers called for the last time. They said, 'We've given the boy back because we took the wrong child.' That was their last message. It gives me the shivers to this day.

I asked Gustavo Meoño to go to Uspantán the following day. He went to my brother's house to talk to Cristina, to verify that the child was well. Gustavo asked Cristina to take the boy's clothes off because she had said he had been wearing the same clothes for a week. After a week a child would at least have a sore bottom. But Kalito was perfectly all right. There was nothing wrong with him. In fact she apparently had to pinch him a little to make him cry.

My friends then went to Miguel's mother's house. They learned that when the police arrived with helicopters, the neighbours began saying that the little boy had never left his grandmother's house. His father and another man called Juan Ajpop had left him there.

We convinced the men to give themselves up to the police, and they were arrested. The neighbours all insisted that the boy had been there all the time. So the grandmother had to admit the truth. She said the boy's father had brought him there at four o'clock on the afternoon of the kidnapping. Cristina had never taken him back to my house after the wedding. She had handed him over to her husband at midday, and given him time to get away. They both admitted it.

They were both arrested and taken to prison, but a few days later Cristina was released on bail. It was a huge amount for a poor family. They also had four defence lawyers. Miguel admitted, however, that it had taken him six months to convince Cristina to co-operate in her son's auto-kidnapping. He says he will go on protecting the friends who helped and refused to name them. He stated that he was solely responsible. He refuses to reveal the identity of his bosses and other co-conspirators. He should be out of jail in two years' time.

After a plot like that, I think Miguel must be mixed up in other things. The people who planned this simulated kidnapping are still free and we don't know who they are. There isn't enough evidence to continue the investigation. They only found three people who actually carried out the kidnapping, and we think there must be more. I'll never know what Miguel and Cristina received for betraying their own kind.

Now that it's all over, I have an even better understanding of a mother's pain; the pain of those who have had children kidnapped, and who have searched for them with passion and desperation. How long will this go on?

If you haven't had first-hand experience, it is hard to imagine the horror of it all! When we become political, everything is superficial, we look for the feet, wings and beaks of problems. Often, as a result, we forget the human-ity, the direct contact, the skin of events. So this was a lesson.

I offered my profound thanks when the little boy reappeared. It may have been a warning to us. We may be living too comfortably, too removed from things that are happening every day. Perhaps we don't believe as we used to? Perhaps we are losing the values of our forefathers? How many children are kidnapped in Guatemala every day? How many children are kidnapped in the world? Who are the degenerates who can kill a child? How many people are still hoping to find their children and never will? Or will find them dead?

This was a time of deep reflection for me. It was so obviously a wicked plot, designed to sap my energy, to make me suffer, to touch the fibres clos-est to my heart and dignity, to destroy me. It was accompanied of course by a slur campaign in the media. From the very first Wednesday, President Ramiro de León Carpio began calling it a family affair, in a very racist way. He stole a march on everyone by saying it wasn't political at all, but a domestic affair. Afterwards he asked me publicly to apologise to the armed forces for having offended them. This was too obvious. He knows I hate the army, at least the type of army that exists in Guatemala today.

When the situation was worsening, certain people in the media vented on me all the rage and the racism that they have in their hearts. They were just waiting for an opportunity. They began attacking me daily, in newspapers that I thought were friends. Maybe they had become used to me always apologising, always bowing my head. Perhaps they thought I should bow my head again.

A lot of them had very macho attitudes. They said things about me they had never said before. Yet in a way that pleased me. At times like this you discover how much educating is still to be done, how human relationships have deteriorated. It gave me many weeks of reflection, study and analysis.

I don't think the Foundation's presence in Guatemala should be criticised. We are not doing anything out of the ordinary. We are just working, and helping refugees to return home. I have been very discreet in the media. I have not highlighted every new story. Sometimes indeed I have been criticised for not speaking out, and I have often felt it is not my place to do so.

It takes courage to live here. You really have to want to. You need courage, a lot of patience and much strength. The bad country we have described does indeed exist; a bloodthirsty, repressive, racist, dirty, backward country. Yet it is also true that we have not always been magnanimous enough to balance the good and the bad. We always say that it is bad or it is good. We have not been sufficiently generous to merge the two.

We owe a great debt to Guatemala. We need to show the world that Guatemala is not the most wretched country on earth. It is not. In the villages there are groups of women, groups of young people, people working together, initiating programmes and showing leadership. And not just the leaders. Each person's work has a value and complements that of other people, and this raises our spirits.

When you see the people and the hopes that they have, you cast a daily vote of confidence in the future of Guatemala. I am convinced that it is worth making a big effort and living here. And anyway, where else could I live permanently? I travel, I come and go, I cross borders. But being in far-off lands is different when I know that this is my home. Plane journeys seem ever longer to me now. The dignity that a real home provides makes me always anxious to get back quickly.

2

COMING HOME TO GUATEMALA,
1988 AND 1994

Kalito's kidnapping would not have happened if I had not decided to come back to Guatemala for good. At the end of 1993, full of apprehension, Gustavo, Dorita, Hugo and I decided to transfer the headquarters of the Rigoberta Menchú Foundation from Mexico City to Guatemala. We wanted the Foundation to be a national institution, with a Guatemalan identity, while still retaining its regional and world role. I returned to Guatemala with my whole family in the middle of 1994.

Dorita Mirón had been in exile for fourteen years. Her two teenage daughters had already gone back to Guatemala. I think they helped to push us into taking the decision to return. Dora and I share convictions and dreams, and a common history. I knew César, the father of her children. He was a *compañero* who had worked tirelessly for the Committee for Peasant Unity (CUC). He had been a fervent supporter of the peasant struggle, and was kidnapped and 'disappeared' in the 1980s.

Dorita experienced the brutality of the repression at first hand. Her parents were kidnapped, and they too never reappeared. She searched for them in the morgues and in the hospitals without success. Then she fled into exile with her two children, as so many others did. I know she knows some of those responsible for her family's suffering. The dangers she has faced and the great humanity with which she faced them bind me to her. We are bound not only by the deep scars the repression has left, but also by a belief in a better future, the dream of a democratic country, and a life-long commitment to our people.

I had already made an earlier attempt to return to Guatemala in 1988. On 18 April that year, I had been arrested at the airport on the orders of President Vinicio Cerezo. You might have thought the police had discovered an atom bomb. More than four hundred police were there to arrest me and Rolando Castillo Montalvo, and other *compañeros* from the United Guatemalan Opposition Front (RUOG), to which I belonged at that time.

We came because the Guatemalan ambassador to the United Nations in Geneva had over-reached himself and invited us, on behalf of his government, to return. It was pure demagogy on his part because the government had absolutely no intention of allowing this to happen. It just wanted to advertise President Cerezo's supposed goodwill, and to avoid being condemned by the international community. It wanted to gloss over the permanent violation of human rights. Of course we were determined to come; a bit like a child who closes his eyes and doesn't know if he's going to be hit over the head. He is ready for it anyway.

Scarcely had we set foot in the airport before we were arrested. When you are in exile, just thinking about Guatemala frightens you. Yet when you get there and are arrested, you have no option but to face the challenge. I will never forget this overwhelming and beautiful experience.

Having spent so long in exile, I had not yet had the experience of being detained by 'the authorities' with such repressive powers, and acting with such impunity. It was now time to pay tribute, through my own experience, to the disappeared, to the kidnapped and to those tortured in clandestine centres. It was time to remember the shadow of death hanging over life. Our fear was all the greater because we were the first political prisoners in Guatemala. We were considered subversives, communists, feminists or *indigenistas*. We were considered to be rebels who, by some mistake, were still alive.

We were arrested at ten minutes past noon at the international airport, and pushed into cars with opaque windows. Nowhere in the world have I seen so many cars with opaque windows as in Guatemala. In other places, normal people driving cars show their faces. In Guatemala, cars with opaque windows are a common and shadowy phenomenon. They stop you seeing who is inside. They have also become a symbol of terror. The *judiciales*, the death squads, the paramilitary groups, and gangs of murderers and kidnappers, all use these cars.

Nobody knew where they had taken us. No one knew what was happening. In fact they had taken us to a building in the capital called *La Torre de Justicia* which housed the law courts. There we were charged, and, for five hours, we tried to find a defence lawyer. We couldn't find one in the whole of Guatemala. Who would have the courage to defend us in those days? No one!

A lawyer was eventually found for *compañero* Rolando Castillo Montalvo. As the former dean of the medical school at the University of San Carlos, he was a well-known figure. Activists among professionals and students had put pressure on the university to provide him with a proper defence. But me? Who was going to defend me?

The judge was a certain Alcides. We were to meet again – the twists of fate! – some time later. He was to be the examining magistrate appointed by the ministry to investigate the massacre at Xamán in 1995, and the first thing he did there was to wipe out all the evidence.

Judge Alcides had exercised his profession in the war zones of El Quiché for thirty years. He had sentenced my father to a year in prison because he considered him a subversive. What wouldn't I give for my father to be able to tell the whole story of this man? How many men and women of El Quiché had been executed on his decision! He was deeply involved in the repression there.

If I had known in 1988 what kind of individual he was, I would have died of shock. Yet when your life is at stake, you trust in your own innocence. Ignorance is bliss. I had no experience of the labyrinths of injustice. I thought he was just another *ladino*. I didn't even realise he was a judge.

Alcides started to question me, but I refused to make any statements without a defence counsel I could trust. I contacted the lawyers' association, and got no reply. I contacted the archbishop, and received no support. Finally I asked the procurator for human rights to help. He didn't have the courage to come himself, though his organisation was the only one represented.

— The University of San Carlos had provided a lawyer for Rolando Castillo Montalvo, but they didn't want to run the risk of defending me. What would it have cost them? Nothing. I was with Rolando, ours was the same case. Yet the university differentiated between us. It would only defend its own people. Perhaps it was because I was a woman, an indigenous woman, a self-taught peasant. Maybe it was just simple racism. If I had dared, I would have had a stream of questions for them.

— So no one came to defend me. I kept hoping that someone would help me before night fell, when I would be taken to prison. Just thinking about the night ahead terrified me.

In the end, I think that Uk'ux kaj, Heart of the Sky, and all the gods of my ancestors, came to my aid. The lawyer there to defend Rolando proved to be a courageous man. He waited until after five o'clock, when he stopped being paid by the university, and then he undertook to defend me on his own account. He was taking a terrible risk, for I was a political prisoner.

I have often expressed my gratitude for the bravery of this lawyer, Harold Vitelio Fuentes. He did not even charge for his services. He knew that I didn't have the university's support, but he acted out of humanity. To take a step like that without the backing of an institution can be a very serious matter in Guatemala. Extra-judicial execution has often been the fate of people who oppose the government, and death threats, intimidation and exile are reserved for those who defend them. How many lawyers must have died for taking a similar decision!

There were three charges against me. One was for public disorder offences in Nebaj, Cotzal and Uspantán, for organising peasants to rebel against the government and putting 'national security' at risk. Yet I had left Guatemala in 1980, and had just arrived from Geneva. Between 1980 and 1988, I had lived in Mexico. I had spent several of those years lobbying at the United Nations in Geneva and in different parts of the world, crossing every border except those into Guatemala.

A second charge was that I wrote Marxist-Leninist ideas, which were prohibited in Guatemala. This too was a threat to 'national security'.

The third charge was more serious. They accused me of collaborating with the guerrilla movement. They said that I had been training guerrillas in two countries, and had camps in Nicaragua and Cuba. They bestowed some rank or other on me, and I was suddenly promoted to 'commander' and 'military instructor'. Other people with similar charges against them had ended up tortured or murdered. Their bodies had been found in clandestine cemeteries, or left on the hillside to be eaten by animals.

The accusations were simply not credible. Thanks in some measure to the clumsiness with which the government handled the case – they made us famous in our own land – the reaction in Guatemala was one of indignation. Three thousand people came out on to the streets to demand our release. I met some wonderful people during this particular battle, strong pioneering women like Rosalina Tuyuc, an admirable Kaqchikel woman, and Nineth Montenegro, a very brave woman who was head of the Mutual Support Group (GAM) for the families of the disappeared. There were also many university students, young people fervently committed to the struggle, and people from trades unions and from human-rights groups. I met Byron Morales, a union leader.

The *compañeros* from the Committee for Peasant Unity, the CUC, also began to raise their heads above the parapet again. I don't know how they dared, since there was still a lot of fear. Yet there was a huge demonstration that afternoon.

The role played by the press in my support was also important. There are always some journalists that wear their pens out venting their racism, but our friends took the opportunity to break down barriers and topple certain sacred cows. We became quite famous in Guatemala. We would never have got such a wide coverage for our mission, for an explanation of the fundamental causes of our exile, had we not been arrested.

My lawyer was present when they questioned me. I was quite careful about what I said. First they accused me of belonging to an organisation that had incited peasants to rebel against the state, an organisation called the 'Committee for Peasant Action'. I said I had never heard of an organisation of that name. I said I was one of the leaders of the Committee for Peasant Unity, and one of their representatives abroad, but not of 'Peasant Action'. I stated quite plainly what I was, reaffirming my membership of the CUC.

At the end of the interrogation, I made it clear that I held the government responsible for my physical well-being wherever I was, inside Guatemala or outside Guatemala. I held it responsible for any type of violence committed against my person.

There were many witnesses. We had brought American senators and European members of parliament with us. It was a very important event. All we wanted to do was to alter the climate of fear that existed.

President Cerezo obviously had his hands tied. What happened to him happens to all politicians who come to the presidency poor and leave it rich. They do not even defend their professional honour. To get rich, they have to toe the line. This has happened to lots of politicians in Guatemala. They become prisoners. They swallow the bait provided by the economic and military sectors of the country – and end up completely hooked, like a jungle monkey who arrives free and wild and becomes domesticated. Their ambition is the medicine that cures their shame. It is the continuous sad story of the impossibility of governing the country. Their personal ambition is too great. They don't have enough courage or conviction to defend the presidency. They simply dissolve, like a spoonful of salt in water, as they pass into history.

The pressure exerted by friends in the international community, especially from Madame Danielle Mitterrand, was most welcome. It was the first time she had intervened. She phoned Guatemala, and was very indignant. President Mitterrand intervened as well. Many other people phoned, and put on the pressure. The affair caught the public imagination.

They had finished questioning us at seven p.m. We then had to wait for the judge's decision. At eight p.m, we were released. They wanted to apply their infamous 'amnesty'.

'Never,' we said, 'we will never accept the amnesty.' The amnesty was introduced specifically for criminals, for paramilitary killers. Its purpose was to allow soldiers involved in the repression and in successive military coups to go unpunished. No less than twelve amnesty laws were passed in ten years, and they all favoured the military. It was another plank in the counter-insurgency plan.

The amnesty had also been applied (unequally, I imagine) to the revolutionary movement, to guerrillas who wanted to give themselves up. They would be obliged to confess their crimes and agree to be used on television and radio, to wage psychological warfare on their former comrades-in-arms. The amnesty was for them too, though no one ever knew what happened to a so-called guerrilla after he had accepted it – if they killed him, if they gave him a house, or if he lived or died. We heard many testimonies about the army's infamous amnesties: how they would capture a suspect, torture him, and then make him confess to having been a guerrilla, even if he hadn't been one.

This was the same 'amnesty' that they offered to us. So we said: 'We aren't generals who stage coups, we aren't ex-guerrillas, we haven't come to wage psychological warfare, we aren't murderers, we aren't criminals. We refuse to accept an amnesty.' The judge insisted. We said no.

In theory, someone who takes advantage of an amnesty law does it voluntarily. He has committed a crime, and he wants the law to pardon him. Yet we had done nothing wrong.

The debate went on for hours. We stayed at the court until the judge finally just released us. He told the public that he had applied the amnesty to us, and they declared the proceedings a great success. It was an example of the kind of unbending arrogance that would not make amends for our illegal detention. Yet we emerged proud to be what we are. In the end, we were just some of the country's many victims, political prisoners with faces and lives. We were the first – living and breathing – political prisoners.

We went to a hotel, though we were still dreadfully afraid for our lives. We felt danger was close at hand. They had released us, purely and simply, so the risk seemed even greater. When we were in custody, we had some kind of guarantee. If something happened to us, it would be the government's responsibility. Now the case was over, the situation was very delicate. The people accompanying us didn't sleep much, and we didn't sleep at all. Every noise had overtones of terror.

I stayed in Guatemala at that time for seven days. My *compañeros* were there for eight. I left early because the situation was getting more risky by the day. An armed man was discovered in the hotel lobby. He was a *judicial*. They grabbed him and handed him over to the national police. We don't know what happened to him.

After that first brief stay in Guatemala, nothing could stop me. I was always finding reasons to go back. That is how, in 1991, we came to organise the second continental conference in Quetzaltenango in opposition to the official Quincentenary celebrations. That was the first massive gathering we had dared to stage in Guatemala. We came and went frequently; not every day of course, but at least three times a year.

So the occasion of the announcement of the Nobel Prize in 1992 was by no means the first time I had returned to Guatemala. I had already begun rebuilding. And I had good reason. In all the chasing around over the Quincentenary I met Angel, the man I am now married to. We had started working locally again, taking up the relentless fight for our land. My *compañeros* in the CUC were determined to rebuild our beloved organisation, although we could never recapture what it had been at the end of the 1970s and the beginning of the 1980s. In 1993, the first group of Guatemalan refugees returned from Mexico. They drove down the Panamerican

Highway, along which thousands of people had been killed, burned and massacred in the 1980s. Passing along it again reminded our people of the reason for their exile. Yet it was also cause to give thanks, and dream of a new life.

My personal decision to return for good in 1994 was due to the huge effort made by my *compañeros* here in Guatemala to convince me. They told me how important it was for me to come. In exile, you live, eat, sleep and dream Guatemala. Your reason for living is your love for that promised land. It is where the memory of your ancestors lies, the place where your childhood memories are. You idealise your country. Yet it was difficult for me all the same. Who would guarantee my safety, and the safety of my family?

All refugees know the immense solitude you feel in exile. Not physical solitude, because you share your daily life with thousands of people around you, but spiritual and cultural solitude. Being Mayan in Guatemala is the norm, it is in your home, on the corner, every day. Being Mayan in other countries is being an exception, you don't fit in. When I was in exile, I felt I was a nomad because I could never put down roots.

Yet I felt that Guatemala was always calling me. When can we go home? Tomorrow, next week, in five years' time? Sometimes we'd even say twenty years. When would be the best time to return? After thirteen years in exile, you have learned many things; you have many memories and many friends. In Mexico I had a big social life, with many friends not connected to politics.

To live in Guatemala is to live in a totally different world. When I agree with people, they will say that I'm an excellent *compañera*, an exemplary woman, a national heroine. When I make up my own mind, they will ignore me, saying that I'm undisciplined, even an enemy. I'm no longer a heroine. Life is hard in Guatemala. It's sometimes difficult to live in this country of mine.

Eventually we took the plunge and decided to return. We discussed it first at home, with all the family. My sister Anita was with us in Mexico by then.

After I received the Nobel Prize, I returned from Oslo to find her at my house with her two daughters, Maya Rigoberta and Juana María. She said, 'I have just come for a visit, I don't know what the future holds.' Anita had spent twelve years in the mountains after my mother's death. 'I'd like to share things with you,' she said, 'but I'm so used to life in the mountains.'

In the end, she decided to stay. She had been in refugee camps for the last two years, and I had had no idea where she was. I was pleased that she had already formed a family. I was happy not just to have found my sister again but to know that she wanted to come and live with me. My sister and her daughters are another reason for living. I love them dearly, they make my life more complete.

Anita and my husband both thought we should go back, but they wanted to take precautions. They love me dearly and couldn't bear anything to happen to me. It all happened very suddenly. One day we said, 'We're leaving in eight days' time.' We started packing our cases. We didn't wait for farewells or tributes or publicity. We left, and we arrived. It was an important day that was to change our lives yet again.

3

THE MASSACRE AT XAMÁN,
OCTOBER 1995

On the morning of 5 October 1995, I woke up with all my muscles aching unbearably. I was in the city of Madison on a speaking tour of the United States. I had had a horrible dream. It was a dream but also a premonition. Then there was this terrible pain. I said to Dorita, who was on the tour with me, 'I wonder how many children were born last night?' I didn't think of death, I thought of life. 'I wonder how many were born and if any were named after me. I feel as though I helped those mothers give birth during the night.'

I ached all over. We began a long day of the usual interviews and speeches, and eventually we went for lunch with a group of friends.

Many people, in different places, have told me that they rarely remember their dreams. I find this strange because ever since I was a little girl I have always remembered what I dream, and I reflect on it. In my distant memories of our hut in Laj Chimel, perhaps even before my sister Anita was born, I remember waking up in the morning and talking about my dreams.

One of my parents, usually my mother, would explain their meaning. She taught us that not all dreams can be told, and not all of them can be interpreted. Some dreams can only be told to the people closest to you; others you keep for yourself, in your heart, to remember and abide by the consequences. Dreams have been very important to me throughout my life; they have often made me reflect, worry and hope.

Over lunch that October day, we began talking about refugees and about Don Juan Coc, the respected leader of the refugees who had returned from Mexico to Guatemala, to the *finca* of Xamán in Alta Verapaz. We recalled his extraordinary zest for life, and the way in which he had combated a life-threatening disease to lead his people back home. He had died not long after, even before he had had time to enjoy his community's first harvest. It was a long conversation.

Then, between three and four in the afternoon, we began getting the first news of the massacre in Guatemala – at Xamán. I was stunned and worried. I felt shivery all over. I could not believe it. The painful news was soon flashing round the world.

My first reaction was of profound bitterness and indignation. I had wanted to believe that massacres and scorched-earth campaigns were now just tragic memories. Yet that day a Guatemalan army patrol had entered the community at Xamán and opened fire on people preparing to celebrate a festival. Eleven people died in this latest massacre of my country's poorest people, including two children. Twenty-five others were injured.

I have known the people of Xamán for twelve or thirteen years. I first met them when they arrived in Mexico as refugees. They had been walking for weeks over the mountains, without shoes, without food, without hope. They carried with them their children and their few belongings. They were fleeing from death. Many said they had buried children, husbands, wives, deep in the jungle on the mountain sides. Some had not even been able to bury them. Only God knows where their corpses lay. They told painful tales of how they had seen their houses go up in flames as soldiers destroyed all they had. All they brought with them was their dignity, their truth and their pride.

I met them as they were first beginning their life in the refugee camps in Mexico, a life of sadness, nostalgia and painful memories. As exiles, victims of war, they faced many years of work and struggle, and always longed for the day that they could return to Guatemala. One of the refugees was Don Juan Coc. I will never forget him. He was a K'eqchi' leader. More than a leader, he was a wise and sensitive man, a man of profound spirituality with unique gifts.

On 8 October 1992, representatives of the refugee organisations signed an agreement with the Guatemalan government allowing the exiles to return. We hoped that the return would be organised, safe and dignified. Don Juan was one of those who signed this agreement. His only wish was for his people to find land to live and work on, and he hoped that life would be normal and stable again. We supported him in his negotiations for the *finca* at Xamán, the place which his people had chosen as the most suitable for their needs.

The Guatemalan government did finally buy the land, but the negotiations were complicated. The brothers and sisters of the new community came from several different regions, and many would have preferred to go back to their own homes. They were from the Mam, K'eqchi' and K'anjobal peoples. They had to spend over a year in temporary accommodation before they could establish their own community; a place to safeguard memory for their grandchildren and for generations to come.

When they finally became the owners of the *finca* at Xamán, they baptised it the 'October 8 Dawn'. There was a tremendous sense of optimism. The Sacred Earth there can provide the people with a decent living: it produces maize and coffee, rubber and cardamom, and many other non-traditional products that do not harm the region's natural environment.

The Rigoberta Menchú Foundation was wholly committed to helping the settlement in Xamán. We worked with many fine and dedicated people, like the doctors from Spain's *Médicos del Mundo*, who organised urgently needed health care facilities. We had to provide education for children with triple identities. They were tri-lingual Mayan children; Mexican–Guatemalan or Guatemalan–Mexican; and they were also refugees with no roots anywhere. When they had first arrived in Mexico, they had asked, 'When are we going home?' Their parents had said, 'Very soon. We're just waiting for the situation to improve a little.' Their little wait was to become twelve or thirteen years in exile.

The two hundred families that returned from Mexico to Xamán found that over fifty K'eqchi' families had settled part of the *finca*'s land some time earlier. Some quite beautiful negotiations now ensued, until those who were living on the land, who were seen as squatters, and those who arrived as the new owners, came to a full agreement. Together they created the Mayan Union co-operative. We were fortunate enough to accompany our brothers and sisters on this road of hope. The message of reconciliation was clear and direct, although the Guatemalan army kept accusing the returned exiles of supporting the guerrillas, and the insurgents mistrusted the people who had minds of their own.

Our interest in Xamán did not begin with the horror of the massacre. We had worked shoulder to shoulder with most of those who died or were wounded. Perhaps that is why the pain was so deep. We asked the same question over and over again. Why?

Xamán had not been an area of armed struggle since 1985–86. It is a peaceful area, and those returning from exile avoided any kind of confrontation with their new neighbours. They offered to share the few resources they had – the school and the health centre – with the surrounding villages. Prior to their arrival, the army had helped to create a climate of tension and confrontation by telling the communities in Chisec (the municipality to which Xamán belongs) that the exiles were guerrillas coming back to restart the war, and were enemies. Yet common roots proved more powerful. The humility of our people, and the dire poverty of both communities, had slowly forged a peaceful relationship between Mayans sharing the same land.

Many misfortunes had befallen Xamán. Don Juan Coc, their guide, their *K'amal b'e*, had leukaemia, a ferocious illness which could easily have killed him years earlier. His strength lay in his commitment to lead his people back to their Mother Earth, where no one would be a foreigner, a refugee or a victim. He was very stoical. It is hard to imagine how a poor peasant, without access to frequent blood transfusions, with his leukaemia slowly taking over, was able to fight off the disease and finally return. Once his people were home, he said goodbye to them. His was the first corpse to bless the graveyard in Xamán.

A few months later, on 6 April 1995, there was a natural disaster. A hurricane took the roofs off all the humble houses, and blew away their few possessions, including the little corrugated iron that they had. It began at eight o'clock in the morning and lasted for three hours. Children were crying, dogs were howling, people were shouting. They were all bewildered. Nature had shown them its majesty, its aggression, its power. They spent a long night of complete helplessness and fear.

I talked afterwards to some of the leaders, and suggested that perhaps Mother Earth needed prayers and offerings. It would be a sort of commitment from all of them to respect their new land, their new community. They should have the humility to bless the earth like they used to in our old villages, burn their *pom* and candles, and offer *cuxa*. 'Ask Mother Earth's permission,' as our elders used to say.

Xamán eventually started to flourish. We had finished dividing the settlement's centre into individual lots, and telephones were being installed. We had been trying to find a better market for the rubber and cardamom produced by the co-operative, and we had started to build decent houses.

At the beginning of September, we met several community leaders and offered our support for a festival to celebrate the community's first anniversary on 8 October. There was to be a big fiesta, and we planned to invite representatives of returned exiles from the different regions and many of the neighbouring villages. They would be asked to play their *marimbas*. There would be football and other sports. Twelve children would be baptised into the Catholic faith, and some of the youngsters would be confirmed. It was all to happen on the day of the fiesta, and the ceremonies of thanksgiving were to begin the day before. Whenever we have this kind of celebration, the community takes the opportunity to change its leaders and reaffirm the nature of their role. Catechists, women and young people all come together. We were all sure it would be a memorable day.

Outside observers and institutions were watching the Xamán experiment to see if it could be a model for other returning refugees. First, because of the reconciliation aspect, and second, because of the speed with which the community had become organised. It might prove a model for the surrounding villages. The new arrivals had quickly begun providing health care for their neighbours who, when they came to get medicine from the new settlement, saw how, with awareness and effort, people can have a decent life. Many came to see for themselves the encouraging achievements of the 'October 8 Dawn'. There was a lot of optimism.

So the massacre, this incomprehensible new atrocity against an indigenous community trying to heal the wounds that had already been so cruelly inflicted on it, suggested some kind of Machiavellian act – an act of pure evil.

On Thursday, 5 October 1995, at about midday, most people in Xamán were going about their normal business. The fiesta committee was desperately trying to finish putting up a huge place in which people could dance. Suddenly there came the first inkling of the presence of armed soldiers in the community. Children coming out of school were the first to see them. Wherever soldiers appear they cause panic, especially among those who have already been victims of their bullying. Some women confirmed that a large group of soldiers had been seen walking through the forest surrounding the settlement. Four community leaders went out to talk to the soldiers, to ask them to leave. This was the first time in the year since the community was set up that the army had come into the *finca*, onto the private property of the co-operative.

The leaders found twenty-five soldiers in the forest, under the command of a lieutenant. The soldiers and the officer were all indigenous and young, like the village leaders themselves. Lieutenant Antonio Lacán Chaclán was told that by entering the *finca* without permission he was violating the Accord signed by the government and the refugees in October 1992. He said that they knew there was to be a fiesta, and they had come to join in.

The leaders asked the soldiers to leave the co-operative's land immediately. They explained that the community could not accept their presence as it would cause great fear. The officer refused their request, saying they had been invited to the fiesta.

Three older women then arrived. It was not right, they said, for the leaders to be talking to soldiers in the forest. They insisted angrily that they should all come to the centre of the settlement and speak to the whole community. So they all went to the centre.

People soon started converging on the central square, where the school was being built. Most were women and children. The leaders used a loudspeaker to call people from the various neighbourhoods, and slowly a crowd of about 250 to 300 people gathered. A Mam woman, a beautiful creative woman called Rosenda Sales, brought a camera. She took several photos of the children, the women and the old people, and of a few young men who formed a semi-circle around the armed soldiers. These photos are very sad. All of them, soldiers and settlers, are indigenous, blood brothers and sisters.

In the subsequent investigation, we discovered that several of the soldiers had been forcibly recruited when they were only fourteen or fifteen years old. The majority of soldiers were young, some barely more than children. The photos show weapons – rifles, machine guns, grenades – ready to be used against an unarmed and defenceless civil population. The frightened eyes of the children can be seen watching with curiosity the soldiers who, minutes later, would be their executioners.

The lieutenant repeated his argument, and the leaders insisted that the soldiers should leave the co-operative immediately. The women, some of whom were very angry, shouted that the soldiers should not leave until observers from the United Nations mission, MINUGUA, could arrive, to verify that the soldiers had breached the peace accord. Terrible memories flooded back into the minds of people who had survived the destruction of their villages thirteen years earlier. The shouting increased, especially from the women. Some demanded that the soldiers put their guns on the ground until the UN observers arrived.

The atmosphere got very tense in just a few minutes. Several witnesses confirm that they saw the patrol's leader communicate with someone by radio. A few moments later they say they saw him give his soldiers a signal with the red handkerchief he had round his neck.

That is when the massacre started. The soldiers began firing in all directions. The first to die were the women who were protesting. Pedro Medina, a much loved young leader, fell wounded and was shot on the ground as he tried to get up. A little girl of only seven, Maurilia Coc Max, was shot in the back as she ran towards her father who was desperately shouting at her to hide. The sound of two grenades exploding was heard among the cries of anguish and terror.

Three soldiers in the crowd of people fleeing in panic were shot in the legs by soldiers further away. They obviously did not care what happened to their comrades in the crowd. There were terrible images of women running among the bullets with babies on their back, holding other children by the hand. They were running all over the place trying to save their lives. Fernando Chop, a young schoolteacher of seventeen, was hit twice in the back as he ran to safety. Several of the wounded were shot on the ground as the lieutenant began shouting orders to withdraw. It seems as if it was not the first time they had shot dying people.

Most of the wounded tried to reach their houses. Some of the most serious cases dragged themselves to the Médicos del Mundo health centre. Though wounded in the foot, Rosenda managed to save the camera and the valuable photos. Someone looked at his watch. It was ten past two on a terrible afternoon; a new nightmare of blood, a new wound in the memory of a Mayan village. The soldiers were running about chaotically, firing indiscriminately into houses on their way.

As one group of soldiers was withdrawing, they came across Santiago Tut Pop, a K'eqchi' lad of about eight. Little Santiago had been fishing in a stream and was carrying a rod with a string. When he saw the soldiers he ran down the path towards his house. A first shot shattered his hand and forearm, but he kept running as he screamed with pain and called for his mother. A second shot hit his back and another smashed his head. Santiago died by the side of the path. Beside him lay his fishing rod.

Over and over again, the survivors and witnesses have told me of the terrible events of that day. Again and again, I have seen the victims and the community crying.

Eight corpses lay in the road at the centre of the massacre. Maurilia died in the clinic where they tried desperately to save her life. Santiago's little body lay by the path. Fernando Chop, the boy-teacher, died the next day in hospital. The final count: eleven dead and twenty-six wounded, on a day that had dawned with such joyful preparations for the fiesta. Two and a half hours later, the helicopters were flying in, and the image of our people's suffering was circling the world.

That night, as the helicopters transferred the wounded to hospitals in the capital, the ministry of defence published the government's version of events. With the utmost cynicism, General Mario Enríquez announced that a military patrol had been attacked by the people of Xamán. He made the absurd claim that certain aggressive women had taken the soldiers' guns and begun shooting indiscriminately with them. It was absurd because they did not know how to shoot. This, according to the shameless general, is what caused the dead and wounded. The general gave this account as if he had been there personally. Of course, nobody believed him, and his version of events only served to intensify the climate of revulsion created by this vile and savage act.

I immediately cancelled my speaking tour of the United States, and Dorita and I took the first plane back to Guatemala. I had asked Gustavo, our Foundation's director, to go to Xamán immediately and show our solidarity with the community in whatever ways he felt necessary. Early the next day, on 6 October, Gustavo found the bodies still lying where they had been shot. The scenes of grief and pain were heartrending. Whole families were crying beside their dead relatives as they prayed and lit candles. The bloody and senseless crime was etched on the minds of the children. Little Santiago was left by the side of the path as a terrible reminder of the extent to which the army had brutalised young soldiers. They will never be able to repay the harm they have done to their own people.

The public prosecutor and the judge of Chisec were soon collecting evidence – in a superficial and careless way. They did not tell the community how to protect and preserve proof of the massacre. They did not cordon off the area round the corpses. They jumbled together in one bag the many cartridge cases people had innocently collected and handed in. Gustavo asked the judge for his name and was surprised to find that it was Alcides, the same judge who had ordered my arrest when I first came back to Guatemala in 1988. Our paths crossed again, but this time in more terrible circumstances. This executioner–judge had obviously not changed much. Several testimonies show that he did all he could to wipe out the evidence of the massacre.

Something else happened that day which clearly reflects the mood of the Xamán community. Amid the general grief, the leaders consulted the victims' families and the rest of the community, and they took the decision to carry on with the preparations for the first anniversary celebrations. Life must triumph over death, they said. The fiesta would be the best way to tell those murderers that they had failed in their attempt to destroy the faith and hope of Don Juan Coc's people.

I arrived in Xamán after announcing that I would accept the community's request to represent them in the court case that was to be initiated. I told the press that we wanted both the perpetrators of the crime and those who had ordered it to be punished under the law. I reiterated this to the community when the long-awaited 7 October finally dawned.

I will never forget the baptism ceremony for the twelve babies alongside the coffins of the murdered victims. Tears were shed for injustice and death, while at the same time thanks were offered to the Heart of the Sky and Earth for the miracle of life. The coffins were covered in flowers and surrounded by candles. Women and children wept. Some prayed aloud, some burned *pom*, others sang hymns or stood in silence. All this took place in an exceptionally beautiful place: a small valley of rolling hills and innumerable streams, surrounded by jungle-covered mountains, and alive with the cries of parrots and macaws and the screeching of the *saraguate* monkeys. The ceremony sealed the bond of commitment between this humble Mayan woman and that model community.

Getting involved in this private prosecution – co-accuser is the technical term – was not an easy decision for me to take. I knew it was a big responsibility and I would be running a considerable risk. I would have to face a corrupt and inefficient judicial system, and I would also be challenging the army head on. Many people thought it was a lost cause from the start.

I thought about it a lot, listened to other people's opinions, and asked for advice. I had to do it for many reasons; for the victims' right to justice, because this was the first time we had been able to take those responsible for a massacre to court; and for the moral obligation to fight injustice and to ensure that such outrages do not go unpunished. Perhaps even more important in the long term was the aim of educating people in the need to reform and strengthen the rule of law. I have fought injustice all my life, but it is a different matter to have the courage to go day after day from one court to another, presenting brief after brief, reading and applying – paragraph by paragraph – the articles of the Penal Code and the Constitution.

At the time of writing, a year and a half has passed since the massacre at Xamán. The court case is still going on, and there is no guarantee we will get justice in the end. Our steps have been dogged with threats, obstacles and traps. We have fought military privilege, and we have won. They have made our life impossible, but we have not allowed them to be the judge of their own crimes. The case will be tried in a civil court. We have come up against corrupt judges and courts used to kow-towing to the powerful and selling justice to the highest bidder.

We have had to overcome the tricks of defence lawyers who for years have twisted the law to ensure their defendants' crimes go unpunished. By carrying out our own investigations, we have fought the disappearance and destruction of evidence by military organisations and officials charged with dispensing justice. We have had to hire advisers and technical experts of our own to contradict the errors and omissions of others. We have incurred debts to cover the cost of a long and complex court case. Yet I want to pay tribute here to some of those state prosecutors and honest judges with whom we have faced these difficulties. Threats and provocation have become commonplace to them in what has become one of Guatemala's most controversial legal cases.

Despite everything, we have gradually achieved the objectives we set ourselves. We formed the Alliance Against Impunity with other brothers and sisters fighting the same battle for justice. It has given us the strength to carry on. The community in Xamán, and especially the survivors of the massacre, have kept alive the spirit of Don Juan Coc. They continue to work optimistically for the future, and believe we will eventually win our court case. On the site of the massacre, they have built a fine school with six classrooms, which the children of the community attend in two daily sessions. It is the only way to ensure the victims of the massacre are not forgotten.

From a legal point of view, we have achieved several important things. We have struck a frontal blow at military privilege. For the first time in Guatemalan history we have brought the perpetrators of a massacre to court. We have made 'extra-judicial execution' a crime in the statute books. We have got some of the soldiers – and the officer in charge – sent back to prison. (Earlier, they had been conditionally released by a corrupt judge. We got this judge removed, although we did not manage to get him punished.) One by one we have avoided the tricks and traps laid for us by the military defence lawyers. I am convinced that all this effort will help to build the Guatemala that we have dreamed of for so long.

I cannot be sure that we will defeat impunity in this case or that we will get justice for the victims. I do not know if we will be able to identify and punish those who planned the massacre. Yet I do know that all this effort has been worthwhile, that there are many of us – the majority – men and women, indigenous and non-indigenous, who want an end to injustice. That is a dream I have had many times before.

4

THE LEGACY OF MY PARENTS
AND MY VILLAGE

The last time I had gone home to Laj Chimel, before going to other parts of Guatemala and finally into exile, was early in October 1979. I arrived without warning and I did not stay long. It was soon after my brother, Patrocinio, had been detained, tortured and killed. My mother was absolutely devastated by his death. When she saw me coming she began to weep bitterly. Not just for the joy of seeing me safe and sound, but to tell me of her terrible grief after the soldiers had killed one of her children – by burning him alive. She was petrified, because she realised that I too was in great danger of being kidnapped. She feared she might lose another child. She was a mother, and her children were her whole life.

The situation in Chimel had become so bad that most families had begun fleeing to the mountains, to sleep in the ravines, to keep watch over the village day and night. Most families were living in terror, fearing that any minute the soldiers would come.

I was twenty years old in October 1979. A new counter-insurgency

campaign had begun. Its main destructive effect was on the lives of indigenous peasants in the rural areas. The hardest things were the intimidation, the destruction of the land, the persecution of our community leaders, the use of torture, and the army's introduction of the Civil Defence Patrols (PACs) which gradually took over our communities. Soon the whole countryside was under the control of the military. My beloved father, Vicente Menchú Pérez, was still alive then, though already, as a result of his thirty-year struggle for our land in Chimel, he was being hounded and receiving death threats. At that time, he was in hiding in another part of Guatemala.

There is nothing worse than living under the constant threat of persecution. My mother's fears were shared by the whole community. I had so little time with her, yet those few hours in my own home made up for the years I was to spend away on the long path of experience. A strange, mysterious destiny awaited me and my mother seemed to sense it. I wanted to devote my whole life to Chimel, and I was committed to the struggle. 'Find somewhere to go,' my mother said. 'You can't hide here.' I felt powerless to ease my mother's pain. It was not possible, even by being there with her. I was so afraid of losing her.

I will never get over the trauma of having left my mother so shortly before her death. It was my last chance to feel a mother's warmth. If I had known, I would at least have paused to look at her, to gaze at her face for the last time. I would have tried, to the very last, to learn more about her. All I could think of in my misery was that I had to go away. There are no words to describe that moment.

I shall never forget Mama fetching a little jar and taking out a red necklace, a medallion of the sun and five *quetzales*. She dropped it all in my hands, looked towards the rising sun and closed her eyes. She wept as she prayed. Then I left. My little sister, Anita, ran after me, crying too. I did not turn back to look at her. I had a premonition I would never see my mother, my little sister or my entire community again. I was almost certain. Never again would I see the humble village where I was born and grew up, where the elders taught us the meaning of the different kinds of birdsong, the meaning of darkness, the place where I learned what it meant to be a descendant of the Mayans of Guatemala.

My mother stayed behind alone with Anita, the *ch'i'p*, the baby of the family. She followed my mother everywhere, still too young to be parted from her. My brothers Víctor and Nicolás, my sister Lucía and many of our community leaders had already gone into hiding. My mother was the one who stayed in the village. She was brave and strong. What was happening was strange and new. Our family was broken up for the first time, so was our entire community and its customs. No one knew how long they would live, and, if they lived, how long they would be away from Chimel.

Some neighbours smuggled me out of Chimel and we set off towards Santa Cruz del Quiché, and walked all through the night. Going through Uspantán was difficult. The neighbours with me were afraid of the soldiers billeted in the village, and we had no choice but to head off for another village, called Cunén. It was raining, torrential rain, typical Chimel weather. It rains for nine months of the year. On some parts of the track, the mud was waist-deep. It poured all night and we were drenched. The cold was unbearable. It was hard to tell the difference between the pain of exhaustion and cold, and the pain of walking towards a wholly new destiny. It is one of the experiences engraved deepest in my memory.

Whenever I thought about my mother, and remembered that last evening together, I was filled with longing and pain. Yet at the same time I could feel the mud, the rain, the sadness. I breathed in the spirit of those thick clouds, the spirit of that wet earth, along with the ugly sensation of fear. Ever since that time, I have had a utopian vision, a determination to go home and live in that little hut in Chimel. I have seen it many times in my dreams, just as I left it. When I dream of my mother, I always have the same feeling. I can feel the fire, the wood, the atmosphere, the sense of a whole life that can never be recovered.

I wish I could have worked some kind of miracle to have my mother with me when Papa died. I felt an almost telepathic communication with her. I tried to guess whether my way of dealing with Papa's death would be the same as hers. When my father was about to die, I dreamed of a little room full of light and heat. He was wearing strange clothes. He looked sad. He told me, 'Take great care of yourself because I am no longer with your mother. We are no longer together.' Then, weeping with sadness, I replied 'But why, Papa? I believe in you and I believe in Mama. We shall only be happy if the two of you are together.'

'You must trust me,' he replied. It was only a dream. Three days later he was dead.

When my mother died, I had a similar dream. I dreamed that I was coming down the hill of Cholá, the crag on the hillside near our village. I saw my mother coming up the hill. She was carrying a heavy basket on her head. Suddenly I saw that the basket was full of rotten meat. I was terrified. About five days after my dream, I heard that my mother had been abducted and was being tortured at the army barracks in Xejul. I knew then that she would not come back.

At the time, I believed that my sister Anita had died with my mother. 'M'in,' she had said to me, 'you are all leaving, but I'm staying with Mama. If they kill us, I shall die here with Mama.' It was a year later before I found out that Anita had survived. She was moved from house to house by people in the districts of Nebaj and Cotzal, and then in El Soch. People took care of her. She never revealed her identity. She did not say that she was a daughter of the Menchú family, although some people knew. She simply went from one house to another, and then back to our own little house. Whenever she could, she would let out the horses and the other animals, and then go back to her hiding place. The few people who had survived were frightened to venture back to their huts. They preferred to hide in the ravines. I felt so helpless when my little sister told me the terrible things she had gone through. At the same time as we faced the terrible truth of the death of my parents, our home and family was broken up, and we had to abandon our culture and traditions. For those of us who survived, this was a real point of no return.

I have discovered much more about my mother over the years since her death. Gradually I have begun to realise that she was far greater than the person that I had known. She was a wonderful woman with many most admirable qualities. She was a midwife and a healer, and possessed many of the virtues of our ancestors. She had brought us up well. I understand that now that she has gone. She was right when she said that her hands were large and invisible. With those hands, she brought babies into the world, naked and confused, and dragging a great umbilical cord. We are born into empty space, and our first contact with the world is with the hands of a mid-wife, and the umbilical cord passes from those hands to be buried in the earth so that it takes root. This is what Mama and our elders told me.

Mama was born into a very odd family. I actually have the same name as my grandmother, not the Rigoberta which I use now; I have only been called Rigoberta Menchú Tum since 1979. My real name, and my grand-mother's, is M'in. My nephews and nieces and all my relatives call me M'in. That's how they know me in Chimel and in Uspantán. When I was born, my father did not have time to register me at the municipal offices. He didn't get around to it for several days. When he went to the office, the offi-cials wouldn't accept the name of M'in. They gave him a list of saints' names, and he chose Rigoberta. I don't know why he chose it. None of my family could ever pronounce it, especially Mama. She always said 'Beta' or 'Tita'. At home, they always called me M'in.

When I was eighteen, my father had a real problem to establish my iden-tity. He went to the offices to ask for the birth certificate of his daughter M'in. They told him that nobody was registered under that name. When he insisted that I was born at eight o'clock in the morning on 4 January, the officials said that no Menchú Tum was born on that date. He had to pay sev-eral fines until he found the name of Rigoberta Menchú Tum, born on 9 January, and names corresponding to the surnames of Mama and Papa. They assumed that this was indeed me, and my legal identity was estab-lished. So that's what they called me.

My umbilical cord was burned. My mother burned it with my compan-ion, the placenta. This is a tradition. We believe that we belong to Mother

Earth and that the earth is sacred. At the same time, a human being should be born free and independent. The earth is our mother because we eat maize that comes from the earth, and Mother Earth accompanies our every step. She is our shadow, our *nawaal*, our personality, our double, our twin soul that will always belong to nature. She is our guardian who protects us and watches over everything we do. She forgives us our mistakes and punishes us for our sins, so that we can grow and set a good example to others. Burning the umbilical cord and my companion is in itself a symbol of our independence. It is like being born again.

There is a reason for burying the umbilical cord. It is as if my cord were my sole link with the energy and life force of Mother Earth. When the umbilical cord is burned it is as a tribute to the natural world. The smoke pays homage to Mother Earth. It is fire, it is energy. It is the union of every man with his environment, of every woman with hers. The umbilical cord will always be the source of energy and life for every human being.

Most people never even think about what might have become of their umbilical cord. I don't criticise them for that. I am simply proud that mine is in Chimel, that it is a part of the mountains of Chimel and Guatemala, shading the ravines and keeping the paths company.

My brothers and I were treated equally in our family. We were also loved equally, although I was the one who accompanied my father as he went about his business. My family didn't follow all the traditional rules. Usually, in indigenous families, the first son is named after one of the grandfathers, preferably the paternal grandfather. The first daughter is named after one of her grandmothers. My brother Nicolás was named after my grandfather, but although I am only the second daughter, I was named after my grandmother. The two people who carry the memory of our grandparents are Nicolás and myself.

Traditionally, we also believe in the duality of life. Even numbers are supposed to be sacred. Yet my parents chose odd numbers. Our family has three people with the same name. I don't know why.

My grandfather was from Chiquimula. In Guatemala, the Chiquimulas are like Gypsies in other parts of the world. They lost their land about 150 years ago. It was part of the province of Totonícapan. Many of them still live in Santa María Chiquimula, but most of them wander around Guatemala. They speak their own language. They wear red-and-black clothes: a red-and-black *huipil* and a hand-woven *corte* with a multi-coloured fringe round the middle. They wear lots of ribbons in their hair and a red necklace, like the red necklace that I have kept with me all these years, my only necklace that marks the passage of time. It's the red necklace of the Chiquimulas.

Their faces are much darker than other peoples'. They have dark skin and prominent cheekbones, so Chiquimulas never go unnoticed. They were the most despised ethnic group. When my grandmother, a pure K'iche', from a very respected family called the K'otoja's, married a man named Tum, which is a Chiquimula surname, there was a terrible row. My grandfather was not accepted by my grandmother's family. They had to do something that goes against the usual custom and tradition, asking for the girl's hand and going through the long ritual that leads up to the wedding. They simply ran away from the family. As they say in our language, '*Xralq'aj rali*', which means he stole his wife.

That's how they ended up in Uspantán. My grandfather said that he saw his first child buried in Uspantán cemetery. When they arrived in Uspantán, they saw that the people there had some very strange customs. My grandfather had a very deep sense of his own cultural identity.

The Chiquimulas have still not died out. They have no land, they have no place of their own. Everywhere they are treated with contempt, and people think they are lazy. They take over a patch of land to set up a market, to sell a few things. They always stay together. They have never given up their traditional dress, even though other ethnic groups discriminate against them.

When I say ethnic groups, I mean all the ones in Guatemala, both non-indigenous and indigenous peoples. We sort of wanted to hide our identity when we were little, and even when we were teenagers, because everybody used to laugh at us. When they wanted to insult us, they called us

'Chiquimulas'. It wasn't a serious insult, not like when a *ladino* tells his pet dog to 'stop behaving like an Indian'.

Our childhood was different from that of today's young. We learned to enjoy nature. It still fills me with a sense of wonderment and great strength. I remember the feeling of cold and the season when there are mushrooms everywhere. We used to go from one end of the forest to the other, searching for a special kind of mushroom, the most delicious kind, the one that tastes like chicken breast. *Moo* was our equivalent of meat. It was a delicacy we never missed when it was in season. Along the track we used to find *slip*, *xik'in mam* and *ra'q masat*, all the kinds of mushroom you can make into a delicious meal. It was so cold!

I remember too the mud and the wet feet. We got 'split paws' as they used to say in the village. During the rainy season people suffer a lot from foot infections. It was so painful. You had to keep burning them, because the next day you would have to go out again barefoot in the wet and the cold and the mud.

If it was sunny for a week, Mama would cure us so quickly that we were soon as good as new, and could start all over again. She knew how to treat illnesses with natural remedies. She taught us *xe'xew*, a cure for minor ailments and the evil eye, *saqchooq* for bad stomach aches, and tender stalks of *chilacayote* leaves to burn the sores on the feet caused by the mud. We were never without *k'a q'elles* for stomach chills or hunger pangs. We used to sleep with wet clothes, and they were often still wet when we got up in the morning.

You never forget those feelings. My grandfather always used to tell us wonderful stories about prophesies and mysteries. One day I would like to put them all together, to tell people the way our elders did things, although I realise it would never be the same.

I also remember the tricks my brother Patrocinio and I used to get up to. We were very close. We learned to help each other when we were little. When he was born I was still being breast-fed and we shared Mama's milk. She would feed him first, and I would have what was left. I remember how we would steal *panela* from home and then go off into the hills to pick mulberries. We would spend all day eating them. Afterwards my mother would say, 'Why aren't you eating?' Looking at our tongues, she would know perfectly well that we had been eating mulberries. What she didn't know was that we had eaten mulberries with *panela*. Patrocinio is the one I remember most from my childhood. We were always together, we grew up together, we shared our fears.

Because of the conditions we lived in, we always had worms in our stomachs. Mama always had *sik'aj* to get rid of them. When tending the sheep, we used to climb trees, although little girls weren't supposed to climb trees. If my mother caught me, she would smack me with a peach-tree branch.

I also remember fear and darkness. I was scared of the dark, of a bird's song, of the way a sound moved. It might have been the K'ox, the dwarf who rides horses at night, the one who plaits horses' tails. I was afraid it was a bad omen, a sign that bad times were coming. I was afraid of animals passing on a bad message. Yet I was never afraid of human beings before I left Chimel – and discovered the fear of soldiers.

Dreams are such a deeply mysterious part of our lives that we can never shake them off. Only animals can see things that exist far beyond human experience. Sometimes, when I'm in a big city I look up at the birds, flying around a hotel perhaps, and I feel uneasy. I feel the same fear I used to have in Chimel. People who live in cities are so strange. They don't know each other at all. When I left Chimel, I took with me bags full of memories.

Patrocinio and I often used to watch for hours as the *zompopo* ants ran backwards and forwards, storing their food, making a communal home. When I look now at a big city, it often reminds me of those ants, though ants don't go around killing each other. They aren't dangerous and maybe they aren't even resentful. Maybe they are better organised than we are. I don't think about them every day, but sometimes they come to mind, just like that. They are with me, quite simply, like a shadow at my side.

Ancient cultures have always recognised the sources of energy from

Mother Earth, sources we can never completely understand. We regard bees as sacred, because they are so fierce. They are creatures that sting, and no one could survive being stung by a hundred bees. Yet they are also as sweet as honey, for although they are fierce animals they also live together collectively, in a community.

Many myths surround bees. They say that bees that live in remote places where there are no chemicals are not domesticated, the rules of nature are unbroken, and they exist very much like a family, united, with the solidarity of a community. One day, when we were still living in Chimel, the queen bee, the one that never leaves her nest, came into our hut. My mother was scared stiff. She thought it might be a bad omen for the family. She was so worried that she prayed and burned some *pom*. She was trying to counteract the omen. We caught the queen bee, and Mama held her so gently as she put her back in her hive. Two days later four hives of bees flew away. Four queen bees left.

We tried to make them come back by making a noise with hoes and machetes. We wanted them to stay. We wanted to appease them. When a whole hive of bees flies away, it's because they are annoyed, because an ant has got into their honeycomb. Yet they usually come back. You pick up the hive, stick it up a nearby tree and then you make a new one. You make a noise with machetes and hoes and burn some *pom*. You pick up the whole honeycomb and put it in their new home. That's what we did to make more bees. When there are a lot of them and there are two queens fighting in the honeycomb, you take out some of the honeycomb, you find a convenient place in a tree close to the house and put it there to attract them. They are like people who need to have a demonstration to solve a major housing problem. You make a new hive and a new family settles there.

This time they took no notice. Swarms of bees gradually left. They disappeared among the clouds above the house. Who knows where they were heading. They finally settled in a nearby tree. When we followed them and tried to keep them there with smoke from the *pom*, they took off again and went to find somewhere else to settle. So, little by little, they flew further and further away from the house. We were all very sad, as if someone had died. Nearly every day we had to chase another swarm of bees, until one day all the bees had gone.

This was just a month or two before my brother Patrocinio fell into the hands of the army. My mother cried every time she went out. She went to the place where the bees had been, and she cried. Bees were very important to us during Holy Week. That was the time when we collected the honey. We always had plenty of honey at home. We got stomach ache from eating so much. We used to share it with our neighbours. We would exchange a little jar of honey for the friendship of the community. We would make a present of an eighth or a quarter of honey to people in the little villages roundabout. It was a custom. That's why it was so sad when the bees flew away. Most of all it was because my mother was very worried, although, like all mothers, she tried not to show it. When my brother was taken away, my mother interpreted it as a message from the bees telling us that the family was about to break up.

On the morning Patrocinio left home, my mother said that first she heard the *xo'ch*, the bat, singing, and then the *tucur*, the eagle owl. It sang at dawn, at three in the morning when Patrocinio went to get his horse to ride with my mother to town. When that bird sang, my mother said, 'Don't come with me. Stay at home, son!' Mama thought he would be safer in the house. My brother wouldn't stay, perhaps because his fate was already sealed.

'I'm telling you to stay at home,' my mother said, but Patrocinio would not listen. My mother wasn't really sure if he would be more at risk if he stayed at home or if he was on the road. Night after night she had dreamed of the shadow of evil. She had seen the signs. You never knew whom the message was for, although Mama was most afraid for Patrocinio. She just couldn't decide what to do. So they went to town.

There they sold all their stuff, and everything was fine until the moment they said goodbye. Patrocinio was going to see his girlfriend who lived near the town. My mother told him, 'Be very careful and come home soon.'

She started climbing the Cholá hill, the hill I remember so well, a really steep hill that takes two and a half hours to climb. As she went up the hill, my mother said she had a very strong feeling and she remembered how afraid she had been when she heard the *tucur* singing at daybreak.

Patrocinio never came back. He was kidnapped by the army. During all that time Mama and the family had terrible premonitions, they had many bad or strange messages that something dreadful would happen. The dogs howled and howled, the bees flew away, and other things happened. We knew there were bad times ahead, but nobody knew what that would mean.

If we had realised how special our parents and grandparents really were, if we had seen the world differently, we would have had fifty thousand questions to ask them. But you cannot change history, you can't go back. We would have to be born again, learn everything over again. I'm sure we will be born again to have another chance.

My world was Chimel, Uspantán, the paths I ran along when I was a child (if ever I really felt a child). The mountains, my people, the animals, the land. Those years were so short, I don't know where they went. They went by so fast!

My world was so big and yet so small. When I first saw Guatemala City, I found it big and ugly. Then I saw Mexico City, and I found that terrifying! It was like a dangerous jungle. Now I know nearly all the streets because I have walked along them. I can't drive, but I can direct a driver round the city. When I crossed other frontiers and got to know other cities, I thought I must be imagining things.

As I have got to know other peoples, I have learned to admire their basic values, and the way they struggle for their rights. I have gained some understanding of their dreams for the future. I admire the way they have managed to survive and achieve more than just eating and sleeping. There is more to life than that, there are a whole lot of things in between. Life is greater and more intense than that.

Some very weird things happened to my mother. In my book *I, Rigoberta Menchú*, I said that there were secrets I would not divulge, and I kept some parts of our culture very secret. I still stick to that decision. Many people have changed our history. Many people have written about us, theorised about us and analysed us. They study us over and over again. They have studied us for centuries. And many of them have even usurped our knowledge. I think it is humiliating when they use us as experiments for their research. I didn't want to reveal any secrets, since some people might like to make fun of what we say, but I will tell just one.

When my mother was very young, she lived in a town called Cholá. That's where her parents lived. One day she was out tending the sheep. According to our elders, especially the tradition of my Chiquimula grandfather, the natural world has masters. We call them *Rajaaw juyub'*, and we also talk about '*el encanto*'.

El encanto is the moment when men and women fail in their duty to Mother Nature. When they ignore moral values and don't show respect for their *nawaal*. Then the Master of the Earth makes his presence felt. He is the *Rajaaw juyub'*, the Master of the World, the Master of Nature, the Heart of the Universe, the guardian of all living things. He is the shadow of us all, our *nawaal*, and can appear to us. He may appear as a beautiful bird. He may take over the body of a pheasant or a *quetzal*, a hummingbird or a rooster. He may take the shape of any beautiful creature, or appear as a creature no one has seen before. He appears to a chosen person, not to just any member of the community.

When he appears, you mustn't make a fuss about it. You have to remember the message and know how to pass it on to one of the village elders, so that they can advise anyone who has had this good fortune. You mustn't try to touch him because he is ferocious and angry, and he might kill you or make you disappear down a ravine. People believe it's a sign of time, an omen, a signal, and a very sacred message.

One day my mother had gone to tend sheep. She took them to the Cholá hill and, on the way, she found a new-born piglet. My grandfather hated pigs, he said he would never have a pig in the house. Mama picked up the piglet and took it with her. She knew that if my grandfather found it he would punish her. So she put it in the *temascal* and fed it in secret. Every time she went out to tend the sheep she took the piglet with her, wrapped in her shawl. It grew and grew, and soon it couldn't go on sleeping in the *temascal*. It grew so fast that my grandfather found out. He was so furious that he told my mother that either she would have to leave, and take the piglet with her, or he would kill it.

My mother was very upset and she didn't know what to do with the pig. She left it in the corral with the sheep. At nine that night, the dogs began to bark. They barked and barked as if the *coyotes* had come down from the mountains. In fact, the *coyotes* did get into the corral and, of all the animals there, the only one they took was the piglet.

When it started to squeal, my mother came out, and my grandfather used to say that at that moment a chill ran down his spine. My mother followed her piglet, and suddenly the dogs did not want to go any further. When dogs are frightened, they stand still and nothing can shift them. They just howl with frustration. It's as though they were pleading for something. This is what happens to dogs when there is a bigger or more powerful animal around that might harm them, or when there is something that is more than their animal instinct can handle.

My mother wanted to continue. The *coyotes* were moving towards a mysterious hill. My grandfather felt his blood freeze; he was terrified he was going to lose his daughter. He thought that this was a powerful premonition of what was going to happen to her. From then on, he was full of remorse, for he had tried to prevent his daughter from doing something that made her happy.

Something very strange happened at the end of his life. We had gone to the little shack where he spent half his time. We called it 'El Aguacatál'. It was a little plot of fertile land in the middle of the hills and rocks. On the edge of the plot, there was a rock that my grandfather used to make a fire, to stop the racoons and other animals from digging up the maize seed. When the maize was growing, and the cobs were starting to form, my grandfather would stay there for ages. That was the time when the animals, the wild pigs, and the wild boar would come, and the racoons would return. Birds would come too, *chocoyos*, parakeets, flocks of *k'el*. They would destroy the baby corncobs.

My grandfather would stay there with his catapult, shooting in the air above the maize. He set traps all over the place, but animals are smart and he hardly ever trapped anything. He lived there, under a rock. All he needed was a plastic sheet, and this was his home. At night, he would make up a fire. When the harvest was done, he would come back to Chimel and the animals would move in and live under the same rock. We never knew exactly what kind of animals lived there. They may have been ocelots or lynxes, who knows? We used to spend time there as well, especially at harvest time. We picked the maize and beans.

Then one day a pig appeared, a great big, red sow, with a very long, wide snout. She had a piglet with her, quite a large one. For my mother, this immediately brought back all those memories. They were so deep and so strong that she was almost convinced that it was an omen. She tried to catch the beast, but it was impossible. It was too huge. In the end, they had to chain it up.

We went from house to house asking neighbours whose it was, but nobody kept pigs that large. Nobody had lost two pigs like that. So when our stay at 'El Aguacatál' was over, we took the sow back to Chimel.

She gave birth to four litters. When she had her first lot of babies, we had to make her a sty with large planks, for she used to chew through the wood and would sometimes escape. When she got out of the sty, nobody could catch her. She was stronger than a mule. We had a dog, an alsatian, and he was the only one that could persuade her to go back to the sty. Who knows why?

There were twelve piglets in the first litter, and my mother supervised the birth as she had supervised the birth of human babies. At around two in the morning, the sow started to show signs that she was about to give birth. My mother took the piglets one by one, moving them so that their mother would not roll over and flatten them with her huge body. The little ones had homes to go to because they had been allotted to neighbours even before they were born. People came from Pinal, Caracol, Soch, Chicamau, from the orchards, from all over the place, asking for piglets.

About six months before all the trouble started, before we had to leave the village for good, the sow had her last litter. When she had finished giving birth, she went mad. She grabbed the piglets one by one and tore them to bits. My mother had to escape from the sty because the pig had gone crazy. We ran and borrowed a shotgun. We had to kill the pig and bury it. We didn't eat the meat because of the way it had died. None of the elders could explain what had happened. My mother was very alarmed. She said it probably was a punishment for selling the piglets before they were born.

My mother always believed that things should be allowed to happen naturally, that they shouldn't be forced. Not everybody receives the marks of time or the signs. Not everybody has to live by the signs they are given. Maybe they are chosen by the universe. Maybe they are chosen by the times they live in. Maybe they are chosen by something beyond our understanding.

When my mother was alive I never managed to understand her completely. I may have admired many things about her, but I didn't understand or imitate her. I didn't learn from her intuitively. Maybe her wisdom was hidden. All those mysteries she told us about came from her own life and experience.

Only in the last twelve years have I realised what she was. For me, she is a constant teacher. Every time things go wrong for me, I always ask myself how she would have coped. I know she would have dealt with things calmly, realistically, simply. She wouldn't have rushed about making a fuss. She is still my teacher today, in ways I can't really define. I can't explain it. I think she is my subconscious, and she solves problems I could never solve on my own.

When I dream of my mother, it's something very special. It makes be feel young again, full of energy and enthusiasm, all peaceful inside. I always remember her saying to me 'You can't fool me, my girl. I'm your mother. I brought you into the world. You can fool your brother, your sister, your friends, but you can never fool your conscience. Your conscience knows the truth.'

Perhaps I idealise my mother, but I believe it is important to idealise mothers because they are the ones who gave us life. It makes us much humbler.

When I recorded the tapes for my book *I, Rigoberta Menchú*, I was still in a state of shock. I was incapable of tackling the subject of my mother. I talked about my father and how I grew up more by his side, but that does not mean my mother meant less to me. I tried many times to talk about her but I couldn't overcome my grief. My relationship with the two of them was so deep! I hardly mentioned her in my first book because the pain of her death was so immense. I didn't give her the space she deserved. She was so brave, so great, so strong.

When they killed her, they didn't just murder a woman, a mother; they also murdered a healer, a midwife, a woman of great knowledge, a carer. Whenever I think of the struggles and the history of my people, whenever I claim my physical and spiritual identity, I admire my mother more and more. I will never stop grieving for her. The hurt cannot be repaired. I wanted to write something but I never finished it.

It's the same with Chimel. I want to write a poem about Chimel. I start a wonderful poem, recalling the rivers, the animals and the stories, and I finish the poem without even mentioning Chimel. I never finish it.

On 20 February 1994, I had a dream about my father. I dreamed he was in Guatemala, in a wonderful place, like a coffee plantation, a place where there were flowers. Papa said, 'Let me help you build this.' I saw a huge building, like a castle. He said again, 'Let me help you build this.'

I doubted if it could be done, so I said, 'Wait, Papa. You can't finish building it on your own.' He replied, 'Trust me, let me try, because it is not being built in the right way. Let's build it together.' I felt sad, and I said, 'All right, Papa. I'll let you build it and I'll help you as much as I can.'

Then I climbed up onto a ridge and watched my father from above. He started to work with so much energy, with so much enthusiasm and pleasure that it reminded me of the time when he was getting the seeds ready to sow. I was on the ridge in the shade of a big tree watching my father work.

After that dream, I went on thinking about it for at least two or three days. It kept coming back to me. It followed me wherever I went. I was absolutely certain that my Papa's message was not a bad one. It made me feel contented and secure. I felt him close to me, watching over me. I think he really loved life.

My mother is a symbol of women and of indigenous peoples. She personifies two kinds of discrimination. Women and indigenous peoples have both been mistreated. It is a debt that cannot be repaid, because there are ills that can never be undone. Yet I have every hope that women and indigenous peoples will come into their own one day, perhaps at another point in history. There will come a time when we are not the most underprivileged. There will come a time when we play a major role.

I am no philosopher. I am simply a granddaughter of the Mayans – not even a daughter, because a daughter is closer. I'm a grandchild of the Mayans and I believe that some day things will be different. Women now have influence in many spheres. Ordinary women have challenged dictatorships, and perhaps they can go on to challenge injustice all over the world.

Women are the mothers of the 'disappeared', the mothers of street children, the mothers of young people destroyed by drugs. They are also the mothers of people who destroy the land. How can they not suffer, how can they not feel?

The national liberation movements in Central America gave women a major role. There was an obvious need to re-establish values, to fight for social change, and to make legitimate claims. The human rights issues – the equitable distribution of land, the struggle against exploitation, discrimination and racism, a just distribution of human resources to serve society, the gulf between rich and poor – these are all still a major challenge to the human race. None of this will be cured by development schemes whereby experts show up with plans under their arms, saying, 'Here is the scheme you've been dreaming of.'

The liberation movements took a different approach, but they had no real understanding of the struggles of women and indigenous peoples either. They understood that privation and poverty were unjust, and they knew that they had to fight for social equality. No one can deny that this profound social awareness marked a big breakthrough towards democratisation. Yet it did not affect the position of women and indigenous peoples.

In most places, there was simply no attempt made to tackle the specific situation of indigenous peoples, what came to be known as 'the indigenous question'. Their analysis and their perception of our indigenous values were wholly inadequate. I tried to get hold of some of the important documents of the liberation movements in order to understand them better. Their theoretical manifestos are really limited. I imagine it's been the same in practice. If they don't grasp the theory properly, they won't grasp the practicalities either.

I'm not denying the contribution of some exceptional women on our continent, women who have taken up the challenge and joined the struggle. Yet the presence of women doesn't necessarily mean that they understand the issue of gender. It doesn't mean they grasp what is involved in a campaign for women's rights. Nor does it mean that they are respected, or allowed to participate actively and effectively at every level.

From personal experience, I know that it is hard to get your *compañeros* to accept your concerns, your ideas and your role. There comes a point when, if they can't think of anything better to say, they tell you, 'Those are women's problems.' As for the huge problems that we indigenous women face in public life! We pay dearly for our mistakes. So do indigenous men.

It is women like my mother who know how to read the signals, the signs, and can perceive what a child's destiny is to be. Being sensitive enough to receive a message from the Guardian of the World, the Guardian of the Universe, the *Rajaaw juyub'*. He is always watching when men and women destroy the environment, or fail to protect natural resources, or ruin the quality of life. Quality of life is material and spiritual, it is humility and respect. The person *Rajaaw juyub'* chooses to appear to must find a way to persuade other people to beg his forgiveness for the damage they have done to the natural world – and to life itself. Or else they must keep the secret that they never talk about. They just burn *pom* and pray. It is a special time because no one ever knows in advance whether the sign predicts disaster; if rains will destroy the maize before the cobs grow, or the *kaqiq*, the air, will bring violent winds. No one knows. It may be an epidemic, some kind of conflict within the community, or suffering that affects us all. *Rajaaw juyub'* might reveal to us a place where one of our ancestors' altars lies, and tell us that we have to look after that altar. We have to revere the altar, pray there for our enemies, for those who do us so much harm.

There is always an *ajq'iij*, a wise person or a Mayan priest or priestess, who can read the signs of the times and the sun. Mama could interpret the signs too, and a lot of very strange things happened to her.

Once, on one of the hills in 'El Aguacatál' near Chimel, Mama was walking along a track and saw a huge snake. She let it pass before she crossed the track. It was as big as a tree trunk. She went to see an *ajq'iij*. He told her to go back to the same place and look for the snake's skin. If she found it, it might be a very important message. Mama went back to the place and found the skin lying nearby, exactly as the elder had said.

She went back to see him, and he said that there might be a *camagüil*, a Mayan altar, there. He said that she shouldn't tell anyone, because the archaeologists who go raking around among our ancestors' treasures might take it away. Mama kept this great vision within herself, for we believe that if anyone reveals these sacred places some misfortune will befall the family and the community. That's why we never talk about such things. There are many things that people will never find out about. Although not everyone respects our secrets, my family and I will never reveal a sacred place.

Papa was a Catholic, but Mama believed more in the Mayan religion. They never quarrelled about it. It was as though they were showing humility towards something greater than themselves. We used to celebrate the

Catholic festivals, though not in the same way as they do in the big cities. Easter is always a big event. It was the only time Mama and Papa bought twenty-five pounds of flour. With a neighbour, who had an oven, they would make bread, and then they would make honey cake. We were lucky enough to have bees then. On Monday, Tuesday, Wednesday and Thursday of Holy Week, the whole community exchanged a little of whatever they had. We would start at about six in the morning, calling at our neighbours' houses to take them a little jar of honey, or honey cake, or a basket of bread. In return, they would fill our jar with honey and give us some of their bread. Everybody joined in. It was nice to exchange gifts with everyone in the community.

Mama stayed at home at that time, for there were always visitors and she felt it to be an honour to welcome them. She only went out to exchange gifts with her *compadres*. It was up to us, the children, to go round handing out bread and accepting something in return. We ate more in those few days than in the rest of the year put together.

In the course of the morning, each neighbour would give us loads of bread and honey, and we had to eat it then and there. We never refused, because our parents had brought us up to accept everything, to eat just enough to be polite and take the rest home. At lunchtime people made white *tortillas*, and white beans with dried fish. They cooked *pacayas*, the shoots of the palm that grows in the deep ravines of Chimel and El Soch, dipped in egg. At midday we would do the rounds again with our earthenware pot of *tortillas* to offer to our neighbours. Once again we would eat something at each place we stopped at.

You can't do it all in one day, that's why we sometimes started on the Monday or Tuesday of Holy Week. Perhaps the nicest thing about Easter was that we knew we would have more than enough bread, and we would eat food prepared by other women, even more than at Christmas. We went to Mass on Easter Saturday and Easter Sunday.

Mama wasn't a Catholic, but she never missed the Easter or Christmas Masses. Sometimes she would go to the services for the local saints' days.

She belonged to the *cofradías* when they were rather different from today. Now they have been influenced by militarism, religious sectarianism and corruption. But in those days the *cofradías* were made up of the leading women of the communities. They would take part in the major festivals, praying and celebrating these special occasions. You would hear the best *marimbas*, especially chosen for the occasion, and dance to them.

Mama always belonged to the *cofradías*. In some respects these groups went against the Catholic Church, yet they didn't reject it completely. The popular festivals were like a mixture of the Catholic and Mayan religions. The Church didn't approve of the *cofradías* where they played *marimbas*, drank *cuxa*, and danced and burned *pom*.

Chimel has always had a strange magnetic sort of power. It's a place where many things have happened. The home where I was born, and where I lived until I was ten, was a little straw hut, with wooden struts, just like all the others in my country. I always dream about the same place. I see a long tree trunk, I see something that looks like the kitchen, I see corncobs dangling from the veranda, I even see rabbits poking their noses out between the bars. I see a bed of wild passion flowers, what we call *karnay' k'oy*. I can see it all, even the apple and peach trees opposite the house. In my dream, the house is just as it was. I wake up with the smell of damp earth, when the sun comes out after heavy rain. I can smell *tortillas* fresh off the *comal*. I always see my mother sitting on the tree trunk. I go up to her and she says 'Xat peetik wal' ('So you've come, my child'.) And I say 'Xat peetik nan' ('Yes, Mama, I've come.')

Sometimes I see her combing her long black hair. I have never dreamed of my mother with white hair. I would have loved to see her with white hair. Our elders say that white hair is a symbol of humility, of the long journey through life, a symbol of wisdom. The house is very clear, the tree trunks in front of the house are very clear, but Mama's face is not so clear. After my dream, I try to remember her smile and her features, exactly as they were, but I can't.

There was a place we were all afraid of, though we used to have to pass rather close to it. There was a chapel high up on a ridge. Our house was way down below. Nearby was a little swamp that once swallowed up one of my mother's bulls. They used to say that the swamp lured things to it, it had some kind of special force. To get to the chapel we had to pass along the edge of the swamp. We used to run past it, especially at night when we were scared of the dark. My mother used to say, 'If there is danger, you must not run away but confront it.' I always dream about that place. It still frightens me.

Chimel has changed a lot. Even before I went back myself, my sister had written to me that the swamp had gone. I couldn't believe it. I thought, 'She's crazy. It can't be true.' She wrote, 'Now it's become pasture land belonging to some landowner who seized our land. All that is left is a tiny little hole, like the belly button of the swamp. I poked a stick in it. I threw a pebble in and heard it sink to the bottom. It isn't big enough to swallow an animal.'

I asked some journalists to take photographs, and it was true that in the place where the swamp had been, cows were grazing. The state land agency, INTA, had sold the land at Chimel five times, and five times the people who bought it had to leave. Their cattle died, their crops failed, they fought among themselves. I believe that when a community eventually settles in Chimel, they will have to be responsible people who respect the dignity of that sacred place. If not, the land will prove to have a power of its own, it will take its own revenge and make them pay the price.

When the military took over the countryside, our traditions suffered great changes, and not just because of the repression, the occupation and the terror. Hardship and poverty were rife, and a lot of so-called researchers and anthropologists appeared. Many of them were arrogant racists who infuriated the local people with their questions. So many people were uprooted (around a million Guatemalans had to flee their homes) that it had a profound effect on their lives and culture. The internally displaced people then went on to have an impact on the culture of the places where they had been resettled.

I hope all our traditions will eventually be revived. Chimel is already reviving them with pride. No one can take away tradition from these people for long, for it is deeply ingrained in their lives. Tradition runs deep, in the paths, in the ravines, in the clouds on the mountaintops. In Chimel it is as if the clouds sing, speak and keep watch.

Nature is much greater, life is much greater, than any project. Indigenous people have soul and great wisdom. The first people who arrived there made sacrifices to make the land their own. Chimel is an indestructible mountain. It has rivers where *quetzales* used to live. They are birds that like to be free, so they probably flew off to somewhere safe. People have said recently that the *quetzales* are back.

Chimel people have always been real fighters. The original community took over a big patch of apparently untitled land where no one had lived for years and years. They made their lives there. Just when the crops were beginning to grow, big landowners came along. That was the beginning of a corrupt system. The landowners and a few ambitious individuals were to blame, but above all it was the fault of the government. Corrupt civil servants were allowed to make money out of the land, and trample on the dignity of the poor. There were the Brols on one side, the Martínez family on the other, and the Garcías too. When they found that they couldn't remove the people who were trying to defend what belonged to them, they stripped them of their land and burned their houses. Over and over again.

Papa went to find a lawyer. The neighbours collected money to pay for his trip, and to pay the lawyer, but everyone was out to cheat him. The lawyers charged a fortune just to write a letter. You were really lucky to find an honest one. Then landowners would turn up and intimidate the lawyers. The whole business would start all over again.

I don't know how many times my father had to start again because he was cheated. One lot made him sign false title deeds to Chimel. Another lot told him they weren't valid. Each new official made up his own rules about the land, and it would all begin again. My Papa was fighting bureaucracy from 1952 until he died.

A little while ago, a new legal process was started for Chimel, through the INTA, the state land agency. They have been issuing new title deeds. I told my brother that I wanted to reclaim a little piece of Chimel, even if it is the only tiny piece of land I shall ever own, and even if I do not live there all the time. The INTA struck out the names of everyone's parents and redistributed the land, more than sixty *caballerías* of it. It is a great mountain where people have been trying to live together without damaging the ecosystem. There had been a plan to build a main road right through it, and the local people campaigned against it. They were willing for the road to run as far as the village, or along one side, but they did not want it to ruin the mountain's entire ecosystem. It's an area that produces beautiful kinds of wood and the animal life is wonderful. You could live well in Chimel without spoiling things. There used to be *quetzales* in the hills closest to the village. If *quetzales* chose to live there, it was because they found peace, safety and food.

The rivers in Chimel could have produced hydro-electricity for the towns and villages for miles around, if we had been given the chance to develop it. We shared all those dreams of development and progress with the communities of San Pablo, El Caracol, Caracolito, Laguna Danta, San Pedro, La Esperanza and El Rosario. We tried to make them happen. My parents were always eager to try new crops. They belonged to the apple growers' association in El Quiché, and the first apple trees had just started to grow when Chimel was destroyed. My father planted a sapling of a very beautiful kind of cypress, and people tell me that it soon reproduced. When they returned to the village, they found the cypress trees tall and green.

My father used to say that when the earth had no plants, it made him feel lonely. He felt he had lost something that made him happy. He always talked about trees with moustaches, not because you could actually see the moustaches but because mature trees inspire respect. The landowners that had the land between 1983 and 1985 cut down many of the trees. They grazed their cattle there instead.

I don't know what it is about Chimel that so many people want to take it over. Landowners, local authorities and their henchmen, and the INTA all have interests there. In 1984, my brother Nicolás went back for a time, and he started to organise the families who still lived there. He was captured. They beat him, and imposed fines on him. They took everything he owned, and stole his crops. Yet he persisted. He is pig-headed, like my father and my grandfather.

My brother says he felt as if he was always being drawn towards Chimel. When he was away from the village, he felt as though a bit of his soul was missing. So he keeps going back. Only recently did he succeed in obtaining a title to the land. When I read the document, I said to him, 'This is a sham, just another trick.' The deeds stated that only my brother was the legal owner, and as soon as he dies his children would have to start the process all over again. The document does not recognise that he has a family and that the land is their birthright.

This is the same thing that happened to our family in the past. My father fought for his land, he acquired the rights to it. Yet now that I want a small piece of land there, I find I have no legal existence. According to his papers, Don Vicente – and his right to his land – only had a legal existence until the time of his death. We have to do something to change these rules so that the land belongs to succeeding generations, as it did in the days of our forefathers.

After I left Chimel in 1979, I went to Chiché, and then on to Cucabaj. There I met Mateo López Calvo, a young K'iche' and a great fighter. He and his girlfriend, Chila, were on the national executive of the CUC, or rather its national co-ordinating committee (CONACO). I saw them as exemplary leaders, compassionate, simple and straightforward. I became very fond of Mateo López Calvo. I was a teenager then. I needed a reference point, someone to look up to. I needed people I could believe in, whose example I could follow.

Mateo was one of those burned alive with my father in the Spanish embassy on 31 January 1980. In the few months that I knew them, I recognised them as defenders of the principles and ideals of the CUC, where I, too, learned to fight. I learned how to hold on to my ideals, to fight for the rights of women and indigenous peoples. I couldn't have become the person I am today without them. I also met Romeo Cartagena, a *ladino* from Huehuetenango, one of my first Spanish teachers. He taught me Spanish in a different way. I wasn't taught maid's Spanish, to say 'What can I do for you, madam?' or 'What do you need, sir?' I was taught that there could be a more fraternal, more egalitarian relationship between my own language, K'iche', and the language I had to learn.

I remember the early years in Guatemala City. They were tough, hard days of persecution and death. I remember the names and faces of many of the people I met, who in the end were not fortunate as I was to survive. They are all with me wherever I go. I have known so many *compañeros* who have died over the years. The rural massacres had a great impact on me. I was to look after the first refugees to arrive in Mexico. My memories of that time are not just of my family, but of a whole nation, a whole society, the whole of Guatemala. I think of the frontiers where our compatriots began their long march, when all they wanted was to return to their land, as I did. I had the dream of returning to Chimel, of rebuilding our home, and seeing our family reunited and working together. Yet my greatest dream was to have the white hairs that my mother never had.

5

INTO EXILE AND BACK,
1980, 1981, 1982

I stayed in Huehuetenango after my parents died, after I had lost track of my brothers and sisters, a time when I thought I was the only one of my family left. I was in a terrible state. I didn't write about it in my book, *I, Rigoberta Menchú*, because I didn't have the courage. I couldn't bear to share my pain; the wounds were still open.

For victims there is no choice. We can't choose. We can't say, 'This is what I want, I have to pay such and such a price.' We can't choose our capacity for suffering. We have to experience what we have to experience, and face what we have to face. You can't postpone your own bit of pain, nor can you share it.

I didn't want to know anything about anything. Not about faith, or life, or prayer. This made me rather ashamed, for my parents and my grandparents, and my people, had taught me faith and hope. They had made me strong. Yet at that time I felt totally empty. I saw the future as an immense darkness. I was very frightened, just at the thought that my parents were no

longer there to protect me, that I would never feel the warmth of my mother's hands again, that I would never be able to tell her all the things I would have liked to say. When you lose your home, you lose a piece of your life.

I was staying in a convent. The nuns asked me to pray with them, but deep down I didn't believe and I didn't want to believe. I had done nothing wrong and I was too humble to deserve this punishment. Yet I will never forget the love and support I received from those nuns of the Sacred Family. Without them, I don't know how I would have survived. They looked after me day and night so that I wouldn't be alone, or commit some unpardonable act, or escape. The truth is I hadn't the strength for anything. I had a peptic ulcer, I was depressed and terribly sad. I felt totally lost.

After fifteen days in the convent, a dream brought me back to life. It was a daydream; it wasn't even night-time. I didn't sleep much at night. The nights seemed endless. Even today, nothing will bring back the happiness of being with my parents. I would drowse a bit during the day, and then one day I dreamed of my father. He was very calm, he looked just as if he were alive. I'll never forget that dream. It was a turning point in my life.

'What are you doing, child?' he said. I replied, 'But, Papa, you are dead.'

'No, child, I'm not dead.' He looked at me, touched my forehead, and said, 'You're not the daughter I know. You've changed. It makes me sad to see you behaving so badly, not like my daughter at all.' Then Papa turned and went away.

I got up and started thinking. I began remembering my *compañeros* in the CUC who had lost me. I thought about my father. I began remembering his strengths; his life of struggle, his courage, his humility, his enthusiasm for life. 'It's true,' I thought. 'If Papa was here, what would he say?' And I started coming to my senses.

That afternoon the Mother Superior, Sister Gertrudis, came to see me. She asked if I wanted to eat something. I said no, I just wanted to go out into the countryside, and have contact with nature again. I remember it well. Out in the fields, my interest in life and what was happening around me returned. I was only there a few days because the army was looking for me. They were searching houses, the convent was being watched, suspicious-looking people were on every corner. Sister Gertrudis said, 'It is very painful for you, but you have to leave.'

One morning, a couple of days before leaving Huehuetenango, I dreamed I was pregnant. I was crying because I was still a girl. I felt my belly was so heavy and I was upset. I was alone, pregnant and desperate. When I woke up, I was sobbing and very afraid, I couldn't imagine what the dream meant. I remember the desperation of that morning as if it were yesterday. Then I told myself, 'You are going mad. Stop it.' And I turned over a leaf of my life.

All the same, it took me years to get over my parents' death. It was always on my mind. I will never accept it as normal, and even less so people telling me it is the price to pay for justice, for peace. For the first four or five years I felt no hope. I grieved and felt almost resigned. Hope came back later when I met so many people with such a will to live, so much energy, such a desire for change. I realised that my own part was so very small and privileged.

I left the convent. The nuns had given me strength. It had been the ideal place for me, and I will always be grateful for what I learned from them. They recommended me to a convent in Guatemala City, and the nuns there managed to get me a passport. I left Guatemala by plane, and one of the nuns came with me. It was her job to find a place for me in Mexico. Although I had a legal passport, I travelled in disguise. I had cut my hair and was wearing *ladino* clothes. I risked putting a *corte* and a *huipil* in my suit-case and was afraid this would give me away. I felt naked, strange with short curly hair. I felt very persecuted. I still have a photo from those days.

I had never seen a plane up close before, let alone been in one. When I was a little girl, I remember seeing planes pass overhead now and again, a long long way away. I would watch a white trail in a blue sky, and was lost in wonderment. I couldn't grasp the amazing knowledge of people who could build or fly a plane. Whenever my father went to Guatemala City he would take me to a place near the airport, and we would spend hours just gazing at the planes landing and taking off. I never imagined the circumstances in which I would get on a plane.

Once in the air, I felt as if I was beginning a new life. I wrote a poem about it called 'The Daughter of *Imu't*'. *Imu't* is a plant we eat in the country. It is medicinal, and cures liver problems, but we eat it as a herb. It is my favourite. In the poem, I wrote that I had no choice, this was going to be my new life. Yet I still couldn't close my eyes and imagine it. I knew the future would be different, unlike anything I had experienced. The nun accompanying me was called Sister Gládis. She was Guatemalan, of the Order of the Sacred Family. She may be living in Europe now.

When we reached Mexico City, we went straight to a convent. I don't remember now which one. I don't think I ever knew. We were looking for a certain Mexican priest, and a bishop. We were told they were in Tehuantepec at a conference of Latin American bishops, priests and lay people. We may have been looking for Monsignor Sergio Méndez Arceo but I don't remember. Sister Gládis said it would be better to go to Tehuantepec, so we left the next day.

When we arrived, a dark man came up to us. He was all smiles and very friendly. He said, 'What are you doing here, sister?' and I could see he knew Sister Gládis. It was Samuel Ruíz, the immortal monsignor from Chiapas. He recognised my dress because I had put on my *corte* and had wound a *perraje* round my head to hide my short curly hair. He said, 'You're from Guatemala?' Sister Gládis said we were. The bishops invited me to tell them about what was happening in Guatemala. They already knew quite a lot about the suffering of the Guatemalan people.

Monsignor Sergio Méndez Arceo told me years later that he still had a tape of that first speech I made in Tehuantepec. 'How you've grown,' he said. 'When I listen to that tape I realise we didn't understand much of what you were saying.'

When I saw all those bishops, I forgot that I didn't speak Spanish very well. I just wanted them to feel my pain. They were all very moved. So moved that they all wanted me to travel on to visit their own countries. I remember the bishop from Venezuela. Another said he was from Peru. There were also bishops from Brazil and Ecuador. They all wanted me to go with them.

I might have gone if it had not been for Monsignor Samuel Ruíz. I kept my eyes on him. I knew he was from Chiapas, in the very south of Mexico bordering Guatemala. I said to myself, 'That's where I will go.'

We stayed in Tehuantepec for two days and when the conference was over, Monsignor Ruíz drove me to his community, in the diocese of San Cristóbal de las Casas. He introduced me to his sister, Doña Lucha, saying, 'This young lady is in a bad way.' They told me to treat their house as if it were my own. Monsignor Ruíz is a wonderful person, he came as if by a miracle into my life and the life of my people. The bishop is immortal in the hearts of so many of us victims. He is certainly immortal in mine.

Like other Guatemalans arriving in Chiapas, I tried to be brave, but no law can make you brave, and no one can be brave for you. You have to face your own situation on your own. First I went to see a doctor. I did not feel ill, but I did feel the whole weight of the repression upon me, this feeling of absolute grief. Every noise I heard sounded like bullets. This terror stayed with me for a long time.

The doctor gave me a sleep cure. He made me sleep for hours and hours. It went on for days. I just slept and ate the food they brought me. I felt embarrassed, but the bishop said, 'We're going to wait on you like a queen. You'll get up only to go to the bathroom. You can just sleep and wash when you feel like it, we'll bring your food and everything to you.'

It was very special. Doña Lucha treated me like a daughter. I spent days telling her everything that I had been through. We ended up crying, from grief and impotence. She was an incredible woman. A great friend.

I slept and slept until the doctor gave me the thumbs up. He said, 'You're well now, you can set to work.' Monsignor Ruíz bought me the Tzeltal and Bachajon clothes of Chiapas, and also wonderful *huipils* and lovely *cortes*.

He said, 'I want to see you dressed in bright colours, as colourful as your own life. Turn all your experiences into life.'

We are very colourful women. When we wear black, grey or dark colours, we feel sad. When I put on my multicoloured *huipils* they cheer me up, they give me life. They clothe your soul as well as your body. The bishop said it was a blessing that I had come to his house because it was in a Mayan area, an area of my people. Only then did I start to understand the meaning of our generic name and that Mayan people are on both sides of the border.

In Guatemala, we had never been told we were Mayan. We were proud of being Uspantecs, K'iche's or Ixils, but we weren't aware of belonging to the Mayan people. I was proud of my identity, yet I had never heard a proper detailed explanation of our history and where we had come from.

Monsignor Ruíz and I became very close friends. I came to call him Tatic, because that's what the Tzeltals say. I never called him by his name. I began accompanying him as he did his pastoral work, preaching the word of God. I was known as Lupita, my third new name. Since I dressed as a Tzeltal, people thought I spoke their language but I didn't. So I started speaking more Spanish. I tried to communicate. Doña Lucha's three children corrected me.

Chiapas . . . dear, beloved Chiapas. It brought me back to life. It also made me aware of the need for change. The poverty, hunger, injustice of the people's lives reminded me of Guatemala. I regained my love of life. I was happy again, and I brought joy to the house.

In Chiapas I got to know many priests. They gave me a lot of support. I went with them and Monsignor Ruíz to the villages and towns. Sometimes he went on horseback, and he said he would get me a horse. I had never been on one in my life. So I said, 'I'd rather walk, if you don't mind.' He also went round the villages with the nuns on foot. The religious community there was wonderful, and the people were so joyful. It made me want to be a catechist again. My father had been one and I felt an obligation to him. I regained my faith and started to learn many new things.

There were health workers who went round the villages too. It was difficult work, and some of them had been killed and disappeared. You had to be very careful. My mother had been a healer, a herbalist and a midwife, so I wanted to carry on the tradition. One day I was in the hospital in Comitán with one of the doctors, and Bishop Ruíz said to me, 'Why don't you become a health worker since you seem to like it? Poor people need them. I'll get the doctor to teach you so you stop being afraid of injections.'

I was really nervous, but I did learn to give injections. It's quite simple, though it was a big step for me. Later I told Monsignor Ruíz, 'I'd like to sell in the shop too.' His sister had a shop of indigenous crafts in San Cristóbal de las Casas. I began selling in the shop.

Then my visa ran out. I began living as an illegal immigrant. I was terrified of the authorities. Monsignor Ruíz said, 'I'll take you to the capital and we'll get your papers in order. We'll ask for a longer-stay visa.'

I said I was afraid they would kick me out of Mexico. That would have left me an orphan twice over, for Monsignor Ruíz was like a father substitute for me. I felt his house was my new home. It gave me confidence and hope. He made me accept people again. He made me want to be a health worker. After six months he had said, 'You should do a first aid course with the Marist Brothers in Comitán.'

I got high marks in that course because I was desperate to learn. Those of us who didn't have time to study normally made twice the effort to learn. Not because we wanted to collect a diploma, but because of the desire for knowledge itself. I learned through listening, because I still had problems with books. I wanted to learn in order to serve my community, though I still didn't know what community that would be. Everything was still very strange for me.

One day Monsignor Ruíz said to me, 'Guess what? The priests in Guatemala say two little girls who might be your sisters have turned up.' I felt life flooding back, but I was afraid it wasn't true. 'How can we find out?' I asked.

'We can try to bring them here,' he said. I begged him to work miracles. And it was true. The priests in Guatemala had found Anita and Lucía, my two little sisters. Efraín Us Contreras, a relative of my parents, accompanied them for a good stretch of the way, and left them near the border. He was murdered shortly afterwards. He was from Cholá, but he was murdered in Uspantán.

The reunion with my sisters was indescribable. I had thought the youngest was dead. After my mother died, she had been lost and wandered from place to place. She walked for hours to see whether the horses and sheep, the pigs and the chickens were still alive. Meeting my sisters again made me feel I had behaved very feebly. I had been weak. My little sister was only ten, yet she had lived through worse things than me and was still happy and brave. My other sister was about thirteen. They were very small. They had not grown very much. They had always been short.

My sisters and I spent the Christmas of 1980 in Chiapas. We were in Comitán at the house of another friend. The three of us agreed, 'This Christmas we're going to get really drunk.' We downed three bottles of rum straight off, and I soon lost any notion of anything. I remember my sister crying and my saying, 'Don't cry, don't cry.' It was our first Christmas without our parents, away from Chimel. I woke up at three the next afternoon. I had blacked out at eight the previous night. Our hangover was the most terrible punishment, because we had never been drunk before. It's the only time in my life I've ever been that drunk. Monsignor Ruíz didn't know, of course. We swore we would never tell him, because it was a venial sin.

After that we went to Mexico City for two weeks. There we met Alaïda Foppa, a great Guatemalan intellectual. An elegant, sensitive woman, courageous and aware, she was a writer and a poet. Many tributes have been paid to her. We were the last people she interviewed before she was kidnapped. Alaïda organised a meal for us. It was like she was, very elegant. Two days later she left for Guatemala. She was kidnapped and never seen again. She remains firmly in our memories although we only saw her a few times. Later on, I learned all about her, about her children, her writing. She is one of those intellectuals who have left their mark on our history, who will remain in the memory of the Guatemalan people.

Through Alaïda we met Bertha Navarro, and that was the first time we were filmed. Bertha said we would be on television. We were given other names. I was Lupita, one of my sisters was called Josefina, and the other Angelina. We spoke on a radio programme too. My sisters didn't say much because they didn't understand Spanish, but I managed pretty well.

By then I'd been with the nuns of the Sacred Family, and six months on my course. Thanks to my Creator, and to the solidarity I had received along my way, there had awoken in me a great desire to learn. I even surprised myself. I slept a mere two or three hours a night. I was very inquisitive. I wanted answers to lots of questions. I tried to practise Spanish, to learn to read and write. I paid great attention to what people said. I listened, listened, listened. I found I could remember things. I was like a sponge. I remembered jokes, funny stories, different ways of saying things. I came across new ideas every day and absorbed them. If I couldn't find words to express them in my own language, I used Spanish ones, and vice versa. So it went on.

My little sisters were terrible. They didn't want to live in Mexico. They talked about Mama and Papa and our old house all the time. They made my life impossible because they kept saying, 'We must go back'. They squabbled like cooped-up chickens. I kept having to separate them. Sometimes I had to smack them because they fought so much. They probably missed the space of Chimel, the clouds, the fields, the mountains, and the freedom. Or they missed Mama's hugs and love. The situation was so difficult. I began wondering whether I would be able to control them better if we returned to our people.

They looked at our tragedy differently from me. Perhaps their experience had made them stronger. Sometimes their feelings would burst out. They would cry and be sad and think of themselves as the most wretched people on earth. Yet they were never bitter. Like all children, they saw things differently.

I was the one who suffered most. I thought I was alone with them. I felt responsible. I didn't know what to do. How long could we keep going from house to house, from convent to convent? What would become of us? They were calmer and stronger. They even used to scold me. When I talked to people I'd start crying and they'd say, 'Don't do that, it looks awful. People won't understand. We don't want them to think we're snivelling little girls.'

My sisters wanted to go back to Guatemala, and my work with Monsignor Ruíz in Chiapas had sparked a new desire in me to carry on working with Christians and peasants, as my father had done. I had been with Monsignor Ruíz when the first refugees started arriving in Chiapas and centres were set up for them. They had walked for days over the mountains. They had no documents, no clothes, nothing. Women had lost small children on the way. They had seen their villages bombed. They had seen massacres. They had seen their houses burned with loved ones inside.

The stories were terrible, yet when we thought of returning, we thought we could be useful despite these risks. To me, that's what human beings are like. In spite of the dangers, they want to return to their roots. They run risks all over again. We decided to go back, and first we took a plane to Chiapas. We stayed with the Sisters of Mercy, then with Brother Vico in a seminary for Central American priests. We just stayed long enough to get our papers in order.

Victims have no choice. I hadn't chosen to go to Mexico in the first place. I didn't know what the future held. I let life and fate carry me along. For a time my mind was empty. I was emotionless. I felt like a child again. When my parents died, I had twenty-five *quetzales*, two *cortes*, three *huipils*, a *perraje* and a pair of rope-soled shoes. That's all I owned. If I had known about the capitalist world I would have died of anxiety.

My sisters and I had made the decision to return to Guatemala, and we went back there to work for the Committee for Peasant Unity (CUC). The three of us swore to carry on my father's principles. I soon realised just how many people knew my father. His name lived on in the peasant struggle.

The *compañeros* shouted the names of Vicente Menchú, Báltazar Ví and Mateo López Calvo. They talked of María Anaya, Regina Pol, and many others whose memory lived on. Working with the CUC was a way of venerating the dead. These great leaders inspired me, and I wanted to live by their principles, their ideas of struggle.

We learned in the CUC to be generous with life and with our people's history. We learned to fight for what many people might consider utopias. Yet those utopias will have a meaning in the future. We drank in the fundamental values of our leaders, their belief in people, in life and in the strength of the people. We learned to share our *compañeros'* suffering, and also to laugh together. We learned to say 'Clear Head, Caring Heart, Fighting Fist of Rural Workers'.

For many people that might sound like just another slogan. Yet our sense of mysticism and our experience of the struggle showed us that having a 'Clear Head' not only showed respect for knowledge in general, it also meant we had to study the underlying causes of problems. With a clear head, I learned to take initiative, propose solutions, think my ideas through and justify my thinking.

When we talked about a 'Caring Heart', we meant showing compassion for others, being tolerant, making our own lives an example of humanity. It meant feeling a *compañero*'s pain as if it were your own, never abandoning your friends, and always being there for them in good times and in bad.

I worked in the CUC throughout 1981. Many things happened in those months. The repression got worse. Many *compañeros* died. It is hard to express the grief you feel when you see such close friends lying in the morgue, when you have to go to identify them. A lot of people disappeared too. When a *compañero* didn't come home, we had to move house. We didn't know if we were going to meet the same fate.

The 'Democratic Front Against Repression' was formed at this time. It was made up of teachers, students, peasants, union leaders, and some well-known figures too. One by one they went into exile. The former rector of the University of San Carlos, Raúl Molina, had to leave the country. Nearly all the organisations lost their leaders, one by one. Others went underground, and changed their identities. Nobody asked any questions. We learned to keep our experiences and what we knew to ourselves. If a *compañero* was captured alive, he would be tortured and might talk. We were all very afraid of torture.

In the midst of all this, I remember making one terrible mistake. We were moving things in a hired van. We had been careless and had not secured the boxes properly. When we set off, one of the boxes broke and the leaflets of various opposition groups scattered on the ground. The van driver went pale when he saw it all fall. We had had to pass three patrols of those soldiers who masquerade as police. If we were caught, we would be dead. I remember how terribly frightened we were. Death was so near, I could feel it under my skin. Of course you always say, 'I want to give my life for my people. I'd rather be captured dead than alive.' But when the time comes, it's as if you say, 'No, not now. I'm not ready yet. Maybe later.'

We made the mistake with the van, and we had to move house. The driver might easily have turned us in because the dictatorship offered rewards to people who denounced opponents. Our leaders didn't have another house for us, and we were severely criticised. I'll never forget it. We each had to find our own place to live. A peasant in Guatemala City is not like a student with a family or friends to call on. A peasant has no family. I just had Chimel as a memory. It was very hard for me. I tried to remember friends of my father and I found a family of Evangelicals for whom I invented a story. They couldn't house me for very long, it wasn't safe. We had to follow certain rules. Especially since I was Don Vicente's daughter.

In the end, my *compañeros* in the CUC said it had become too risky for me in the city, because I was becoming too well known. Yet I couldn't go back to the countryside. The repression had intensified, with the Civil Defence Patrols and the increased militarisation. The army was rounding up peasants, forcing them to denounce any strangers in their villages. There was a reward for anyone who did. The massacres had begun.

My sisters decided that they would go back to El Quiché, and join the guerrillas. It was a big step for them, and very sad for me, yet in a way I was relieved that we wouldn't be together. At least they couldn't kill all three of us at the same time. Before she left for the mountains, my sister Anita had said, 'If we're together, they can kill us with just one bullet. If we're apart, they'll have to fire lots of rounds to kill us.' I had no idea if they'd be able to endure the hardships of guerrilla life, or what the conditions would be like. One day they themselves will tell how they survived.

Now my *compañeros* told me, 'You have to leave.' It was very hard for me to leave Guatemala again. I felt guilty about leaving my sisters, and I would be alone without a family again. But I had to agree.

We went overland. We crossed Honduras and I asked for asylum in Nicaragua. Two people travelled with me. One drove and the other accompanied us. There were no problems at the customs although my passport was in my name. The others said, 'We're going to Tegucigalpa.' They were pretending to be businessmen, and they continued to do so until we reached Nicaragua.

There they searched us thoroughly. The Sandinistas were taking very strict precautions. I didn't have a visa to live in Nicaragua so I had to declare myself a refugee at the UN High Commission for Refugees. They gave me a passport. In those days, the UN had a formal passport for refugees, with a person's details on it. I travelled on it for a long time until the UN cancelled it.

When I arrived in Nicaragua, the place was bubbling with solidarity. The Nicaraguan Committee for Solidarity with Peoples organised a press conference for me. Because of the fear and anxiety of the journey I had just made, I completely forgot what I was going to say. Faced with a sea of journalists with cameras and tape recorders, I was so nervous I couldn't speak. I even forgot my own name.

From Nicaragua I embarked on a pilgrimage that was to last for twelve years. The most time I ever spent in any one country was a month. I just had one suitcase. I felt that it contained all that anyone would need in life, particularly the Mayan keepsakes that my mother gave me.

Eventually I decided to leave Nicaragua, and to return to Mexico with the international committee of the Committee for Peasant Unity (CUC). I also worked in the Christian Co-ordinating Committee for Solidarity with Guatemala. The main reason for moving to Mexico definitively was the news filtering out about the Communities of the Population in Resistance (CPRs), living high up in the mountainous jungles of Guatemala.

We didn't know very much about them until 1983 when we learned for certain that large numbers were hiding in El Ixcán. They were the survivors of massacres, mainly orphans, widows and old people. Almost all of them were Mayan. They had long used up the few things they had scrabbled together from their houses, and lived in dire conditions. They had no connection with the normal population of Guatemala. They were gradually dying; from malaria, infections, malnutrition and hunger. On top of all that, they suffered constant harassment from the army. They were chased from place to place, often in torrential rain. Any crops they had managed to plant were destroyed. The army thought they could starve them into surrender. Aerial bombing was also used to try to wipe them out.

From 1982 I was a part of the Guatemalan Committee for Patriotic Unity. It consisted of about sixty professionals, all moved by the great suffering of the Guatemalan people. Most of them were *ladinos*. There were ex-university rectors, ex-ministers, poets, writers, journalists, prominent political leaders, the odd retired military man, and other Guatemalan figures with democratic and patriotic leanings. All of us longed for our country with the same sense of nostalgia.

My relationship with them was very important. Many are still in exile, others are dead. Some went back and took jobs in the government, others went back and continued fighting for a democratic Guatemala in political parties, in human-rights organisations and in the indigenous movement. The committee had two indigenous people in it: Pablo Seto and myself. We weren't important intellectuals or personalities. Don Pablo was an Ixil, a believer in freedom and a great fighter for justice. He never grew old, perhaps because he had grieved so much.

Our president was a great Guatemalan writer, Don Luís Cardoza y Aragón, who died in exile after a long life of honesty and integrity. He was a great friend, teacher, *compañero* and brother to me. I used to visit him and his wife and life companion, Doña Lía. We often talked about the indigenous question, for his view and mine did not exactly coincide. Yet this helped me to hone my arguments and express them better. He taught me to reflect, to ask questions, to exchange ideas. I had enormous respect for him. It wasn't easy discussing with a great humanist of his stature. We indigenous people have not had the time or the opportunity to reflect on our own culture and our identity, and to present our arguments. We haven't always been able to think about our aspirations or to consider how we would bring them about, given the chance.

Don Luís used to maintain that the long-term future of the indigenous people lay within a unified nation, living side by side with the rest of the population in a strong democratic country. In those days we had not developed the concept of national unity, let alone the notion of ethnic and cultural diversity. He was very radical in his conviction that indigenous peoples had to go through profound changes in order to meet this goal. We didn't know then the effect that technology would have on indigenous peoples, or on the rest of the population for that matter. It could either help to consolidate a common culture, or indigenous people might be afraid of it and would resist. There was always the fear that they might take up arms and fight for their heritage.

Don Luís had been pondering over these matters for a long time. I used to think that his view was rather rigid, and he died before we could finish defining this idea of a multi-ethnic, multi-lingual and pluri-cultural country. We kept modifying our positions over the years. We got to know each other and our ideas evolved. We always used to talk about our beloved *tamales*, about the smells of Guatemala, and the paths of Panjachel. He would tell of the towns he had known long ago, and his love for his country. We returned again and again in our minds to the labyrinths of the immense rainforest in Chimel.

We also talked about his experiences and his many hopes during the democratic regime between 1944 and 1954.[1] I didn't know much then about that particular democratic process but I soon became familiar with the term. We discussed his opposition to the military, and his profound rejection of military government. He always maintained that whenever the armed forces were in power and decided the fate of the peoples of America, the continent was lost. We used to end up weeping for our people. In the view of Don Luís, the armed forces represented a major obstacle to progress and were largely responsible for the tragic fate of millions of people in the Americas. Holding views like these meant that it was impossible for him to return to his country. He recognised with great sadness that his return was less likely with each passing day.

He had vowed never to go back while the civilian government was merely a front for the armed forces. He died before he realised his dream. He never went back to Guatemala. When he died, certain Guatemalans came to Mexico to take his ashes back to Guatemala. I was at his tomb and heard the row that went on. I thought they were cowardly, for they didn't respect his views when he was alive and now they wanted his ashes when he was dead. Don Luís Cardoza y Aragón was a wonderful example of commitment and justice to many of us looking for a mature person upon whom to model ourselves.

I also met Julia Esquivel, a Christian poetess, and many other compatriots. That's how I made friends with Raúl Molina, formerly the rector of the University of San Carlos. I also became a friend of Rolando Castillo Montalvo, a man with pale skin and white hair, who looks Swedish or Norwegian. He had been the dean of the medical school at the university. Both of them had had important academic posts in Guatemala before going into exile. I became very fond of them.

Later I worked with Frank Larrué, a Guatemalan lawyer, and with Marta

---

[1] A reference to the final years of the left-wing government in Guatemala, led by Jacobo Arbenz. It was overthrown in 1954 by a US-backed military coup.

Gloria Torres, a simple woman with a wealth of knowledge. All have been, at one time or another, leaders of popular movements or prominent in their particular areas of work. They all survived, but they mourn their many friends who were killed or disappeared. I learned a lot from all of them. They corrected my Spanish, altered the view I had of their culture, and gradually helped me write in Spanish and answer the telephone.

Another important influence on me was Arturo Taracena. I met him in Paris. We weren't working together then, but he was the one who persuaded me to write my book *I, Rigoberta Menchú*. We were on a speaking tour of ten European countries. With us was a Dutch priest called Mario Colen, who had worked in Guatemala for ten years, supporting the CUC on the south coast. He had had to leave Guatemala and had returned to Holland, but he was still very involved and helped to organise Guatemalan solidarity movements in Europe. I also travelled with a *ladino compañero*, a union leader called Mazariegos.

I spent most of my time listening on that tour; I didn't know very much. Mazariegos did all the talking about Guatemala. It was good training for me. Gradually I learned to speak, and trembled less each time. When you're born in a racist country, you have no sense of your own worth. You're afraid of everything and think that everybody is superior.

At the end of the tour, Arturo and I started work on the book. He wanted it to reach as wide a public as possible. Recording my testimony took about twelve days. The Guatemala Solidarity Committee in Paris helped with the transcription. There I met Juan Mendoza, a dear friend to this day. Dr Taracena introduced me to Elisabeth Burgos. He said that if he and I wrote the book, an exile and an indigenous woman, it would seem like a sort of family pamphlet. He said we needed someone with a reputation and an *entrée* into the academic and publishing world.

Arturo had convinced me that narrating the story of my life could turn into an interesting book, above all because of the tragic death of my father, mother and brother. He had followed the whole story and thought it would be an injustice to a time and a people if we didn't relate it. The only way of constructing a historical memory of a people was to write it down. He had a significant hand in the book, though he is a modest man and was not interested in self-aggrandisement. After the text was compiled, I spent about two months trying to understand it. Seeing it on paper is very different from talking into a tape recorder.

I realise now how shy I was. I still am, but not as much as I used to be. In those days, I was innocent and naive. When I wrote that book, I simply did not know the commercial rules. I was just happy to be alive to tell my story. I had no idea about an author's copyright. I had to ask *compañeros* in Mexico to help me understand the text, and it was painful to have to relive the content of the book. I censured several parts that might have been dangerous for people. I took out bits that referred to my village, details about my brothers and sisters, and names of people. That is why the book lacks a more specific identity and I feel it will be my duty to provide this before I die. That is what I still hope to do.

My dream is to recover the rights to *I, Rigoberta Menchú* and to expand it. I want to give it back to Guatemala and the coming generations as part of their history. I took out names, above all names of family and neighbours, because, although I assumed they were dead, there was always a tiny doubt in my mind. Giving their names away in a book could have had them killed.

I also left out the details of my life in the Committee for Peasant Unity (CUC). It was there that I learned to fight, as a woman, for women's rights, and for fundamental human values. I also met a number of people in organisations working for justice, democracy and human rights, and for the respect of our indigenous identity. All these experiences and struggles should have been in my book. I had originally given details of life in the CUC but, when I saw them written down, I was so frightened for the lives of the leaders and other *compañeros* that I took them out. Yet I was left with the feeling that I should have talked about them.

I am grateful to my Creator that I am alive, and I hope I can still finish the story, and regain the rights to that important part of the patrimony of my people, *Ixim Uleew*. It should belong to no one but them and

Guatemala. One day I will tell the whole truth. It will be my small contribution to the educational and cultural resources of future generations.

Arturo Taracena knew this was important. If I had listened to him, we might have improved the book. In any case, we would have done it differently. Yet you can't change history. You can only learn from experience, and not make the same mistakes again.

Around this time I was invited to the United States. I went as a representative of the CUC. This first invitation began my battles with visas. It is hard enough for anyone from a poor country to get a US visa, and with a refugee passport it is almost a miracle. I had to go through endless interrogations and checks that I found intimidating and humiliating. When they would not let me in, there was an outcry from solidarity committees. The State Department opened a file on me which was still there as recently as 1992.

In the United States I met my Native American brothers and sisters for the first time. I thought that they didn't understand me, for I was very shy. Yet they received us in a very affectionate and friendly way. The story of my father's death affected a lot of people. Descriptions of the terror the Guatemalan people were facing made a huge impact. I met Bill Mean from the Ogtala nation and Ingrid Washinawato, and I made a special friend, Bill Wahpepah, from the Kickapool nation.

Bill Wahpepah became one of my most important teachers in how to lobby at the UN. He has since died as a result of discrimination in San Francisco. He had a heart attack, and being poor, old and an Indian, he was left for three hours unattended in a hospital emergency ward. He died from lack of care, just one of hundreds of thousands of indigenous people in the world who die from curable illnesses. When they die in places where there are no doctors or hospitals, we are sad. When they die in emergency wards of good hospitals because a non-indigenous doctor didn't come, or because the hospital wasn't for us, our pain is eternal.

I also learned of the case of Leonardo Peltier, a man who has unjustly served seventeen years in prison for claiming lands in Lakota, Minnesota.

The US supreme court gave him three consecutive life sentences. In 1973, our indigenous brothers had occupied Sak and Fox lands that they had been evicted from in previous years. The battle lasted for seventy-three days. The federal police intervened and two policemen and an indigenous youth died. Without proof or any serious investigation, they accused Leonardo Peltier. His crime was to be the leader of these nations.

Despite appeals for clemency from all over the world, despite thousands of us appealing to President Clinton for the case to be reopened, Leonardo is still in prison. His people are men and women of few words. Their expressions are grim. Their faces and voices encapsulate their history. Life is hard. A smile escapes them only on special occasions. Listening to what they have gone through, I feel very indignant. I realise that our grief is shared.

All these men had fought in the Vietnam War. Many of them had been drafted, recruited by force. They later started the American Indian Movement (AIM) which has been involved in several battles over identity, rights and land ownership. In the past they also suffered repression on other fronts: sterilisation of their women, contamination of water, expulsion from their land, and the massive introduction of drugs and alcohol that would destroy their communities. Yet they have resisted, and this is why they are still alive. I did not speak English and they hardly understood Spanish. We managed through interpreters. Despite this and other obstacles, our indigenous souls united.

Yet the North American Indians were different from me. I had never seen a man with long plaits, and I wondered, 'Why are they so fat and so big?' Then there were their customs. In October 1982, I was privileged to take part in the special conference of the American Indian Movement and the International Council of Indian Treaties. It was held at Duke University. This was the main indigenous platform in the US. I was shown their *temascal* known as Sweat Lodge. A *temascal* is for purification and for prayer, for passing the pipe and venerating the greatness of life. It means asking for the strength and courage to carry on. It is proof of friendship.

Inviting an outsider like me into the *temascal* means being put through a test. It shows that there is the beginning of trust. If there is no trust between people, life is not complete. Yet their trust has been betrayed many times. They have learned not to trust easily. They have learned to invoke the Creator to purify their trust. Sweat Lodge is for praying together, calling up good spirits, venerating ancestors and purifying relationships.

I thought they were wonderful people. They were an example to me, for their profound mysticism and for their struggle and their resistance. Yet they were being more and more isolated by the day. I began to realise how valuable Guatemala is in this sense, for we are many. We indigenous people are everywhere. We are the majority. We live in the big cities and the hills, in the mountains and the jungle. Our achievements are growing by the day.

My experience in the United States was like a reaffirmation of the need for resistance. This was the first time that the leaders and the people of the North American Indian nations, young and old, had heard the story of our people in Guatemala. Many of them cried. They felt our grief as if it were their own. They felt it as if it was happening to them. These indigenous brothers and sisters were the first to invite me to Geneva.

6

HEIRESS TO AN ANCIENT CULTURE
AT THE UNITED NATIONS,

1982

In August 1982, shortly after I had met the North American Indian chiefs, I went to the United Nations in Geneva, invited by the International Council of Indian Treaties. I asked the leaders of the Committee for Peasant Unity (CUC) if they would let me go. I couldn't move a finger without their permission in those days.

I went off to Geneva, and was immediately lost. I had no knowledge of the international scene, no idea what it was all about. The Council of Indian Treaties had paid for my ticket, and the *compañeros* in the Guatemalan CUC had given me a hundred dollars to hold in reserve. They told me that a friend would be waiting for me at the airport. Everything had apparently been arranged.

Nobody was waiting at the airport. I didn't know what to do. The Swiss authorities took my bag and went through my things, one by one. They looked carefully at my face, my size, my eyes. They were all huge men, just

their eyes were enough to frighten me. I didn't understand what they were saying, and I prayed to God that they weren't thugs like in Guatemala. I don't know how long I was there.

They tried to question me but didn't want to say a word in Spanish. The Swiss officials I met were all like that. They only spoke French. I was very scared, but finally they let me go. I didn't see anyone I knew. I looked for Roxana Dunbar. I looked for anyone who spoke Spanish, but I couldn't find anyone to help me. I went to find a bank and changed my hundred dollars, with no notion of the value of the money. People told me later, laughingly, that it wouldn't have got me very far.

Then I thought of something. Even in the middle of the jungle, you will always find a way of surviving. My father always told me that. There is always a sign of life. I asked myself, 'What shall I do?'

'Go to the Nicaraguan embassy,' I answered. In those days, the Nicaraguans were our best friends, people who would help us, no matter what. We called them 'los Compas'. They were revolutionaries who had spent their lives fighting to overthrow the Somoza dictatorship. In a place where you were lost, finding a Nicaraguan seemed like your salvation. So I got in a taxi and asked the driver to take me to the Nicaraguan embassy. I had to spell it for him. Thank God 'embassy' is almost the same word in Spanish, English and French. If not, I'd have been in trouble.

It was about four in the afternoon, and they told me the ambassador was busy. I said it didn't matter. Now that I was there, no one was going to turf me out. The people spoke Spanish so I was confident nothing would happen to me. I told the secretary my life story, that I was lost and needed humanitarian aid from the Nica *compas*. I don't think she believed me at first. In Mexico, it's normal for people to arrive in their thousands needing emergency aid. Institutions go crazy trying to avoid them. In Geneva, it's not so common.

The ambassador in those days was César Vera, a nice, chubby, little man. He said they couldn't put me up at the embassy because it was small. He offered me his house, and that wasn't large either. He already shared it with other Nicaraguans. I said I didn't care, I would be fine in a corner or a corridor. I promised not to take up much space.

When we arrived at the ambassador's house, he asked if I had any friends. 'Not in Switzerland,' I replied, 'but in Mexico I know Don Luís Cardoza y Aragón.' He passed me the phone and I spoke to Don Luís in Mexico and asked him to help. 'You're in luck,' he said, 'because I have Julia Esquivel staying with me. She's a Guatemalan poetess who lives there, in Neuchâtel. She might have some friends who can help you.'

I had not met Julia then. I spoke to her later and she said, 'Go to Neuchâtel. Some nuns will meet you at the station.' I didn't get lost this time, but it was difficult being in a train and not knowing where I should get off. I had never been in a train before. I wanted to cry, and I kept thinking the train was going to crash, especially when we reached the tunnels through the mountains and when we passed other trains. European trains are fantastic!

I couldn't even pay the fare. I knew I owed money, but I had no way of getting any. I got there somehow, and the nuns were very kind to me and lent me money. Then I was called back to Geneva, where I was introduced to a man called Luís Necate (I don't even know if that is how you spell his name). I didn't know at the time, but he was an important person. Everyone seemed the same to me, and I thought they were all important. I treated everyone with a lot of respect.

Señor Necate introduced me to a woman with a well-guarded house with double locks. It had three storeys. They gave me a very big room. The woman spoke very good Spanish and called me '*mi momin*', I don't know why. She warned me not to touch anything. There were earrings and mirrors lying around, as if someone was living there. She said, 'Don't touch these things. Don't move anything.'

Then I noticed there were armed guards nearby. I could see them using walkie-talkies. My fears at once returned. It is incredible how traumatic figures of authority can be if you come from Guatemala. Authorities means repression, ill-treatment, death. If someone was watching the house, it was suspicious. Surveillance and armed men would mean they've discovered you. 'I've been caught!' I thought.

The following Sunday, the lady of the house said, 'Come and eat with us.' Her family came to lunch at her mansion. 'Is that house yours as well?' I asked, pointing to the house with the armed guards. 'No,' she said, 'it's the residence of the US ambassador.' I nearly fainted!

Later I learned that this woman's daughter had died twelve months earlier in Nicaragua where she had been working as a volunteer doctor. Someone coming to her house from Central America on the first anniversary of her daughter's death was an omen, a blessing. Especially after I told her my story. It was like a message from her daughter.

Although I had everything I needed in that house – I didn't need food because the fridges were always full – when I heard who my neighbour was I was frightened. I started looking for somewhere else to live. In those days, the *gringos* for us were all in the CIA, dangerous accomplices of what was happening in Guatemala. For us, the United States was the major symbol of repression.

One weekend I made a French friend, Louis Joinet. He was one of my teachers at the UN for many years. He said, 'Good, we've got a Mayan here at last, we've finally got a Guatemalan. It'll be the first time Guatemala is discussed. Come, I'll invite you to a reception.' I didn't know what a reception was, but I accepted. I was more confident now because I had found Roxana Dunbar, and I always went with her.

There were three very elegant women at the reception, wearing lots of jewellery and long dresses. 'Are you from Guatemala?' they asked, and I said that I was. 'We are great admirers of Guatemala,' they said. I said, 'My name is Rigoberta Menchú Tum.' It was all I had learned to say.

'Really? What a lovely name!' they said. 'Very Mayan!' They knew a lot about Guatemala and I thought they were very nice. Señor Joinet came over, and I told him, 'These ladies know all about my country.' And I introduced them. He then said, 'Why don't you invite your friends to come and have a pizza with us?'

So we all went off to have a pizza. There were a lot of us. Señora Odi Benítez from Costa Rica; Señora Souza from Panama and her husband; the Vietnamese ambassador; Señor Augusto Willemsen Díaz; Louis Joinet; a representative of the Farabundo Martí National Liberation Front from El Salvador; Ricardo Cordero; a representative of the Palestine Liberation Organization; a Chilean by the name of Mário Ibarra; and the women I had met that afternoon. Louis Joinet said, 'Let's toast to the presence of a K'iche' Mayan among us.' Don Augusto and Don Louis were great admirers of our Mayan culture.

After Don Louis's toast, it was my turn to say 'Thank you'. 'It's thanks to your friendship that I am here.'

Then one of my new friends got up and said, in Spanish, 'We prostitutes admire Rigoberta very much.' I thought, 'Good God, what on earth are prostitutes doing here?'

I froze up completely. I didn't know what she meant. Señora Odi Benítez said, 'Perhaps that's not how it's said in Spanish.' She said it seriously in a low voice.

The other woman went on: 'I'm the president of the Association of Swiss Prostitutes. We're delighted to be here celebrating with you.'

I thought either their Spanish was very poor or perhaps this was a provocation. I knew the mentality of the other people there – several of them were Latin American. I didn't know what they would think. A hush fell over the table.

The only person who didn't hear what was said was the representative of the PLO. 'What did she say?' he asked. 'What did she say?' But no one wanted to translate.

The women clearly felt bad. The atmosphere was rather strained. Then they got up and said, 'Well, we'll be going. Nice to have met you, Rigoberta. You know we have a room for you whenever you need it. Come and see us.'

I felt I couldn't stay either. The atmosphere was not right. I was afraid of my enemies. I knew the Guatemalan government was quite capable of doing anything to undermine the space I had so laboriously carved out for myself. The Guatemalan ambassador in Geneva then was the daughter of General Lucas. My Chilean friend said as I was leaving, 'I'll walk you to the door.' Then, as we were going out, he said, jokingly, 'Nice friends you've got! How's business these days?'

I burst into tears. I don't really think I had much idea what prostitution was. It just seemed bad and sinful. Yet this was the first gesture of solidarity that I had received, from a group that is also badly treated. Prostitutes are always rejected and discriminated against. I was familiar with the Latin American mentality regarding prostitutes, and I had never heard anyone in America speak up for them with such courage. Talking about prostitutes is a social gaffe, you would only do so in whispers. Our continent will never recognise that prostitution has a lot to do with the social situation, and the lack of respect and opportunity for women. Prostitution can often be understood in the context of an area of work that enables women to survive. I am not saying it is good or bad, only that it is something that exists in our societies. We have to study it and find a solution. We have to respect the people who lead that terrible life.

This happened on a Friday, and I spent the whole weekend pondering my problems. My next-door neighbour was the US ambassador and I was very afraid of him. Then the incident in the restaurant happened. It would have been helpful if I had had a community to discuss things with. I was obliged to turn it round and round in my head on my own.

The first thing on Monday morning, I went to see Louis Joinet to apologise. In our culture, I said, if something is not clear we have an obligation to explain it. He agreed to explain to the others what had happened. I was very doubtful that he would, and I dogged his footsteps all day. It did me no good, and I'll never know what was said. I don't know to this day whether the incident had any repercussions, but I will never forget it.

I left the house I was staying in and found some new friends. For ten years, the house of Pedro and Sally was my home in Geneva. Pedro is Spanish and Sally is English. They are a beautiful family. All the

Guatemalans who have been to Switzerland on any kind of mission have passed through their house.

I gradually got to know the officials at the United Nations. The International Council of Indian Treaties helped me with accreditation, but little else. I hadn't a clue at first. There were very few indigenous people at the UN in those days. A Working Group on Indigenous People had been set up, and there were about five or six *pelones* lobbying for it. We looked like oddballs and we were treated as such. Some officials were offhand and rather suspicious, as if we were making things up. I think they were embarrassed for us.

Others were curious to find out what we had come to the UN for. Non-indigenous friends fighting for indigenous rights were few and far between in those days. For many people, we were insignificant, though for others we were important. People with similar causes and similar sensitivities welcomed us into their homes and gave us the best of what they had to offer.

My indigenous brothers on the Council told me the history of the indigenous struggles at the UN. The first conference of non-governmental organisations (NGOs) had been held in Geneva in 1977 and included representatives from indigenous peoples. Over five hundred people came on that occasion to discuss the problems facing Indians in North America.

I kept going to the UN and listening to the speeches. I loved the language. I spent almost all the sessions listening to the richness of the language and learning all the tricks of the trade. I also learned to listen to English. Thanks to Louis Joinet and Señor Elde from Norway, I had gone to a meeting of the Working Group on Indigenous Peoples. I told them all about myself, the situation in Guatemala and the need for a Guatemalan presence at the UN. They invited me to speak at one of the sessions.

I had hardly begun before the ambassador from Guatemala called for a point of order. She was seconded by the delegates from the United States and Morocco. The Moroccan delegate had been at the UN for thirty years. I imagine she knew all the tricks to intimidate anybody from Morocco speaking for the first time.

The president of the session had to give way. I no longer had the floor. There was uproar, and the session had to be suspended. Then, as always happens at the UN, they began negotiating. I was afraid this incident would affect the International Council of Indian Treaties. Telling people about the scorched-earth campaign in Guatemala was urgent and necessary, but the fact that it might damage the interests of my Lakota and Hopi brothers and sisters made me think it might be better not to talk about it. Most Guatemalans scattered round the world are reserved and respectful, even rather withdrawn and shy. The indigenous mentality is to be patient.

The Guatemalan delegation wanted to appeal to the statute book, and it threatened to remove the consultative status of the International Council of Indian Treaties. It was a very aggressive reaction. They probably thought that if they could kill twenty indigenous people in El Quiché, they could shoot a few at the United Nations with the same arrogance. Their principal international ally was the US, which had been annoyed by the presence at the UN of Navajos, Hopis, Lakotas and Yaquis. It was sad to see these governments closing ranks to defend their repressive colleagues.

After the session was suspended, my *compañeros* in the International Council said, 'Don't worry. If they want to kick us out, we'll all go. We won't let them kick you out alone.'

Half an hour later the session restarted. To my great surprise, the president arrived and said, 'Miss Rigoberta Menchú, the representative of the International Council of Indian Treaties, has the floor.' They told me later that I began speaking as if nothing had happened: 'Mr President, in my country they speak twenty-two different languages . . .'

I went on to lobby the UN and the human-rights organisations in a group with other Guatemalan exiles; we were called the Unitary Representation of the Guatemalan Opposition (RUOG). There were five of us: Rolando Castillo, Raúl Molina, Frank Larrué, Marta Torres and me. They helped familiarise me with the various areas of the UN. At first, when I saw a high-ranking UN official, my hands would sweat and I would lose my voice.

Sometimes you feel overwhelmed by things, you feel helpless. But my friends practically forced me to speak. During important conferences they would say, 'Now let's hear from our *compañera*.' I couldn't escape, and that's how I learned to speak in public. It wasn't a punishment, it was just a challenge I had to meet.

The Guatemalan group was a strange phenomenon. We did not have consultative status at the UN, but we always found an NGO to help us lobby. We weren't in a political party, yet we always had the ear of political parties. We were not spokespersons for the Guatemalan guerrilla movement, the Guatemalan National Revolutionary Unity (URNG), and we did not play the role that Guillermo Ungo played for the FMLN in El Salvador. Yet we were listened to in the same way. We had our own space. Foreign ministries listened to us. International human-rights organisations listened to us. They saw us as the voice of the popular movement that had been destroyed. We were considered the channel for different shades of opinion in a Guatemalan civil society that had been eliminated, and we were treated with respect.

Our group all lived in exile, but in different places. Marta lived in Canada, Raúl in New York, Frank in Washington, and Rolando and I in Mexico City. But we were well organised and had a very close relationship. Our main task was to call the attention of the international community to the serious and continuous human-rights violations in Guatemala. We were always trying to get delegations from city councils or universities, or influential individuals, to go to Guatemala. We hoped that they would be able to send a different message to the world about what was going on there. We monitored the situation in Guatemala all the time, and we did not concentrate solely on massacres and repression. We tried to make people understand the whole panorama.

Gradually we carved out a niche for ourselves. We never had any proper status, and we never bothered going through the formal channels. Yet we kept going year after year. We had two annual meetings. A good part of my work on speaking tours round the world was on a joint agenda. I was a representative of the CUC abroad. But when I wasn't representing the CUC, I was representing the RUOG.

Raúl, Frank, Marta, Rolando and I all did the same kind of work. Nobody had a higher position or tried to appear cleverer than the others. We rotated. If a delegation went to Geneva, Raúl and Rigoberta would go. If a delegation went to the Organization of American States (OAS), Frank and someone else would go. We were interchangeable, and played a different role according to the platform. Not a meeting of the OAS passed without us being present, even if we had to get in through the kitchen door or had to challenge the security guards.

Human-rights issues were often discussed in the conference halls or in smart drawing-rooms, without the victims being present. For on many occasions, we were not allowed into meetings because we were not considered sufficiently important. But at least we were present in the city where the meetings were being held, and we had friends to pass the information on to us. We always had a resolution to put forward: a strong condemnation of the Guatemalan government.

Much the same would happen at the UN since we did not have official status. On countless occasions they had to throw me out of the main conference hall. The police would come and tell me, 'Madam, this is a government area, you can't come in.' I would pretend that I didn't understand English, but they would throw me out anyway. Then I would go back in again. For twelve years I steam-rolled – literally steam-rolled – down the UN corridors, battering down all its doors.

When you are convinced your cause is just, you fight for it. It is not pleasant, the role of the losers. It is humiliating. One day, Marta and I had been waiting three hours to see a particular diplomat. She was looking tired when Rolando arrived and said, 'D'you realise how pointless this is?' His words summed up how she felt. Having to explain a people's suffering in diplomatic language is outrageous; we're talking about lives, women's lives, children's lives. To see a diplomat you would have to ask for an appointment over and over again. The diplomat would only come to be polite, and often wouldn't even listen. It was always obvious that he had only agreed to the meeting in order to get rid of us. Some governments guilty of human-rights abuses would take fright when they saw us coming. They knew that we would always challenge their version of events. The Guatemalan government looked at us as they would any other opponent of their regime, except they couldn't punish us in the same way.

I have always been amazed by the way the United Nations operates. When a vote is taken, some delegates press the 'yes' button, some press the 'no', others abstain and some walk out. This happens after months of negotiations, without a single item of information being given to the millions of people round the world on whose behalf they are voting. They would do better to say a prayer for humanity. Indeed it might be more ethical, moral and honourable to do just that. It would also do them good spiritually. It is good to stop for a minute and pray for other people. But the UN is not about praying for humanity. It is more concerned with the important political, economic and military matters at stake.

When the Guatemalan situation – a tiny, absolutely minute case – was being negotiated, it was our job to highlight the existence of Guatemala, Central America and the whole of our continent. To the delegates it was all much the same whatever place you came from, whether you were K'iche', Aymara, Mapuche, Apache or Garifona. It was all called the Third World, and everyone from that world seemed to be committing the same sins.

We didn't talk about all of Guatemala's problems, only about the right to life, to freedom of organisation and to freedom of expression. The scorched-earth campaign passed down the corridors of the UN as if it had never happened. When we first arrived there to lobby, our hearts sank, we felt intimidated, we felt so small compared to the great monsters of political intrigue already there. Every day, there was something new and strange to discover or establish.

We tried to talk to diplomats or bureaucrats one at a time. All the governments reacted in the same way. We would ask for an appointment with a diplomat, and it would be three days or a week before he gave us one. During that time, we had to remind him five times a day that he had promised to see us. He would dash off or escape through a side door. He would be busy coming and going. When he finally saw us, he would sit down and say, 'So, what can I do for you?' with his watch in his hand, looking distractedly at people walking by. He would always conjure up a smile, but he always seemed to have more important things to do. In our precious five minutes he would shake hands with five colleagues who happened to be passing.

Then he would leave, saying, 'Don't worry. Leave it with me. My government is committed.' Usually, we knew that these were empty words, we knew there was no commitment. Not just to us, or to the Guatemalan people. There was no priority given to defending human rights at all.

I used to say, 'Oh my God, what a hard life!' Not to be downhearted, but to emphasise the need to carry on. I then began to understand that ethics were not on the agenda of many of the people making decisions.

This went on, year after year, the excuses were always the same. The bureaucrats would say, 'Well, the situation is improving because I have reports from the Guatemalan government saying that fewer people have died this year than last. They have shown goodwill. We have to give them the benefit of the doubt.'

Lives became a game of statistics. We never knew what number would impress which government official, and we had the impression that all governments had their feet under the same table. The bureaucrats seemed very self-important, well-off people. They pushed paper around. The photocopiers were busier than the diplomats. There was always a line of agitated people waiting for the photocopier and, if it was not done in time, it would make a regrettable difference to somebody's vote.

Some officials come and go, you can hardly tell the difference. Some are veterans who know the ropes and can find their way through the maze. The rest of us were all trying to discover the secret of those unforgettable corridors. Even if officials know you, they shake hands and have a coffee as if it were the first time. It was a cold, cold place, as if the cold of the snow had penetrated the bodies of the diplomats when it came to the subject of human rights. If four hundred villages burned in Guatemala didn't move them, what would?

We were the ones making the fuss, but who were we? Nobody. Our only credentials were to have been born in Guatemala. And it wasn't just us. There were El Salvadoreans, Colombians, Burmese, Timorese, Afghans, Tamils and Kurds. All had hair-raising stories of killings, of children being raped, of land and property being destroyed. Many of the witnesses had suffered the savagery of systemic human-rights violations in the flesh. The various human-rights NGOs worked tirelessly to get these victims a chance to speak, to try and move government delegates. They rarely even managed to finish the few minutes they were allotted.

We all had a common cause and were all doing the same lobbying. We gave each other moral support and sympathy because we had a common language and a common history. If some group or other was successful, we all felt strengthened and optimistic, and it raised our hopes for our own particular cause. Some NGOs were more lost than others, but as the Bible says, 'There is great variety in the vineyard of the Lord.'

There came a time when I simply couldn't carry on with my work at the UN. I had always been asking for new *compañeros* to join me. I wanted them to learn about the circles I was working in, and to understand why we had to be at the UN. I wanted to prepare people to take my place, for no one is indispensable. It is sometimes better to teach people to walk along an old path than to build a new one.

In 1984, I insisted that my *compañeros* in Mexico should send new people. A group of us went to try and convince them that the UN was a very important forum and that we shouldn't neglect it. It is where a people's destiny is forged. We need to be there, if only as moral witnesses.

The new *compañeros* who came would often become depressed, for it is lonely work. They would miss life away from Guatemala in a place where they can't eat *tortillas*, where they can't understand the language, where they don't have friends and where there is no *marimba*. They would say, 'I want to go back to Guatemala, I can't stand it here.'

In 1987, the experience was interrupted. None of them understood the importance of learning about things outside their own frontiers. Then another couple of *compañeras* came, but they too got depressed and had to be sent back. You can't keep people in a place against their will. They must want to stay because it gives their life meaning, because they feel it is right, not because they feel obliged to be there. It happened over and over again. A lot of Guatemalans feel terribly lonely whenever they leave their community and their land.

A UN resolution critical of human rights in Guatemala had existed ever since 1979, and it had been tabled year after year. It involved an incredible amount of work; three months of negotiation in Geneva, and then three more months at the UN General Assembly in New York. It was work Raúl, Marta and I devoted particular care to. There were no winners and losers, it was simply a text that needed hard negotiation. We liked to think that it would help the victims, and avoid further deaths.

The Guatemalan mission was made up of ten to fifteen top diplomats. Their job was to soften the clauses, find euphemisms to describe the terrible abuses that their government committed. Our organisation, RUOG, and other non-government representatives would then try to ensure that the document would at least mention the existence of human-rights violations. Getting this clause taken out would be regarded as a victory for the government.

This is one of the major drawbacks of the UN. The war is fought in the lobbies, and, after the lobbying, still more years pass. No one person ever sees the project through, or knows whether the resolution is finally carried. At first I found the whole thing very difficult to understand, though we eventually became procedural experts.

The negotiating process at the UN is often so extraordinary that if you told people who didn't know anything about it, they would be outraged. They would think they were dreaming, or that this was a brilliant work of fiction. Negotiating is the worst issue because human rights can never be negotiable. Guatemala was never punished for its human-rights violations because, despite the massacres, they were not of much interest to the majority of countries. The fact that more than four hundred villages had been destroyed touched neither the conscience of the UN, nor that of the international community as a whole.

I knew the UN was the preserve of governments, but I had never seen a Guatemalan government delegate up close before. I only knew the representatives of the INTA, the Guatemalan state land agency, who in my experience were just thieves who imposed fines on peasants. Sometimes the delegate might be an army officer. I was used to the army too. We knew that if the soldiers, the *pintos*, came after us, our lives were in danger and it would be a miracle if we survived. I had never seen soldiers wearing a tie before. Seeing them in a tie, without batons in their hands, seemed strange to me. I didn't really believe they were soldiers. They could be any other human beings but not soldiers.

In the diplomatic world, you see a soldier and you even smile at him, or nod 'Good morning!' We could be two equal human beings. It was at such moments that I began to understand the importance of disarmament, the importance of disarming the military by denouncing the horrors they commit. One of the hardest things is to make a speech for the first time in the presence of a senior army officer.

I heard Guatemala's UN delegate reciting the Guatemalan constitution and I have to admit that I didn't know it at all, not a single article. They talk so much at the UN about the law, rights, international standards, the Universal Declaration, accords and protocols, that I thought I ought to read the Guatemalan constitution. I now began to realise that laws exist that are not applied in real life. I felt extremely angry and indignant. I realised there were international laws to regulate a government's obligations to respect its people, and I thought of how many times those laws had been violated.

The UN sessions lasted for two and a half months. Human rights were always discussed. The contradiction was that although the issue was human rights, many of the bureaucrats were not prepared to hear stories of human-rights abuses at all, and even less to respect the feelings of the victims.

Most of the people lobbying were victims and had lived through traumatic experiences. Many had been persecuted. Most of the time, the people were not heard: the dramatic case of Colombia, the case of Peru, of Haiti, Burma, Kurdistan, Afghanistan, to mention but a few. Certain other cases were lucky and had a UN resolution passed, and were taken up as special. Ours was one of those. I say lucky because, in the end, it happened more by accident than conviction.

When the resolution on Guatemala was being discussed, they examined every comma and full stop with a magnifying glass, so as not to offend the Guatemalan government. Many sectors of the international community never saw the tiny case of Guatemala as a serious problem. Yet we knew that in a few years' time we would see many more things happening in Guatemala: refugees, exiles, internally displaced people, people fleeing to the mountains, populations in resistance. We would see large numbers of orphans and widows – and more torture, disappearances and clandestine graveyards. Yet the diplomats had to endlessly examine the small print. We waited as if we were at a funeral – or at a birth. Waiting for a resolution on Guatemala sometimes seemed like waiting for someone to be born.

Yet finally the vote was taken. Our people won. It seemed extraordinary, and we were amazed at what we had achieved. We were very happy with our work. In the end the morality and ethics on our side won the day. It was a victory for life. We hoped that one day this would contribute in a small way to ensuring our history would not be forgotten and injustice would not triumph. We did not think that the Guatemalan government or the armed forces would take any notice of a UN resolution, nor did we think that fewer of our compatriots would die. I never believed that. Yet every little thing is significant.

Whenever I talk about the Guatemalan resolution, I always remember the Mothers of the Plaza de Mayo, the Mothers of the Chilean *carabineros*, the Mothers from El Salvador. I know now that the struggle for human rights can not be fought by just one or two people. It's no use having figureheads. Human rights have often been the preserve of a couple of figureheads while the people whose rights have been violated have not been seen. The day when different sectors of society take control of their lives, and are able to keep a more careful check on their governments, will be the day when the world will return to its natural rhythm, and public morality and ethics will prevail. Things must change. We need different reference points if society is to improve. The struggle for human rights is endlessly frustrating and demands a permanent commitment.

I believe in people, and in people's power. If we all joined human-rights organisations, big and small, in fighting corruption, injustice and greed, then the huge gulf between North and South, between rich and poor within nations, would be bridged and the world would change. If society recognised that the suffering in El Quiché hurt the whole world, then humanity would recover its true meaning.

A large part of my education was acquired through lobbying at the United Nations. I really appreciated the chance to learn about bilateral organisations, intergovernmental organisations and the world of the NGOs. I never missed a single session.

A disagreeable person said to me one day, 'You are the UN pet.' I did not really understand what he meant, and I said simply, 'Well, that's your opinion.' But I grew up politically while lobbying at the UN.

I followed everything that happened with regard to Nicaragua very closely: the negotiations, the problems, the pressures. I knew the role played by the Latin American Support Group (GRULA). I knew the role played by the West. I knew how our continent's diplomats brought up issues, negotiated and blackmailed. I saw how they hounded Nicaragua. It was incredible. The role that the UN played in protecting US interests in Nicaragua was patently obvious.

I also saw how difficult it was for Cuba at the UN and how it affected that country. I soon understood that the anti-Cuba statements coming from various countries had nothing to do with a genuine concern for the Cuban people's human rights. The question of Cuba is one of independence and autonomy. Some countries are just not prepared to respect Cuba's right to self-determination. The United States considers Cuba a part of its territory, another Puerto Rico, another Dominican Republic. To them Cuba is another piece of land, one of the many it has invaded, except that Cuba is a rebellious piece that has remained outside their control.

The United States has never been particularly interested in civil society. The attitude of the current US government may have changed slightly, but previous US governments actively supported militarisation. Latin American countries would often cover up for each other, because their own record on human rights was so bad. Colombia, for instance, could never agree to human-rights violations being condemned because their situation is similar to Guatemala's. Peru is the same. Brazil as well. We could go through all the countries of Latin America, one by one. There are few countries on the continent without a history of serious and systematic violations of human rights. They are, as my mother would say, birds of a feather.

I spent so much time at the UN that I learned the phoney expressions of goodwill repeated each year by heart. 'The situation has improved', or 'the government has assured us that next year will be different'. Always the same old phrases. You learn to understand the organisation, to read between the lines, to recognise the decisive moments. You learn, and you guess. Everything carries a message. If this person has coffee with that person, if this delegate lunches with that delegate . . . At first I found all this rather shocking, yet in the end I began to understand that the answer doesn't lie in abandoning the UN platform. The need is to keep banging away at it, even at the risk of seeming an oddball. It is better to do that than to leave it in the hands of the same old diplomatic hacks.

All in all, I still have a high regard for the work of the United Nations. The NGOs certainly have a job to do there. They are the organisations closest to the victims. I think all the world's civil movements should get more involved with the UN. They should contribute, criticise and demand the changes that are necessary. Civil society can bring them about. Every country should be obliged to send a human-rights specialist. How can a diplomat who does not have the words 'human rights' in his vocabulary defend them, either as a professional or as a human being? Many of the bureaucrats who arrive at the UN have inherited their positions from a family member. They haven't inherited much knowledge of what is really going on in their own countries.

If governments were to take the trouble to appoint new diplomats from time to time, and were to choose people who were more educated – in the deepest and broadest sense – they would be doing the world a great service. Only recently have diplomats begun to be more objective. You used only to hear wonderful things about their countries. When a government made a report about their country, it was to say that they were paying 90 per cent more attention to women's issues, 80 per cent more to young people's issues, and 100 per cent more to employment issues and the education of indigenous peoples. A general improvement in everything! A society without defects!

Government reports always seemed to be talking about a world without problems. Yet there has never been such a thing as a perfect society. Wars, the fall of the Berlin Wall, new conflicts all over the globe, have proved this. So has the increase in world poverty. So where is all this wonderful progress?

At least governments now talk about 'combating poverty'. Yet how can they achieve this if they don't know any poor people, and if the poor have not been consulted about any of the big decisions taken about them? I didn't learn these things from books. I learned them from the people themselves, from their experiences.

I really admire people who never lose their humanity despite all the obstacles. There are people of sincere good will in all echelons of the UN. There are good people in the NGOs. Our paths have crossed over the years and I have the same respect for them as I did when we first met. There are people who have worked with great dignity and in the true belief that things will change.

I am sure the UN will gradually meet these great challenges. It is after all the only international instrument today with authority to deal with matters that affect and help humanity.

One important thing I have learned in these years is that you have to listen to the victims and to sympathise with them. This is where the human-rights NGOs have an important mission to fulfil. These organisations have devoted many years to investigating abuses, taking down testimonies, tracing victims and their families and trying to identify the world's areas of conflict. At the same time, chronic contagious diseases like cholera have re-emerged and new ones, like AIDS, have appeared. These affect the most destitute and long-suffering populations in the world, especially those that do not have clean drinking water, health centres or a minimum level of sub-sistence. AIDS does not just affect large numbers of people, it also brings discrimination and racism. It has come to be seen as a mortal sin. People die in isolation, because others think that divine punishment has been visited upon them – and even more so when the sufferer is poor.

Organisations now exist that are beginning to urge respect for homo-sexuals. Defending any kind of minority and fighting discrimination is the responsibility of all of us, and especially of the UN. Yet concentrating on these issues, because they are new, sometimes obscures more traditional issues – like dictatorship, repression, militarisation and injustice in different parts of the world. We have to campaign for human rights as a whole. The victims of new incurable diseases, the victims of social injustice, and the victims of war and impunity – all these are equally important. Often when we talk of human rights we get stuck in the particular. I don't think the nations of the world have ever really thought of human rights in global terms. The UN does not always apply its own universal principles consistently.

I have always considered the UN a great challenge. I am not against it, but I would like the whole nature of the institution to change – so that the issue of human rights could be given a decent hearing.

The UN should take a fresh look at all its work, and introduce a series of reforms that would put the Universal Declaration on Human Rights into a global context. Social inequality would not occur if the UN ensured that its own Declaration was actually applied. The issue of human rights – connected with their systematic violation, with cholera, with AIDS, or with political repression – is often used as an excuse for not tackling the global issue of a people's economic, social and political rights. In many instances they are both judge and interested party. In this sense, the work in the UN is very frustrating for the victims. Tyrants in one part of the world defend victims in another part, and they are the ones who are supposed to apply sanctions.

If everybody had the chance to discover the UN the way that I have, we could probably change a lot of things with the laws already in existence. I managed to learn all this without having any diplomas or university degrees. I have never studied international law and I never will. I simply learned by following UN diplomats and bureaucrats around.

The UN is supposed to be the world's main problem-solving body. Yet it is difficult for the victims of the world's problems to gain entrance. Not many of them can make a fuss, as I did, and get in. Worse still, victims have no protection after they have told their stories. Governments take note of the witnesses who testify and from then on they are marked men.

We need to review the role of the UN and devise a process by which the NGOs have a bigger say. Their stance is impartial. We cannot change the nature of the UN, but we can try to make it serve the world better and make it work more efficiently.

I thought the UN was the principal guardian of peace, but it is the Security Council that has always made decisions about the weapons used in the world. The Security Council is made up of a small group of countries with a right of veto and the right to use force. In a sense the UN has authorised armed conflict in many areas. Its function has gradually deteriorated and regressed. Under the sacred banner of the Universal Declaration of Human Rights, the UN has donned the blue beret and gone into combat.

This has been the lowest point in the crisis at the UN. I think it is sad that certain countries fight each other with the approval of the UN. The Declaration means something important to people. Its original principles should be upheld. If they were, the Balkans, Central Africa, and Central America, would not have had to go through such horrendous times.

The UN is still the highest authority for the millions of people in the world who watch its decisions. We must appeal to the UN. We must make our criticisms known. We must urge the signatories to the UN Charter to play the role originally assigned to them. There are people alive today who were involved in the early stages at the UN. They too should use their moral authority to appeal to the UN.

I feel part of the UN, not just because I have lobbied there, but because I have heard the testimony of thousands of people who, like me, believe the role of the UN is fundamental. I am also part of it because I agreed to be 'Goodwill Ambassador' for the International Year of Indigenous Peoples. I would accept any work to do with the UN. These close ties do not mean that I have to modify my opinions and criticisms. Other people should do the same, if we are to further the cause of human rights.

7

FIGHTING FOR THE RIGHTS OF
INDIGENOUS PEOPLES

I went to the United Nations year after year for twelve years. At the beginning, many governments denied the existence of indigenous peoples in their countries. One day I heard a Guatemalan speaker saying that in Guatemala there was only one people. He recognised that certain Guatemalans felt discriminated against, but he explained that this was a psychological problem. There were no differences, according to him, there were no ethnic groups. He began to deny everything that was happening in Guatemala. There had never been racism or discrimination, let alone violations of free speech and freedom of movement. He gave what was practically a lecture on the Guatemalan constitution; everything was perfect! This was at the time the government was waging a scorched-earth campaign!

Indigenous people had first appeared at the United Nations in the middle of the 1970s. After long-drawn-out bureaucratic procedures, the International Council of Indigenous Treaties was officially recognised in

1976 as an NGO with consultative status. Today there are now eleven indigenous organisations with consultative status at the UN. But we should pay particular tribute to Chief Descage. He was the first indigenous leader to go to the League of Nations at Geneva, as far back as the 1920s. He tried to get his voice heard, but no one listened to him. He was the first indigenous leader to try to use an international forum to express his ideas, and perhaps the first to understand that international organisations might some day defend the rights of indigenous peoples.

Later, in the 1970s, the native peoples of the United States and Canada – the Navajos, the Sioux, the Hopis and the Lakotas – also went to Geneva. They travelled on their indigenous passports to challenge the US and Swiss authorities. The 'indigenous passport' is only supposed to be used for Native Americans to cross the border between the US and Canada. Our indigenous brothers used it to leave the US and to enter Switzerland.

They arrived in Geneva with their passports, musicians, drums, pipes and rattles. The authorities only realised when they were already on Swiss territory. They set off to march to the city from the airport. Their slogan was 'We come with respect, we come in peace. But if we are not received peacefully, we are coming in anyway, kicking and screaming.'

They wanted to reach what they called the 'House of Glass'. There they would proclaim their names, and the names of their lands. The 'House of Glass' refused to recognise what lands they were talking about. They were referred to the US and the Canadian authorities that had embassies in the city.

Their demonstration was very moving, for their only weapons were their prayers, their offerings, their music and the sound of their drums. They defied the authorities of both the United States and the United Nations. The police would not let them into the UN buildings, and wanted to arrest them, but they insisted that they had come in peace.

As always, there were negotiations. A UN representative went out and received their offerings and listened to their demands. Their principal demand was for a minute's silence, and for a prayer to be offered, in the seats of the governments that took decisions in their name. They sat down, prayed for a minute in silence, and left.

There were colleagues at the UN whose main task was to recover the treaties that had been signed hundreds of years ago, treaties which were never honoured and were gathering dust in government archives or indigenous communities. Some treaties involving land are valid today. We waited with bated breath for the report by Cuba's Miguel Alfonso Martínez to find out the current state of these treaties. Don Alfonso, and Erika Daes from Greece, had spent a lifetime trying to find an answer to our dreams, they will always be in our memories.

In 1983, the UN considered the issue important enough to set up a system to centralise these documents, so that they could be used as the basis for a future international agreement to ratify the treaties. The centre was called the UN Centre of Indigenous People's Documentation (CIPD). We invested all our hopes in it, and over the years we added to the Centre's archive. Brothers came down from communities up in the mountains to deposit copies of their treaties. Sometimes they even brought the originals. It was to be indigenous people's memory bank in Geneva. That is what we all understood it to be. What we did not understand was the risk.

We handed over our patrimony, unconditionally, blindly and trustingly. For almost a decade we had put all our people's documents there. And then we heard that on one August dawn in 1989, the Centre had burned down. Nothing was left but ashes.

Many people have given a lot to the cause of indigenous peoples. I would particularly like to honour Augusto Willemsen Díaz, who wrote a remarkable document known as the 'Martínez Cobo Report'. This is three huge volumes, and its vast number of pages specifically set out the rights of indigenous peoples. Don Augusto was a Guatemalan mestizo, a great admirer of the Mayan culture, and a world expert on the rights of indigenous peoples and ethnic minorities. People like him put pressure on the United Nations to recognise the issue of indigenous peoples.

The Working Group on Indigenous Peoples was finally recognised officially in, I think, 1982. There was also a separate platform for ethnic minorities; the Sub-Commission on the Prevention of Discrimination and Protection of Ethnic Minorities. This had a higher status than our Working Group.

This was not achieved without a great deal of patience. Whenever we went through the check-in desks at the UN, they looked in our bags and passed their gadgets over us – to see if were carrying knives and guns. This did not happen to others coming in; they just had to show their credentials. We had to undergo more specific checks. We were always very friendly and courteous to the police. I have always made a point at the UN of greeting the employees and the guards, and of talking to them and asking them where they were from. We made friends with them.

Our Working Group had five experts, one per continent, elected through the Sub-Commission. More and more of our people began arriving, and by 1984 and 1985 the Working Group had become an effective platform. We eventually began to learn diplomacy and were able to express ourselves in diplomatic language, so that we did not get expelled. We began to explain courteously and diplomatically the dreadful problems facing our people in Guatemala. We were the first to denounce the Civil Defence Patrols, the occupation of our villages, the scorched-earth campaigns, the massacres, the burning of more than four hundred villages. We placed it all on record. We were very diplomatic, so as not to offend the Guatemalan government or their allies. People gradually got to know us.

Governments participated in the Working Group too, especially those governments that expected to be denounced for human-rights abuses. In a way this enriched the Group, for it would have been worse if there had been no dialogue and each side had spoken in a different forum. The governments came as observers, but they were lobbying at the same time. They got very involved. This meant governments and indigenous peoples were not buried in hostilities, but searched together for a consensus on which to base dialogue, *rapprochement* and, in some cases, alliances. Eventually a process of negotiation began with government representatives. It was a worthwhile lesson that we should value, for the new relationship we are proposing to governments is based on dialogue and negotiation.

Governments and indigenous peoples have to trust each other. Their relationship has to be regulated. Governments can no longer make laws behind the backs of indigenous peoples. They must include them in the decision-making process. The Working Group has been the only forum in which both indigenous peoples and their non-indigenous governments can be heard.

The concept of 'indigenous peoples' was one of the first things to be discussed in our Working Group. The issue had been raised by brothers and sisters from all over the world. They concluded that it was important to accept the name 'indigenous'. A large number of indigenous peoples live on the American continent, and it was amazing how many of them sent representatives to the UN. They came from the Andes, from the mountains of Bolivia, from the deserts of Peru. Many came from Ecuador, Brazil and Chile. Some came from Central America, for the question of the Miskitos in Nicaragua was being discussed.

The United States was manipulating that particular debate. They set themselves up as protectors of the Miskitos. Yet this same government was trying all sorts of manoeuvres to marginalise the Lakotas, one of the first Native American nations in their own country. This kind of thing created divisions among us. We felt the fall-out from the Cold War. Although we were defending common interests, we had our own particular political and ideological identities. The Cold War affected us as it did everyone else. There were a lot of divisions, and the legacy of fragmentation continues to this day.

One of our aims was to secure a Universal Declaration of the Rights of Indigenous Peoples. If the UN were to declare indigenous people legal, they would have a legal framework within which to work. At present, national constitutions do not recognise indigenous peoples, nor do international law and institutions, because we don't appear as specific peoples in the Universal Declaration of Human Rights. We simply do not exist; we have no rights. The UN, however, could recognise our legality.

The year 1984 was a watershed for our Working Group, though we didn't really understand this at the time. We were rather divided, with several different positions and different interests. But the UN realised that the Working Group had become a powerful platform. They decided to cancel it, supposedly for lack of funds, and a big battle ensued. The NGOs supported us, and so did the environmentalists, and we forced the UN to reconsider. Finance or no finance, we said, we were not going to let our forum be shut down. So the Working Group survived, and continued with the Universal Declaration project. This, we hope, will now pass to higher levels of the UN, and some day indigenous peoples will have universal principles to enable them to live on their land and demand their rights.

I consider it a privilege to have been on the UN's Working Group on Indigenous Peoples. In an ideal world, I would like to embrace everyone's cause, that of every people on every continent. But I know my own limitations, so I just defend my own patch: the Americas and the Caribbean.

I realise too that recognising the rights of indigenous peoples creates problems for many countries. In Spain there are Basques, Catalans and Galicians. In Ireland there are deep divisions. The Balkan countries maintain a very precarious equilibrium. India faces problems of a similar kind, as do the countries of Africa. This is a huge area of controversy. Yet the justice of recognising the rights of indigenous peoples must be universally accepted. The proposed Universal Declaration of the Rights of Indigenous Peoples would light the way to respecting all the world's minorities. I am sure of that.

Yet it will be a long haul. It would be much easier and more gratifying for me just to defend my own village, Chimel, just one of many such cases in Guatemala where generations have fought for a piece of land and have never been recognised as the owners. Landownership remains a problem all over Latin America, and some governments must be made to be more flexible. I know the Brazilian representatives in Geneva very well, their attitude is very rigid. Costa Rica is still considering whether indigenous people are citizens or not. In North America, our indigenous brothers live on reservations, their tribes have either been wiped out or they have suffered continual harassment.

Attachment to the land is common to indigenous peoples throughout the continent. Some peoples have been treated better than others because they signed treaties many years ago, and the treaties are still valid. Our Canadian and North American brothers have such treaties, though they have not always been respected. In the case of Guatemala, there have never been treaties. Ownership of land is simply under review. According to laws made by the non-indigenous, the people have never owned the land. Even today, the government is trying to sell land that has been claimed for generations by indigenous people.

Few governments tackle the land problem through legislation. Mexico declares itself to be pluri-cultural and multi-ethnic, and this suggests the process could be different. It certainly is in Chiapas, a new form of development that we must watch carefully. If Mexico manages to make it work, if there is a lasting solution to the armed conflict there, it would be a great example for the rest of the continent.

An initiative was taken in Brazil to demarcate indigenous lands, but with a change of government the proposals were shelved. The Atlantic coast of Nicaragua remains interesting because they are talking about an autonomous government within national borders.

In Guatemala, big steps are being taken which we hope will bear fruit. We are working there for a multi-ethnic, multi-lingual and pluri-cultural nation. We are convinced the solution lies in cultural diversity. We have to recognise that there has been progress in many areas, but there has been no significant change in the way in which the government responds to the needs of its peoples or to their just demands. Guatemala is the epicentre of America. One day our achievements will shine out like a beacon of hope for the whole continent and for indigenous peoples everywhere!

Fifty years after the world's nations adopted the Universal Declaration on

Human Rights, we indigenous peoples are still clamouring to be heard. We want a Universal Declaration on the Rights of Indigenous Peoples, to end the ethnocide, massacres, destruction and contempt in which we live. For more than fifteen years we have contributed to the discussion at the UN on the draft Declaration. We have pinned huge hopes on it being adopted as soon as possible.

Our hopes go further. Our ultimate dream is an International Convention on the Rights of Indigenous Peoples, ratified by all the nations in the UN. Only then would our existence be fully recognised, and would the active participation of our peoples in determining our own futures be guaranteed. At the moment, there are many places where we have no legal identity. Our ultimate objective is that our children should grow up within their ancient identity and culture, that they should live in freedom and dignity, without fear of persecution, and that they should have the right to live in a pluri-cultural world.

The fact that the definition of such a Convention is complex does not mean that it is unobtainable. It would have to go hand in hand with national political struggles, since nothing can be achieved internationally without them. That is why it is so important for indigenous organisations, and indigenous people who have played any kind of political or social role, to unite to take control of our destiny in our own countries. Otherwise the UN might define a set of international norms that would be ignored at the national level.

This is easier in the case of Guatemala because the Mayans, Xincas and Garifunas are the huge majority, and the *ladinos* are beginning to realise that they themselves are only another ethnic group. There are few areas in which indigenous people are not now in evidence. There are Mayan refugees, Mayan displaced people, Mayan widows, Mayans in the NGOs, Mayans in the co-operative movements and Mayans in the peasant movements. Since 1993 there has been considerable Mayan involvement in the electoral system, both inside and outside the political parties. They are also present in civic committees and religious congregations of all types. A synthesis of this process will determine new relationships in society – in the economy, politics, the military and the law. Every day we fertilise the seed to build a new relationship between indigenous and non-indigenous peoples, between the *ladino* government and its multi-ethnic, pluri-lingual and pluri-cultural people.

This is one of the reasons why the struggle of widows and peasants against compulsory military service is so important. Conscientious objection offers solutions for the whole of society, and is not just an indigenous demand. We must make this type of struggle the norm. The debate will eventually be very fruitful, and we will be able to consolidate a national identity based on mutual respect. The Guatemalan – the *chapín* – will exist within this plurality. This is not a utopia, for one day we will eradicate the roots of racism. This is the true nature of Guatemala, though it may still be difficult for some to accept it.

It is important that this debate should take place before the end of the millennium, for its seeds will flower in the next century. Mayans believe that our debate about identity, rights and the indigenous struggle is like a bridge over which we will pass to join the next millennium. It is like a prophecy. I believe in prophesies and I also believe in the international conscience. I believe that it is not going to ignore the indigenous question in the way that it has done for the last five hundred years. The Quincentenary celebrations were a focal point for resolving many things.

I believe the next millennium will not forget the people massacred in Panzos, in El Ixcán, the women raped and burned alive in this land of maize. It will not forget Chiapas, it will not forget the Guatemalan Mayans, our Andean brothers, the peoples of the Amazon. It will not forget something that will be embodied in a Universal Declaration of Principles. It will continue fighting to legislate at an international and national level for the rights of indigenous peoples. Our children have the right to the truth. I'm sure it is inherent in them to seek it.

In 1989, the year the Berlin Wall fell, a new and complex issue arose at the United Nations. It concerned the difference between 'indigenous peoples' and 'ethnic minorities'. Many different groups appeared for the first time, all desperate for an international platform. The Working Group on Indigenous Peoples swelled. Groups arrived from all over the world – from Japan, Tibet, India, Thailand, and many other places in Asia and Africa. The ethnic minorities from Eastern Europe came for the first time too. Environmentalists joined us, and, as if that was not enough, the issue of the Columbus Quincentenary celebrations came up too.

This was to be a difficult time for indigenous peoples at the UN. Defining the concept of what is 'indigenous', what is 'ethnic', and what is 'a minority' is not easy. Everyone uses the terms in his own way. Some ethnic minorities are indeed original peoples. There is not necessarily a religious connotation, it could be an ancient culture that has forged its own identity and created a specific character. Saying 'Indian' in the sense of 'indigenous' in India is a paradox. They are Indian in the true sense of the word. Calling them 'indigenous' only confuses the issue. In India, it is better to talk of 'original peoples' who, within India's cultural diversity, have a specific character. If we mix the issue of indigenous peoples with groups that are considered minorities within their territory, we get into a debate that has no solution either in the short or the long term.

The majority of countries are not willing to make declarations about minorities, or to recognise that minorities have specific rights. One example is the situation of the Caren and the Mons in Burma and Thailand. They are not even mestizos. They have the same identity. Some peoples' cultures are so deep-rooted that their values give them a specific identity.

We had a wonderful experience recently in Thailand with refugees from Burma. When I saw them I said, 'These are my people!' I felt as if I was in a Mayan camp in Quintana Roo, or in Campeche or Chiapas. The problem is to find norms to establish what exactly is 'a people'. The important thing is that these norms are just and defend the rights of the people.

There has been an endless discussion at the UN about the difference between indigenous peoples and ethnic minorities for almost two decades. I believe there is a fundamental difference between indigenous peoples and other minorities as such. When we talk about ethnic minorities, we are talking about a very wide-ranging concept that includes all the religious and cultural diversity that exists in Asia, Africa and also Eastern Europe. They are people with origins and characteristics very different from those of indigenous peoples.

Some governments like to confuse the issue, in order to demonstrate their power and authority, not only over indigenous peoples but over other diverse groups that they lump together. They think that by complicating and distorting the indigenous issue, and confusing it with the ethnic-minority issue, they can delay the legislative advances made on the rights of indigenous peoples at the UN. In this way they thwart the recognition of, and respect for, the rights of indigenous peoples as well as the rights of minorities.

In the Americas, we have taken indigenous peoples to mean those whom Christopher Columbus confused with the inhabitants of India more than five hundred years ago. Our brothers in the Pacific, Australia and New Zealand also have ancient cultures with very deep roots. These indigenous peoples were under formal colonial control until recently, and in some cases colonisation still exists. We talk about 'original peoples', or 'founding peoples', or 'peoples from regions of ancient culture'. On the American continent and in the Caribbean, you don't have to be educated to know who is indigenous and what an indigenous people is. We are talking about thousand-year-old cultures born as part of the great civilisations of humankind.

The rights of minorities go beyond political or economic claims. There is a religious element, there are group characteristics that have evolved to form specific identities. This is a serious and complex subject. Minorities do not come under a simple academic definition. They have proliferated because capitalist society is one that fragments national unity, and makes certain groups increasingly marginal.

Minorities are not just of an ethnic or a religious nature. They are often made up of those who survive and resist in a society that excludes them. Many minority groups do not have historic roots. They are created as a means of self-defence, and they fight together for a common ideal. Collectively, they create a specific mystique and identity. Refugees, for instance, constitute minorities with specific demands. In many parts of the world there are new religious movements that try to convert poor people into small sects. These use diversity as a weapon that goes against the natural harmonious relationship between diversity and national unity. This is a situation we know only too well in the Americas, where the specific objective of some new religious movements is to fragment our society, and divide us.

If we talk about minorities in Guatemala we have to identify exactly who they are. First there are the different religious sects. Then there are society's most vulnerable groups, the poorest of the poor: street children; handicapped people; crippled war veterans and widows. Then there are AIDS sufferers, or people afflicted by rare diseases. These minorities include people from different ethnic groups, both indigenous (Mayan, Xinca, Garifona) and *ladino*. There are also minorities created as a result of the war and the doctrine of national security.

The fragmentation of society creates minorities, and many of the struggles of these vulnerable and marginalised minorities are similar to those faced by indigenous peoples. Both are misunderstood, devalued, despised and oppressed. There is a bond between them for they are both discriminated against. Both dream of living under a new and fairer judicial system. I see their struggle and ours as one. We suffer from the same racism, exploitation and distortion of our reality. The end of this century is marked by an economic crisis that favours the growth of racist and neo-fascist attitudes and organisations. In these circumstances, women, indigenous peoples and minorities must join hands and fight for their common interests. While aware of our differences, we must embrace this cause together.

One of the characteristics differentiating an age-old people with an ancient culture from an ethnic minority is that it has a cosmovision, a philosophy of life, one that is rooted in history. It has laws and norms of its own that govern its existence. The Mayan world, for example, is composed of three basic elements: society (individuals, community, family); nature (physical spaces or territory); and the sacred (divinities, ritual). Harmony between these three elements is central to the cosmovision. The Mayans belong to the planet's great ancient civilisations, to the very first nations. We are not an ethnic or religious minority.

A religious minority is different. Although it may have a philosophy of belief, it does not necessarily have an ancient people's roots and culture.

The distinguishing feature of an indigenous people is the elaboration of a whole area of thought about the earth. An ethnic minority, on the other hand, can live in urban centres or indeed anywhere; it does not necessarily need to be in a community. An ancient people needs to live communally. Their thoughts centre on the universe: the earth, the sea, the sky and the cosmos. Their community guarantees the continuity of the transmission of thought down the generations.

Mother Earth, for us, is not simply a symbolic expression. She is the source, the root, the origin of our culture and our existence. Human beings need the earth, and the earth needs human beings. This balance of co-existence on earth has been slowly eroded. According to our forefathers, the ancient civilisations, the 'first peoples', possessed these values. In all aspects of life there should be harmony and one of the most important sources of this harmony is the community. That is precisely what has been lost today. People do not remember that the earth is their mother. They no longer remember their duty to the community. They do not remember that it is the source of so much energy and so much wealth. So a distance has been created.

We humans are so arrogant we think we do not need the earth. We think we do not need other people, we think we can rely on our own talents. Or we simply forget that the earth exists, and when we do remember we forget that it belongs to all of us. This is important. If there is disharmony, naturally there are terrible consequences; like individualism, wars, cruelty, intolerance, racism and ignorance. The cause of wars is the inequalities and imbalances that the human race invents.

Land, nowadays, has an exclusively material meaning. In Our America, especially in Guatemala, land means wealth for those who have grabbed it and dispossessed its original owners. Eviction and intimidation have meant that the land is now in very few hands, and is exploited only for commercial purposes. In Guatemala there are two kinds of relationship to the earth: that of people who exploit the land for purely material ends; and that of people who see the earth as their mother, the origin of life and source of their inspiration.

This is not to say, however, that the earth has no economic meaning for us. We need the earth, of course. It provides us with our living. It gives us our maize and our beans. It gives us all its fruits so we can live. Inasmuch as we live in a so-called modern world, in which no one can escape the modern influences and the global politics that govern humanity, indigenous peoples also need material benefits from the land. We have never refused to accept a decent life from the riches that the earth produces. The only thing our people ask is to be able to use our own knowledge to secure and enjoy the benefits of the earth.

We human beings are alone responsible for the earth's bountiful gifts. In Guatemala there is a great desire for development and progress, for a better use of the earth's resources. Guaranteeing respect for the earth and the environment does not mean getting rid of the people and leaving the monkeys to roam the countryside.

A great indigenous brother, Flod Westeman, once told me, 'Rigoberta, when men and women return to their Mother, rediscover their Mother, they will have a different kind of energy to use for the future.' I have thought about this a lot. I believe that our people have never seen the universe solely as a source of wealth. They never replaced the creative hand, the tender hand, with destructive hands. They respect animals as Mother Nature's creatures, sharing the right to exist with human beings.

This is not a romantic view. These are not just empty words. This is a different way of viewing creation. It is harmony. I find in my childhood an example of how we interpret life. Our games when we were little were recognising a *zaraguate* and learning the song of the *zaraguate* that forecast rain. Just turning our eyes to the sky and seeing a cloud also confirmed the *zaraguate*'s song. So we knew when to expect a storm, sunny showers or drizzle. Our tactile sense, our very existence, is still close enough to that mysterious nature we think of as the *zaraguate*'s mother and our school of life.

When there is sun with showers, we believe many deer have been born. Our dearest wish is to see a baby deer beside the swamp. At sowing time, the racoons, the wild boar, the birds which peck our seeds, are like clairvoyants or seers. As soon as we began cutting the undergrowth, preparing the land to sow our maize, they appeared as if by magic. It was a fiesta of animals. It was truly weird and wonderful. We all went to protect our seeds, to do battle with the hungry animals over what we had sown.

In the same way, when our maize and other food was finished, we had to go into the mountains to share their flowers, herbs, lianas and different roots. The racoons, armadillos and *taltuzas* calculated their food supply. They knew in which months they couldn't share our maize, *ayotes* and *chilacayote*. They knew they had to eat something else. They made calculations.

Our life followed the seasons. Time becomes our own, the time of animals, and the time of life. Everything has its own precise time. When food, water and work is in short supply, when what was plentiful is scarce, we become frightened, and realise just how limited the human world is.

My mother always used to say, 'Time is wide and long. So wide and long that we are but a tiny dot. Our forefathers passed this way, they trod our paths, they used the shade of these trees, ate their fruit, and we will walk that path too and leave it safe for our heirs to pass after us.'

Even paths teach us things. An old path is there for ever. It holds the history of all those who have passed that way. Even if it becomes a road, it was an old path before. The different stages of our world also pass through us with great intensity. I feel this deeply even at my young age. From the time that we are very young we know that we pass through the world very quickly, in a trice. Nothing is completely ours, yet everything belongs to us.

The world has no notion of how small it is. It is a tiny point in time that is long and wide. Yet almost all human beings, from about the age of ten onwards, start feeling they own this world and nature. That is why they think they can do with it whatever they please.

They have no notion of continuity, no notion of grandchildren, great-grandchildren, no notion that human life blooms in the midst of nature on a grand scale. Anthropologists, sociologists, so-called social scientists, can analyse this all they like. They might even want to be part of it. Yet it is not like a recipe that you can follow. It is in your blood, your memory, the universe. In spite of all manner of oppression, indigenous peoples are still here. They have a tremendous desire to live and flourish. Our cosmovision gives us the permanent chance to recover what has been lost. We have to recover it, because it does not belong to us. We are only its trustees.

Our forefathers were very wise when they discovered years ago that the earth was in grave danger from chemical experiments. We were altering the natural order in a way that would be harmful to generations yet to come. We need agreements that transcend governments. We need solutions that can be urgently applied to save our earth from destruction. We need a definite commitment to save the earth from men and women's greed, and to return it to the natural rhythm of our human race.

Not only were indigenous peoples born of the earth. All humanity came from the earth. We are her children. As the human race is gradually enslaved by its own progress, it attacks the holistic nature of the earth, ignoring the safety of the generations to come.

An indigenous people's cosmovision is centred on their relationship with Mother Earth and Mother Nature. In contrast, the majority of the world doesn't give it a thought, doesn't know what the source of life is. They pollute the earth and do more and more damage. One day the earth will exact a price for this disdain and destruction. When this happens, we will see that the earth is not just good and bountiful, it can also be vengeful.

Indigenous people see Nature as a living mother, not as an inert organism that would allow itself to be destroyed. All those who violate its laws

155

must accept the consequences, because it is alive and will react. My grandfather always used to say that the day human beings violate our universe, they will receive signs and messages. These messages will be very forceful, and will bring severe punishment.

The central premise of the cosmovision is that harmony depends on human beings themselves. We are responsible because we are aware. We have to respect the community, but we also have to demand respect for the family and each one of its members. Not everything is collective nor is everything individual. There is a balance. The process of 'development', on the other hand, has shown an apparent disdain for the origins of humanity, in which the community and a sense of co-operation were very important.

We view the end of the twentieth century with considerable trepidation. The future is uncertain, even threatening. Relationships between men and women have broken down. The education of children has been disrupted. Old people are no longer respected. The nuclear family has disintegrated, causing deep rifts in society, as if men and women were not created to share things. I am not saying that women's struggles have not been valid, but there have been excesses and contradictions.

The same has happened with children and old people. Children's minds today are being deformed by the advertising that goes into their eyes and ears. Children imitate the world around them, and since that world is filled with vice, violence and hostility, children are imitating a contaminated environment. The damage is incalculable. I think current generations will have a lot of difficulties, not only as children but as adolescents. I only hope they have the strength to survive.

Old people also suffer. Far from embodying wisdom, being our walking Bible, and the possessors of experience and values, old people today are rejected and shut away in old folks' homes. Their children rush off after new challenges, like birds abandoning their nests, never to return. This is Western progress: discarding old people like products that no longer sell.

This disharmony affects every aspect of our lives. It dominates ethics. Many people no longer love their work, which used to be their main function in society. This damages the community as a whole. Many professional men and women leave the university swearing to defend the downtrodden classes, the most needy and underprivileged, yet after a few years their professional ethics have disappeared. The same thing happens with those in positions of power. Power is a myth and a reality at the same time. Those who govern us are just a handful of people who dictate everything, both the laws and the way they are applied.

Among ancient peoples, however, the situation is different. The leader, our *K'amal b'e*, is not to be found among the most corrupt and devious members of the community, or the most tricky and opportunist, or even the richest. He is not among the most grasping, or the most sectarian. Our leader is traditionally the person whom the rest of the community most respects, the person who has distinguished himself by his service to the community. His authority derives from his ethical behaviour, and from his experience of life. In modern times, however, the vast majority of people are merely spectators, not actors, in life.

8

SCORCHED EARTH

IN GUATEMALA

While I was in exile from Guatemala in the 1980s, working at the United Nations on behalf of indigenous peoples, going on speaking tours round the world, and helping refugees in Mexico, the military government at home was carrying out a 'scorched-earth' campaign in the rural areas. The reasoning behind the campaign was that the destruction of whole villages would lead to the elimination of all witnesses to their crimes. Witnesses included people from the villages who, by chance, happened not to be there at the time. Like me. If the soldiers had caught me, I could not have told my story. It's as simple as that. They hated us so much.

In their eyes, killing a leader was killing ideals in the people's heart; killing a mother was killing an unborn child who could turn out to be a rebel; killing a young person was killing a potential guerrilla fighter; and killing a child was terrorising the rest of society.

They knew that leaders are not formed quickly. Like fruit, they need time to mature. It is a long process. Every time this process reached maturity,

they picked them off. There was no middle way. You couldn't be a leader without ending up as an outlaw, a widow, a clandestine orphan or a dead guerrilla. This government policy, and the military tactic of eliminating leaders, severely damaged the country's democratic process.

The aim of the scorched-earth policy was total annihilation. They didn't care if they sacrificed fifty people in order to eliminate ten potential guerrillas. They knew they were not destroying actual guerrilla bases, but they wanted to prevent them from being created. They shot pregnant mothers, children, men and women of all ages. They killed them in the vilest manner, and deliberately tortured them as an example to others. There were numerous clandestine prisons and cemeteries. The regime considered every poor person, every indigenous person, to be an enemy. This experience has now become another part of our people's deep memory, and it will be an important source of struggle in the future. No one can leave a loved one forgotten in a communal grave. Burying our dead, with all the respect they deserve, is part of our tradition. People may think I am exaggerating, but I am not. I had to have a tragic life and relate it in a book for people to become aware of our people's plight. My mother was kidnapped, raped, tortured and murdered. My father and little brother were burned alive. Each one of my steps in exile is buried in my memory. The scars do not disappear with the years. They last for centuries in the memory of generations. Victims' wounds remain open. Mine still are. Although the harm done is unpardonable, many governments pardon by decree. They expect the victims to forget by decree. I, as a victim, say no. The decision to forgive belongs to the victims and to them alone. We go on fighting so that the cruelty we suffered never happens again.

Our elders say that the majority of the killers can never be happy afterwards. They fight among themselves and kill each other, they catch diseases and die in agony, they drink themselves to death, they become ashamed to face their families, they commit suicide, they end up alone and friendless. Some killers go mad. Others pray night and day but don't feel God's pardon. They change religions all the time, but they still don't find peace.

Some of those thugs even end up frightened of the dark. The ones that try to live happy lives keep on killing, or await their punishment. That has been the story of our people. The murderers will always be fugitives. They flee from God's justice, and from human justice too.

The scars left by the scorched-earth campaign are so dreadful that it is almost impossible for other people to imagine its impact. One thing is to know about it, another is to actually experience it. We must never forget that this campaign was directed at indigenous people, at the poorest, most humble of peoples. Yet what emerged once again was the courage of our people. They repudiated the system of militarisation, the violence, the creation of nucleated villages. I am sure this courage will some day be the basis of a true culture of peace for our people.

The Communities of the Population in Resistance grew out of the resistance to government atrocities. Some villages, like San Pablo el Baldío, San Pedro la Esperanza, and Chimel, had not been in existence for long when the repression started. The communities in El Ixcán had been going for about ten years when they were destroyed and the people massacred. Who knows how many thousands died there?

People had come from different cities to live in the area. They formed co-operatives and established new rules. The land was fertile and they worked hard. They had managed to introduce new crops there, like coffee, sugar cane and cardamom. If they had been allowed to continue, El Ixcán would have been a commercial centre by now. With hard work, the people found they could have a decent life. Their economic prospects were improving fast.

Yet in the 1980s, ten years after they had come to the area, their production was being wasted because the government did nothing to provide the infrastructure that would have enabled them to get their products out to the market. The people were trying to find new outlets themselves. They even hired light planes. The co-operatives in that area were models of their type, and they really served the community. Significantly, they had had the support of Father Guillermo Woods, who was later killed by the army in El Ixcán.

With the success of these new communities, the army thought it had lost control of El Ixcán. So they destroyed them, and the potential they represented. Yet far from feeling defeated, or saying 'I don't want to know', the people understood the need to fight, to fight a just war to defend their lives and dignity. So the first Communities of the Population in Resistance (CPR) emerged at the beginning of the 1980s. They came from politically aware communities with a deep sense of social responsibility and desire for freedom; they had no desire to submit to military control. Over the years, whole communities – including the sick, the old, orphans and widows – took to the mountainous jungle and tried to adapt to Guatemala's great natural world.

Some of them were there, night and day, for almost fifteen years. Protected by the enormous dense jungle, they survived because of their spirit of community, and by living collectively. They had no salt, maize or beans. They tried sowing *malangas*, *chilipines* and *camoles*, but army patrols found them and destroyed them. They had no cooking pots, clothes or medicine, but improvised by using the things they found.

When you are in a village near the jungle, you don't always realise the useful things the jungle contains. It is an unknown world, and it's not easy to learn how to survive. You have to eat new things, and recognise different plants. You must eat flowers and roots, and even the animals that live in the jungle. In many cases, our people had to break with their own taboos. In many villages, people used to be told that they should never kill birds unless they had to. People who had never lived by hunting now did so. They had to compete for food with the animals, those that survived the daily bombing. Sharing the food in the jungle with animals is not easy. You can't plan it together; you can't organise joint survival under those conditions.

The CPRs developed a kind of alternative health care, based on traditional Mayan knowledge. A disease like malaria can't be treated in the mountains with natural medicine, but the people soon developed treatments to prevent it killing large numbers. They had ways of keeping the fever under control and containing the worse effects of the disease. It is very contagious, for there are millions of mosquitoes.

They had other diseases too, notably the one caused by the *chiclera* fly. Mountain leprosy, too, can be fatal. It kills slowly. Our people would never have been able to get medicine to cure it even if it had been available in Guatemala, which it wasn't. It would have been impossible to bring enough medicine from France for a whole population, since each case needed forty injections. So our people developed new ways to contain the disease. They didn't cure it, but they discovered new treatments. Over fifteen years, both old and young died from malnutrition, intestinal infections and skin diseases. The natural medicine of our healers saved many people, but it was never enough.

They also had to find new ways of holding wedding ceremonies. If Ixils married each other, there was no problem. But living together in the mountains were K'anjobals, Mams, Ixils, K'iche's, K'eqchis, and *ladinos* as well. They all had different ceremonies and customs. These were not easy to perform for a population in a permanent state of emergency.

They say that the story of the Communities in Resistance in Guatemala is the only example of its kind this century in the Americas. There had been something similar during the Spanish Conquest when the indigenous peoples fled to the mountains to escape enslavement. It took years for the conquistadores to reach them. This ferocious war was repeated in the 1980s in Guatemala, when we imagined the world was more civilised.

In our communities, defending your neighbour's life is like defending your own. Without him you can't survive. The two lives are inseparable. This collective experience is the source of life. Hence the experience of the Communities in Resistance has a special validity, both for the present day and for the future development of Guatemala. Their history is the story of all the survivors of the scorched-earth campaign.

I think it is these people, coming from different ethnic groups and different religions, who will determine the future in Guatemala. They have a different sense of freedom and are profoundly democratic. They said, 'I am free. I can cross the jungle and climb the mountains as I please. If they start bombing, I will hide.' These people have a different sense of commitment, both individual commitment and a commitment to a cause. They have a different sense of development and different time scale. They kept the struggle going, year in and year out, in the hope that one day they would have a decent life and see social justice. They could never live now with the system of corrupt mayors and military commissioners that the war created. This corruption would be incompatible with their spirit of freedom, progress and democracy.

It's amazing that this spirit survived, despite the scorched-earth campaign that drove them to the mountains. They saw their children die for no reason. They lived with continuous militarisation through the Civil Defence Patrols. They saw their rights to freedom of speech and movement curtailed. Their traditions were undermined by the invasion of new religious sects. The terror was such that they even started to mistrust their parents, and their friends and neighbours. They feared forced military recruitment because the army computers had details of all their sons, from the oldest to the youngest.

The scorched-earth campaign, however, accelerated the opposition. CONAVIGUA, the National Co-ordinating Committee of Guatemalan Widows, was born. The widows were very brave in organising themselves. They denounced the murder, torture and disappearance of their husbands and sons, and they went further. They demanded decent funerals for their men-folk who had been tossed into communal graves. This meant forcing the government to investigate the whereabouts of clandestine graveyards. That was where the bones of their loved ones lay – and still lie.

I remember the time when the first secret graveyards were discovered. The government and the army were denying everything. They denied the scorched-earth campaign, they denied the secret graves, they denied all their crimes. This offended Guatemalan dignity, our sense of morality, everything we stood for. All that army officers could do was to shut their eyes when the television showed communal graves being discovered. They didn't have the courage to watch the bodies being dug up, for I can't believe soldiers could be so insensitive that they would not have been affected. What would their children, their wives, their mothers, have said? What would their consciences have said? Yet who knows? Human beings can be so cruel. It might just have been routine for them.

My hopes lie with young people. I'm sure the sight made an indelible impression on them. You could see the family's grief when each body was brought up, and they identified the belongings of their loved one. It was a solemn and moving sight.

I admire the courage of CONAVIGUA's leaders. They were abused and threatened for years before they succeeded in getting the graves opened. They finally got Masses said and decent funerals for the victims. Thousands of obstacles were put in their way. The army intimidated the families, the judges and the forensic scientists. Knowing how difficult it was for these women makes us appreciate them even more.

In 1990, President Vinicio Cerezo said that all these bodies were those of guerrillas and subversives. Yet even if they had been, it would not have justified the crime. I believe all human beings have human rights, whatever their beliefs. Prisoners of war have a right to humane treatment, too.

Soon other civil-disobedience movements arose. The most controversial issue was conscientious objection to compulsory military service. In many advanced democratic countries round the world, people can choose the way in which they best serve their country. They can choose service to the community. They are not perceived as unpatriotic since military service is no longer the only option. A long time will have to pass in Guatemala before any of us, the victims, could be proud of being in the army. The conscientious-objection movement is headed by CONAVIGUA, by the families of the disappeared and by the communities opposed to the Civil Defence Patrols.

For years, our young men have been captured and forced into the barracks. Many, from the age of fifteen, go into hiding to avoid it. They are brutally beaten when found. No one has been able to change the system. Many of those who have tried have died horribly. One day, we hope that young men all over the world will be able to serve their country without shedding each other's blood.

President Cerezo claimed he was 'the first civilian president' in recent Guatemalan history, and he promised the army that he would change their image. He tried to give his government a civilian facade, and he sought to co-opt certain middle-class intellectuals who had been in exile for a long time. He guaranteed their safety and offered them good jobs if they would come back to Guatemala.

For many of them, this was the moment they had been waiting for. They were tired of being in exile. They weren't really committed to the struggle, they had just wanted to save their skins. The most important thing for them was to have a guaranteed job and a nice life for their families. They weren't fighting for equal rights for indigenous peoples, or because they wanted our nation to be democratic. Their struggle was for schools and careers for their sons and daughters. Many *compañeros* who I thought understood our indigenous struggle let me down in the end, though not everyone. President Cerezo invited Luís Cardoza y Aragón to return to Guatemala, and Don Luís always refused.

9

THE QUINCENTENARY CONFERENCE
AND THE EARTH SUMMIT,

1992

I have been going round the world for years, to house after house, to town after town and to different countries. I have got lost in airports, in buses and in train stations. I have been invited to many places. People have gradually got to know me. I am like a drop of water on a rock. After drip, drip, dripping in the same place, I begin to leave a mark, and I leave my mark in many people's hearts.

Over a period of ten years, from my first visit to the United States in May 1982 until the end of 1991, I had the good fortune to meet an enormous number of people – in solidarity groups, in women's organisations and in ethnic groups. In the early days, I was happy if there was just one photographer or journalist at my press conferences. I had no complexes. I talked about Guatemala and about indigenous peoples. I told my life story, and discussed my childhood, my youth and my first book.

I learned a lot by listening to other people. I did not learn from reading

but by listening to young people's problems, marital problems, society's insensitivity and people's intolerance. I listened to the voices of other victims of oppression, and sometimes we would end up crying, not just for Guatemala, but for all the things they had gone through too.

If I talk about specific problems in other countries, it is not because I have read about them in a book, but because people have told me about them. People usually start by asking me about Guatemala. Then they compare it with their own reality, and soon they begin talking about their own uncertainties and hopes and aspirations. People cry out in pain all over the planet.

All these speaking tours have come about quite spontaneously. We never had a particular itinerary. There was no decision to follow a particular line. Somebody had to do it. If no one had done it before, it was because no one had had the opportunity. They weren't as privileged as I was. Nothing was planned. If it had been, it might not have got very far. These things are like footprints on a path, like the smell of the earth after the rain; they happen by themselves.

In 1993, we went on a tour of twenty-eight countries. It was very hard work. In each country the days were packed with arranged meetings and activities. On top of that, there were the unexpected events. We might suddenly have to go to a special function with presidents, ministers, royalty, celebrities, 'important people'. Even though we had had twelve years' experience of using elegant knives and forks, we still found it difficult. In contrast we might visit Burmese refugees in Thailand, or indigenous people in Santa María del Este in Argentina or Chimborazo in Ecuador. We might get to countries where they eat and live differently, or where we had to take our rubber shoes off and walk through the mud.

You have to be with people, live the lives they lead and feel how they feel. We might go to elegant houses and feel very tense, and have to be careful about what we did and said. From there we'd go to a world of poor marginal people. We'd feel so weary and conscience-stricken, and also so full of admiration for these people's courage. That happened everywhere we went. Sometimes, after fifteen days with a team of workers, I felt I needed to change them so that we didn't all get tired together. I would return to Mexico, leave one team behind, and set off again with another. There was no alternative. It's been like that for the last few years.

In 1992, there were the celebrations of the Quincentenary of the Spanish 'discovery' of America. I learned many things that year. It's no secret that I had many problems with the official Spanish Commission on the Quincentenary, especially the team dealing with indigenous peoples. The commission included a particular racist whose name I choose not to mention. He defended the most indefensible positions.

We had started organising a counter-campaign in 1989 when we first heard that the Spanish Commission was bent on celebrating the Quincentenary. Our people said that there wasn't anything to celebrate. On the contrary, the occasion offended us and generations of our ancestors. It was no cause for celebration, and even less a meeting of two cultures. We wanted to commemorate our ancestors, and remember them with a dignity worthy of the coming century. If the Spanish Commission thought the date was so important, they should have given us the opportunity to participate as protagonists in our own history.

In 1989, we managed to hold our first continental Quincentenary Conference in Colombia. The original idea came from the indigenous movements in Ecuador (CONAI), Colombia (ONIC) and Guatemala (CUC). The first conference, organised initially to support the landless peasants of Brazil, brought together all the active indigenous organisations in America and began the 'Five Hundred Years of Resistance' campaign.

By the time of the second conference, held in Guatemala in 1991, we had included not only the Caribbean, but also popular movements throughout the continent. We changed the name of the campaign to 'Five Hundred Years of Indigenous, Black and Popular Resistance'.

By 1992, we had decided to change course again, to make it a continental movement and not just a campaign. Hitherto we had followed the approach that governments were taking to the Quincentenary. Now we wanted to approach it in a different way, looking towards the year 2000. In our struggle, we always follow a star – a long-term vision – in this case, the prospect of a better life for oppressed and marginalised sectors and the achievement of full recognition for the indigenous peoples of the world.

The financial resources for organising these activities came from thousands of people: solidarity committees, women's groups, youth groups, human rights groups, small institutions in Europe and the United States. A large part came from the Evangelical churches and from the National Council of American Churches, the World Council of Churches and the International Lutheran Federation. Collecting this money was not easy. Certain institutions put us through a kind of Spanish Inquisition first before they would part, reluctantly, with a thousand dollars or five thousand dollars – when they could have given us so much more. To powerful institutions like the Catholic Church, our activities smacked of subversion or communism. It was as if we were the Devil undermining their belief. They could never understand why our people criticised the Quincentenary. They thought we were just being aggressive, and they were suspicious of us. Yet, as always, we also found good and generous allies, and these we will not forget.

We indigenous peoples live in different parts of the American continent, we have different experiences and identities, and we also have diverse and multiple dreams. Each of us has survived alone, in our own nations, without contact with other indigenous peoples. Just as I was not aware that there were other Mayans before I went to Mexico, the indigenous peoples of Latin American have not known a great deal about each other. Yet the fundamental bases of our culture unite us, because they are ancient cultures.

We discovered that indigenous peoples have always contributed valuable things to society through their labour and culture, their art and medicine, their wisdom and patience. They have contributed their own blood and pain to build the so-called democracies, a contribution that has never been recognised. On the contrary, a good number of our mestizo children have been denied participation in our ancient culture, and have been made to feel ashamed of the earth which bore them and of their roots.

By the time of the Quincentenary in 1992, the indigenous peoples of America had begun to have a common vision, shared demands and a sense of solidarity. The majority of our peoples have a vision. They foresee a great future. They have dreams, and the determination to see them take shape, for the sense of community is sacred, and something of real value in this day and age. We called our third conference, which took place in Nicaragua that October, 'The Conference of Self-discovery'. The huge majority of our people are poor. We discovered that if poor people unite they can achieve results. Before we got funding, we had to take a few *centavos* from each family, from our children's mouths, for our projects to materialise. The expenses of our early meetings were borne by our own families.

Our community is the reason why we are still alive, why we are still here five hundred years after the Conquest. We have survived amid the rubble of endless massacres. If our peoples had disintegrated, if they had lost their languages, if they had lost their communities, their collective way of life, their concept of leadership, they would have died out. We discovered that if we unite, if we recognise our organisations' leaders and avoid rivalries, we will achieve the results we seek.

We also discovered that we have not simply been spectators during these five hundred years. We have been protagonists as well. We realised how often our intellectual rights have been usurped, how our thinking has been manipulated and distorted. Since 1989, the world has rediscovered indigenous wisdom. This is a source of pride for us. I am pleased that the thoughts and lives of our peoples have become more widely known. Yet the more they are known, the more they have become a commercial product.

Our profound appreciation of the relationship between Mother Nature and people's lives has been exploited over and over again, by environmentalists, writers and celebrities. Voluminous works plagiarising our thinking have appeared, apparently magical works pulled out of the air by famous brains, the sole authors of indigenous thought. They have stolen these concepts from us and not given us credit.

They don't say, 'This is what the Yanomamis think, or the Mayans, or the

Aztecs.' Or, 'This wisdom comes from the native peoples of the Pacific, or the Maoris.' They don't say, 'This is the wisdom of ancient cultures, therefore we respect it, we borrow it to share with other people.' No, these are simply great brains who have suddenly discovered the importance of harmony.

When I read a poem about nature and find that it is actually a Hopi or Navajo saying, and that the poet does not recognise the source and presents it as his own work, it makes me very suspicious. They never say, 'Chief Descage said this.' Or, 'A Mayan chief said this.' Or, 'A Chorti woman, a Chamula woman, said this.' They never explain that these concepts had ancient roots. That is why people often think that indigenous peoples have no body of thought. I know that a people's experiences, values and wisdom do not belong to any one individual and should be universal patrimony. It offends me when this patrimony is simply used to benefit certain individuals.

I don't like saying things like this, but sometimes you have to talk plainly in order to be understood and to make friends. It teaches you who your real friends are, and I want my friends to know what I think. In our culture, our word is our bond. This does not just refer to the spoken word, it also means commitment, feelings, responsibility, frankness. These are values one receives as a child, and we should reaffirm their importance. I go back to the time when I learned our culture from my elders. Yet paradoxically, to be able to talk about it, I had to physically leave my village and my wider community.

By the time of the third conference, we were delighted to see that the exchanges between our leaders had reached a qualitatively different level. Our efforts had given dignity to the human race. The Quincentenary taught me something: that the young five-hundred-year-old culture of the invader (a bloody culture with many inherent problems) had wanted to rapidly eliminate the memory of a culture that was thousands of years old. Yet five hundred years is nothing. It takes a lot longer to destroy an ancient culture. Cultures have roots, a heart, a meaning. Hopefully, in the future, one culture will not impose itself on another in this way. Cultures will fuse, not by massacres, sterilisation, repression and destruction, but through mutual respect.

I happened by chance to be at the Earth Summit held in Rio de Janeiro in 1992. I had been invited to Brazil by various church organisations for another conference, and I was curious to see what the Summit was like. So I paid my fifty dollars entrance fee and went in. I couldn't get through the security barriers that prevented ordinary people from going into the official conference, so I went in what was called the 'global arena'. It was a very disappointing spectacle. Indigenous people were dancing for the public in a sort of folklore show. It turned out to be a load of blond people pretending to be Amazon Indians.

Some journalists came over to interview me, not because they recognised me but because I looked indigenous in my colourful costume. They asked me what I thought. I said, 'It's entertaining. There's a lot to buy. I've enjoyed myself, I've watched Indians in feathers dance. I've seen lots of T-shirts, plastic bags and postcards being sold. But I wonder how many trees were cut down to make them.' I didn't tell them my name because it wasn't important.

I had gone to find out what their idea of the earth, plants and nature might be, and what I found was a commercial version of ecology. There were T-shirts with tigers, lions and parrots painted on them, and plastic bags with animals' faces. It was a case of businessmen making money out of the environment. They usurped indigenous wisdom, and made films to sell to make even more money. They prostituted the thoughts of the indigenous peoples. I had the feeling that the organisers weren't very clear about the difference between indigenous people and wild animals, between protecting the jungle and exploiting it. A love affair with nature has its limits when it comes to making money.

Yet the Earth Summit undoubtedly did a lot of good. It made young people think about environmental issues. Intellectuals devoted a moment of their time to studying the problem, and the views of representatives of ancient cultures were listened to. It was a big success for us, it had world-wide exposure. The danger is that protecting the environment has become fashionable; it is a fad that may not last.

I walked around the streets and went into neighbourhoods, and I was recognised by certain nuns and priests. We went to see what they call 'street children' and people lost in the precarious life of poverty. We heard many sad stories. People said, 'There used to be lots of children on the streets but they had a clean-up before the Earth Summit.' We asked what they meant by a clean-up. 'Well, they rounded the kids up and took them a long way away.' That's what we were told.

A great many people assured us there was a city where all the children had been taken. I would have liked to find it. In some corner of Brazil about thirty thousand kids who had been cleared off the city streets to prepare for the Earth Summit? Did it mean they were in some centre, or in a special barracks, or in a hospital, bottled up and ready to be sold? What did 'taking them away' mean?

A lot of people said they had been killed. 'Well, they weren't any use,' they declared. 'Why weren't they any use?' I asked. 'Because they were layabouts, they hung around the streets, and they stole. Some were ill, and they probably weren't given medicine. They're bound to be dead.'

I felt so impotent. I didn't know what to do. I felt guilty just knowing about it.

They were also holding an indigenous people's conference which if I remember rightly was called the Carioca Conference. It was being held simultaneously with the Rio Summit. It aimed to produce an indigenous model for the next decade. I was curious to see what the model was, so I went along. If our houses were like those on show, it would indeed be a gift from God. Perhaps by the end of the decade our people will live in houses like that. They had concrete foundations that made them very stable. They were well built and attractive. Their architects had studied various types of houses in Brazil and had come up with this model house, large and spacious too.

The difference between the two conferences was that the Carioca one was more authentic. Much of the folklore had been organised so that indigenous people performed for each other rather than being put on show as exotica. Even so, there were plenty of dirty blond people with long hair who were pretending to be Indians, or wanted to be indigenous, or sympathised with indigenous peoples. I came to the conclusion that we don't need handouts or charity. We just want the chance for people themselves to take the decisions that affect their future.

After that I went to an ecumenical conference. Priests from various countries, of varying origins, and with various levels of social commitment, were there. This conference raised my spirits because it dealt with problems rigorously and critically. They looked at environmental issues from a moral point of view.

I stayed on in Brazil a few more days, doing my usual lobbying: cornering people to ask to be allowed to put our case, giving my opinion on issues they were tackling, finding out whether one thing was more important than another, and generally investigating what was going on. I spent still more time consolidating ties with indigenous groups and getting in touch with peasant organisations that were possibly there for the same reasons as me, but just a bit lost.

I often ask myself what the point is of our being here, we who are part of nature too. How will we be able to buy air and water, how will we be able to live? Human beings should think more carefully about the damage they are doing to life. Brazil has a very significant role because of the immense natural wealth it has available to sell to powerful trans-national companies. How much wood did it sell despite the conference? How much bargaining went on? How many deals were signed? And how many economic and political concessions were made before they reached agreement?

I didn't get answers to a lot of questions I asked that year. There are defining moments in our lives that raise our awareness. It is a different kind of awareness from what you get from books, it comes from direct experience. I was lucky enough to have been to the Earth Summit because it made me aware that the struggle of indigenous peoples to protect the environment is different from the struggles of other peoples'. Ours is not just a passing fancy. We protect our environment, our air and our water by the way we live. It is our very life.

The solution to our problems of poverty is not just more money. It lies in more equal distribution. It may also mean eradicating fundamental inequalities, abolishing privileges and purging the development agencies. At the moment, we have government bodies full of experts with money in their pockets, who believe they hold the key to development. We also have poor peasants who have nothing and whose only value is as a theoretically developable object. This is a situation that has to change.

I have been very critical of the International Monetary Fund (IMF) and the World Bank. I think these organisations deal very badly with problems of human-rights violations and the environment. If they didn't deal with them so badly, the scorched-earth campaign in Guatemala could have been prevented, and new laws governing land distribution introduced. How can the World Bank allow huge areas of land to be used to pasture a few cows, so that land-owning and bourgeois families can spend their weekends killing deer? How can they allow this at a time when millions of people are starving because they have no land? How can it permit huge land concessions that destroy the natural world by trafficking in wood, rare animals and archaeological remains?

I continue to think that the IMF and the World Bank have a direct responsibility for the extreme poverty that plagues the majority of the world's population. I still hope these institutions can bring about change, not with words, but with actions. There must be forms of economic planning and concrete measures that demonstrate to poor people the good will and generosity of these institutions.

In the absence of such large institutions, indigenous people have developed a spirit of co-operativism. This has been a way of instilling collective responsibility. It is not based solely on economic progress. I defend co-operative values wholeheartedly. It is a system of organisation, a way of life, a culture. Throughout the world, poor people are able to survive because they co-operate. They need to organise to combat social injustice and the unequal distribution of wealth. They need solidarity. Day after day, in their neighbourhoods, villages and municipalities, they face adversity – a brother's death, a relative's illness, a child being orphaned – in the tangible way that only the wretched of this earth really know. Charities programme their aid, but poor people contribute twenty-four hours a day. Charities choose which of the poor they want to help, but poor people don't have a choice. They are born with a caring heart. It is not only indigenous people who have this sense of solidarity.

That's why I argue that the struggle of indigenous peoples has a purpose – to represent all oppressed people in the world. If we were the only ones, we might act differently, because we have been wise enough to realise what was being done to us. Yet the fact is that poverty does not only affect indigenous peoples. It affects black people, mestizos, and all the world's dispossessed. Suffering knows no frontiers.

In recent years, in their haste to control indigenous peoples and change the way they live, and perhaps to avoid internal conflicts, international agencies have tried to undermine the value of co-operatives. One of their strategies has been to create phoney NGOs. In our own experience, most of the experts in these NGOs are foreigners from the developed world. If they are not actually foreign, they tend to think and act like foreigners. They come with the idea that indigenous peoples understand nothing about development, and have no projects of their own. They believe that they have to educate them, like a species that can be trained to understand the principles of development. Their arrogance and deep paternalism so blinds them that they are unable to see the positive things and solutions that are already there. This has meant they have made many mistakes. In the end they merely create what I call 'parasites on society'. These are harsh words, I know. Not everyone is like this, but all suffer the same consequences.

We are talking about people who have made careers out of promising development. I had travelled all over the continent and visited most of the countries in the Americas long before I received the Nobel Prize. I know most of the local development agencies. I am not wrong when I say that these bodies undermine the people's own organisations and leaders, imposing on them groups or organisms that just serve to channel funds. A lot of money has gone to poor countries without anyone bothering to investigate properly whether it actually reaches the people. In the majority of cases, ridiculous, paternalistic and discriminatory policies are in force. How can you explain the fact that an expert lives in an area for fifteen years and then, when he leaves the community, it is poorer than before he came? What development has he taught?

The problem usually occurs because two different languages are being used. One is the language of the expert who comes from, and thinks in terms of, the First World. He earns an absurd salary; he earns in a month what poor people earn in two years. The other is the pragmatic language of local people. As a result, oppressive situations are re-created. The problem facing these agencies in the coming years will be for them to win back the people's trust. Poor people are not for sale, our poverty is not for sale. Yet the great craving for development that has been awoken in our people still has to be satisfied.

Government agencies have to realise that our people can contribute knowledge, techniques, wisdom and labour. We could perhaps work on projects together, ones that are more humane, sensitive and respectful of the environment. We might have to find criteria for training experts so there might be a point at which our knowledge and that of the expert could be mutually beneficial. The development experts need our people and we need them. We could both contribute to a more secure future.

I got these ideas about the dialogue between different cultures from having stayed in the houses of many different people all round the world. I always ask a lot of questions on my solidarity tours. I have taken part in countless conferences about development and the eradication of poverty. I have spoken to audiences of hundreds of people.

These last few years have brought hundreds of new experiences. I have earned the affections of many people. I have been given flowers and wonderful hospitality. I don't have a single bad memory of any of the homes I visited, and I don't think any have bad memories of me. I tried to be respectful to all my hosts. I respected their food, their homes, their customs. I tried to learn things that were not easy for me.

It was hard for me when I discovered the consumer society, the society of waste: to see food and objects thrown away; to go to a vast supermarket and see all the food for cats and dogs, at incredible prices; to think of all the protein that this food contains, and to know that we never had food of that quality.

I also learned a lot about women and children. It was strange for me to discover about feminism and Islam, and about all the other beliefs I had not known about in the mountains of Chimel. Some of the things I discovered, I just couldn't understand. I couldn't understand how a woman could be with another woman. I had never heard of homosexuality. I was like a child who doesn't understand, who questions and asks. It was hard to understand how people complicated their lives so much. I found lesbianism very strange because it has nothing to do with the way I was brought up. Yet in the end I don't have to understand it to respect it. Respect for others is bigger than my small world. I have talked to several women friends and they have told me a lot about their lives. Theirs were very unusual circumstances. I have come to realise that each person's life comes from their own experience and is the result of their own decision.

I have a great friend who is homosexual. I met him in New York. He is openly homosexual. He is a wonderful man, very courteous and refined, and with a simplicity that shows his pureness of heart. I was always very curious, but I never enquired about the details of his life. I was naive about such matters, though I knew it was a controversial subject. I have always thought it is better to be reticent and not get involved in the whys and wherefores. I was more interested in understanding than in passing judgement. This is perhaps because we indigenous peoples have always been misunderstood, and many people think that our difference is a reason to despise us.

When we fight for our rights, we are called indigenous, but if we take our demands further than indigenous rights, then we are called communists. If we include women's rights, we are not only indigenous communists but feminists too. They put labels on us to devalue our struggle. This hurts us deeply, so our understanding of others comes from that too. We know that other underprivileged or misunderstood groups face similar problems. They are marginalised like us.

In indigenous societies, homosexuality might exist but it would probably be integrated within our society. Most of our people get married between the ages of fourteen and sixteen, and they lead a very close-knit family life. In recent years, however, some women live alone or some men don't get married. The indigenous community absorbs differences, be they sexual, mental or physical.

Disabled people in our villages are integrated into the community, that is, they are looked after by their family who treat them as equals. Everybody treats them with respect, because disability is considered normal – because it is Nature's work too. We are taught from the time when we are very little that making fun of a disabled person brings a curse from Nature upon our heads. It is like offending something sacred.

The same goes for pregnant women. You can't eat in front of a pregnant woman without offering her some of your food. Otherwise you would hurt her feelings and those of the baby she is carrying. So disabled people and pregnant women are thought of in the same way. In this respect, I think Western society has lost its sense of balance. Human beings are different from animals, there is something more profound in them than in animals. An animal doesn't care what it does in public, whereas human beings are more discreet. Not for any moral reason but because there are sacred aspects of life which must be given total respect.

Mayan women are very hardworking. The sense of family, the feeling for life, the duality of life, is a philosophical and conceptual principle that governs their existence. Yet the position of women is very unfavourable at present. We too are fighting for better treatment and better conditions. We are fighting to achieve full and effective political participation. This doesn't mean sterilising women so they can't have any more children. Our problem is not our children, but having access to science, technology, knowledge, development and the legal system. We want equal opportunities, and to have them within the norms of our own culture.

As we near the end of the century, we can see all too clearly how some categories of human beings have been marginalised. An outrageous example of this is the war in the former Yugoslavia, where it was women who suffered the worst kind of violence. Throughout history women have always been raped in war. The very nature of motherhood, the very basis of femininity, has always been used as a weapon of war. What has happened as part of ethnic cleansing in the former Yugoslavia is horrifying and shameful, not only because it is a repetition of crimes committed fifty years ago under the Nazis, but because it has been happening at a time when everyone is preaching development, progress and modernity.

I was deeply disturbed when I realised what was being done to women. Forcing a woman so that she gives birth to the fruit of an act of violence is too terrible to imagine. If we, the women of the world, were to unite and organise, we could break down the frontiers of silence with our cries of condemnation. We could raise the cause of these women as a battle cry that would live forever in our common memory as a gender, as the givers of life and creators of hope. We must never forget these women.

It is almost as if there were a curse on them. Those Muslim mothers will never be accepted by those of their religion because they have been raped by strangers. It is like a human sacrifice. The rape of a Muslim woman is like making a human sacrifice to the Gods of War, Capitalism and Power. What hope is there for the children when they are born? It is all bound up with the distribution of wealth, individual ambition, men and women's alienation and the abuse of military power.

How would I feel if I were a Muslim woman in that situation? How could I even bear the touch of my own skin? We have to put ourselves in their place. I am astounded that people dare tell them what to do. All those arguments we hear so much of, about whether they have the choice to abort babies conceived as a result of rape. There are world leaders who tell them that abortion is a sin. I have the deepest respect for the determination of these women, and I have to confess that I never agreed with those who begged these women not to have abortions. I respect world leaders, but this time they made my blood run cold. Their message went right against my own ethics, and my experience as a victim. If a woman has been raped, she and she alone knows what this act of cruelty means, and she alone must decide how to deal with it.

When the Spaniards arrived five hundred years ago, they raped our ancestors, our grandmothers, our mothers, to breed a race of mestizos. The result is the violence and cruelty that we are still living with today. The Spaniards used a vile method to create a mixed race, a race of children who doubted their own identity, with their heads on one side of the ocean and their feet on the other. That is what happened to our culture.

Admiring other cultures is fine, but the imposition of one culture on another is not. Mestizo society in America is not the result of a process of understanding within that society. I don't mean that the mixing of races is a bad thing; it is just that cultures must learn to live together.

Intellectuals like José Carlos Mariátegui defied the rules imposed on them by a society that devalued their roots and their reality. People like these make history, because they are part of our identity as a continent. Their ideas and their struggles have transcended society. The past cannot just be about myths. It must be a source of strength for the present and the future. All the good things that have come out of our continent, even the ideas that we once regarded as superficial and useless, must be re-examined. We have to blend our two cultures, the ancient and the modern. We should not be trying to eradicate anything or anybody because we think one is better. We should be trying to find a way of living together, combining the ancient culture of our peoples with the culture of the colonisers. That is the strength of our American identity, the privilege of having roots that go back for thousands of years.

The crises that a society goes through are also part of its history. They show us the way forward, they shape our culture. You can't go back and change history, nor can you make it an excuse for not changing the future. We can make the future different, we can make it better.

Looking back, I think perhaps it was a mistake to turn the Quincentenary celebrations into a kind of battlefield. Many people want to return to the old Inca and Mayan ways of five hundred years ago. It is impossible to do that! How can we go back and be the same? Indigenous tradition itself says that time is long and wide, and it has its own signs. Each sign has a different meaning, it may mean the time has come for a generation of great leaders or great achievements. That is a sign of the time and you cannot go against it. On the other hand, it is wrong to simply praise the victors. We should accept that things can always be improved.

Many people believe that indigenous peoples have been no more than spectators over the past five hundred years, that we are the conquered people. It is true that we have been the victims of racism, discrimination and oppression. We know exactly what colonisation means. It means terrible exploitation and humiliation. But people should remember that indigenous peoples built great cities with our own hands, we created the most wonderful works of art with the sweat of our brows. All were carefully designed and built in our own distinctive way. We have contributed so much to the richness of our peoples in America that it is impossible to say where indigenous culture begins and ends.

Culture isn't pure, it is dynamic, it is a kind of dialectic, it is something that progresses and evolves. As for purity, who can determine what that means? I don't think our peoples were ever passive bystanders. The advances made have just as much been ours, for we contributed to them, just as we have contributed to the enormous ethnic diversity. I think the whole idea of purity is damaging, it leads to sectarianism, intolerance, segregation and racism.

A lot of different attitudes emerged during the Quincentenary. Some of our brothers believed that the purity of the Mayan, Inca and Aztec cultures still exists, others proclaimed that the times favoured the ancient cultures. Then there are those who believe that human destiny is intercultural, that unity lies in recognising differences. I believe that the revival of ancient values does not benefit indigenous peoples alone.

Our *ajq'iij* had the right idea. They didn't argue over whether our ancestors were better or worse, whether one person was purer than another, whether *ladinos* were purer than us, whether *ladinos* should live like Indians. They taught us that war destroyed indigenous dignity and unity. They didn't say if you belong to our tribe you are pure, and if you don't belong, you're not. They didn't waste their time on nonsense like that.

The *ajq'iij* were simple men, and wise at the same time. They said, 'Now is the time for the rain to fall and make the seeds grow on our soil and make our culture flourish, so let there be no more discord.' They told us when the rains would come and when there would be light, to light our path. This light would make us recognise our identity, recognise who we are, make us think in a different way. When one cycle is completed, then we are in a new cycle.

This is very closely bound up with the issue of the environment that seems to be one of the main themes in this new cycle. The most important thing about the Earth Summit in Rio de Janeiro was that it generated debate everywhere, from the indigenous communities to the most elegant salons. I attended countless women's conferences and youth conferences. Young people are beginning to care much more about the environment. People are becoming more environmentally conscious, and when there is awareness of a problem, there is positive action and solutions are found. Sometimes this sort of thing may just be a fashion, and this can prove negative. But I think the past few years have been very fruitful as far as environmental awareness is concerned.

Indigenous peoples have always cared about the environment, we learned about it from our elders. Now we can make a much bigger and better contribution. We have to say to the world, 'Listen, we want to have our say, because we love Mother Earth and we love life.' I think the future looks good, but we must remember that the fruit only comes when we have had time to sow the seeds and bring in the harvest. It may be some time before many of us see how the world reacts. Maybe a lot of what is being done now is simply reclaiming the living seeds. It is these living seeds that will germinate and flower again.

10

THE MAYAN SPIRIT

In 1980, when I first left my country and went into exile, I was weighed down with deep sorrow. My parents and my brother Patrocinio were dead. I didn't know what had happened to my brothers Nicolás and Víctor, or to my sister Marta. I guessed that my sisters Lucía and Anita, the little one, had fled to the mountains.

Later I discovered that Nicolás and Víctor and their children had taken refuge in the mountains too, and had become part of the Communities of the Population in Resistance (CPRs). They couldn't sow beans or maize, so they lived on roots, grass, lianas, whatever they could find. For four years they stayed in the mountains, without a home, with only the clothes they stood up in.

My sister-in-law María, Víctor's wife, was kidnapped by the army, and butchered soon after in 1980. They found her body near my parents' house in Laj Chimel. She was fat, smiling and very affectionate. A very healthy woman.

Víctor was in the mountains alone with his three children. They were growing up. He remarried and his second wife was also captured. I still

don't know what happened to her. I think they had another son, also called Víctor, but I have not found him yet.

My brother Víctor was shot by the army on 7 March 1983, after being interrogated and tortured in the church at Uspantán. The army offered him an amnesty but he refused. They tried to persuade him to confess to being a guerrilla leader, and the man responsible for all the local guerrilla attacks. They were trying to use him as a weapon of psychological warfare against the guerrillas. In exchange, they would not only spare his life but pay him a reward. They wanted him to accuse the members of the Communities in Resistance – men, women, children and old people – of being guerrillas. He refused, so they shot him. The execution was carried out in public, to frighten people.

Víctor's eldest daughter, Regina, the one who got married in 1995, would have been about seven then. She and her two little brothers were held in the army barracks until my half-sister, Rosa Calam de Chivalán, rescued them and took care of them. Rosa is my father's daughter by his first marriage. When my father was captured and forced to do military service, he was already married with three children. When he came back from the army, his first wife had remarried. Then he met my mother.

Rosa was so poor she couldn't afford to feed all three children. The two little boys were already completely bloated from malnutrition when she took them from the barracks. They only survived a few months with Rosa. We believe that when children are in a state of shock, even if you feed them, they will die of grief. That's what happened to those two.

Because she was trying to save the two little ones, Rosa passed Regina to another family. She asked around to see if anyone would look after her. In the last thirty years of civil war in Guatemala, many orphans have been taken in by new families. It's one of the great strengths of our communities, that orphans can find a new home. The only problem is hunger and poverty. Every family sees one, two, even three children die of malnutrition, and the orphans suffer the same fate. The same happens to old people and disabled people; to all those who have no way of providing for themselves.

During the war, frightened as they were, our people were very willing to care for the massive numbers of orphans left behind. There are more than a hundred thousand of them in Guatemala. Families offer them to the community to see if anyone can give them some kind of life, some kind of future. So Regina was passed from house to house in Uspantán. She didn't fit in anywhere. My sister tried to give her to the nuns in the village, but they couldn't take her in.

About three years ago, my sister rescued her again and took her home to live with her. I didn't find out about her until after I had received the Nobel Prize.

My sister Anita, who lives with me now, had joined the rebels in the mountains. When I left Guatemala for the last time, my two sisters had taken up the armed struggle. They were so young. I was terrified just thinking what might happen to them. Who knows how many kids end up in guerrilla graves?

I couldn't talk to anyone about this. My closest friends had some idea, but it was a constant heartache. In the end, Anita went into exile in Mexico. She was already pregnant. She only just managed to get to Chiapas after walking many days and nights. Her daughter, my namesake, little Maya Rigoberta, was born there.

I had always thought of my baby sister as a child. When I met her again in Guatemala, it was a surprise to see she already had two beautiful little girls of her own. She had learned a lot from her hard life. She had become politicised, she was a woman of vision, and she spoke Spanish well. She had spent more than twelve years of her life in the mountains and the refugee camps of Chiapas. Twelve years! She hadn't had a home since they burned down our hut in Laj Chimel. She had spent the first six months going from one house to another until she found friends.

My whole family had fallen apart. Soon after Víctor was shot, my brother Nicolás, his wife and six children, were all captured. They were held in the church at Uspantán for about six months. That was in 1983. The soldiers had occupied the church and turned it into a barracks. They only moved out recently.

Nicolás was transferred by helicopter to the barracks at Santa Cruz del Quiché where they tortured him for six months. He saw many people tortured to death, he saw about sixty die right there in the barracks. All those who came with him were murdered. From the moment he arrived they beat him. He was also subjected to psychological torture. They didn't let the prisoners sleep. At five in the morning, when the cold was most intense, they would throw buckets of cold water over them. They gave them filthy food, and interrogated them for hours at a time. An army officer there said, 'I'm not going to kill you, you piece of shit, because I owe your mother. I'm going to let you live a few days.' We don't know what he meant about 'owing' my mother. Later, he told my brother he was in Xejul when Mama was tortured and murdered.

Then they moved Nicolás to another unit. Every day he was threatened with knives. They stamped on his feet, they sat him on the floor, and they jumped on his knees. Prisoners were tortured in a tiny cell. He could hear the screams of people being tortured in the cell next door. Every morning at dawn, about four in the morning, they would bring out sacks full of corpses. My brother never knew whether they buried them or just threw them down a ravine. My brother could hear what they did to people before killing them. Who knows why they did it? Maybe it was part of their punishment.

That's how he lived for six months in the El Quiché barracks. They told him they had killed all his brothers and sisters. They showed him photos of my little sister Lucía. She was still fighting for the rebels, but they told my brother they had taken her prisoner. Then they told him that if he went to the town, and said everything they wanted him to say, they would spare his life and release his sister and his children. He was to tell people that children captured by the army were well looked after, that they were given food and medicine, and that the soldiers behaved well. So he went back to the village. They wanted him to say that he had seen the army treating people well. This was meant to demoralise the CPRs and, so they claimed, to undermine the guerrilla movement. He didn't say anything.

When my brother came back, his children were horribly bloated through malnutrition. The *tortillas* they were given in the church where they were held were hard and mouldy. They were released, and my brother set out to seek shelter for them. They had suffered so much, and they still bear the scars of their ordeal. Nicolás and Juana took their six children and went to the *fincas*.

They went from one *finca* to another, putting up with all sorts of inhumane treatment. But they had faith and hope. They really believed their children would survive. They were close to death many times, but they survived. Thanks to our Creator, thanks to life, and thanks to the power of our ancestors, they are still alive and are witnesses to the cruelty of war. My brother is deeply religious. Perhaps he survived because he prayed day and night.

My brother never lost his political consciousness. He still wanted to fight for Chimel, but the authorities made his life impossible. They imposed fines on him just for the right to live. They invented things, saying, 'Pay this fine or we'll accuse you of being a subversive.' He was left with nothing. He went from house to house, working in other people's maize fields. That is how he, Juana and the children survived.

Today they live in Uspantán. When they were finally released, they were told they weren't completely free, that they could be re-arrested at any time. Sure enough, the army soon showed up again to frighten them. They accused my brother of supplying the guerrillas with food, and they took him to the barracks again. They interrogated him for hours. From 1983 onwards, he suffered nearly a decade of harassment.

When I went back to Guatemala for the first time, in April 1988, Nicolás and his children were arrested and held at the barracks. The soldiers claimed they had caught the guerrilla supremo – meaning me – and I was going to be shot. When they were released, the soldiers claimed that I had accused many families of having links with the guerrillas. They said they had released me because I had given information about the guerrillas. That is how it was for years.

When it was first announced that I had been nominated for the Nobel Prize, the military started turning up every two weeks at Nicolás's house to try to intimidate them. When I was awarded the Prize, they took him in again, on another trumped-up charge of selling maize to the guerrillas. Each time he was arrested, my sister-in-law had to sell the few things she owned to bribe the authorities. It was the only way to get him released. Corruption was rife among both the military and the civil authorities. I have all the documents connected with this persecution, every certificate of arrest, every certificate of release. I have a whole file of certificates they gave my brother, all signed, although sometimes they didn't bother to give him anything in writing. They always made him pay for his arrest. Even the mayors, the so-called justices of the peace and the local military and civil authorities, were involved in this intimidation, as were judges and former judges, members of the Civic Action Patrols, army officers and sons of landowners.

Impunity was the norm in that little town. Victims and perpetrators of the crimes came up against each other every day and justice was always on the side of the people responsible for victimisation. No victim ever plucked up the courage to speak the truth. But these things did happen. Maybe one day the victims will speak, when it is no longer dangerous to speak the truth, when impunity is a thing of the past.

A few days before the Nobel Prize was announced, Nicolás took an enormous risk and came to see me in Guatemala City. It was wonderful to be together again. It was the best prize of all. I knew he and his family were alive but I never said anything. Nicolás was terrified when he came to see me. We met and talked in secret and never let anyone know he was my brother. We went to great lengths to hide our tears. Only the *compañeros* of the CUC, the *compañeras* of CONAVIGUA and Rosalina Tuyuc knew that he was my brother. I had learned to weep in private, so as not to demoralise anyone.

He couldn't stay with me because of the continuing terror campaign. It was too risky. It wasn't until after the Nobel Prize that my brother and his family and the people of the village could enjoy a little more peace. But the harassment continued. He kept receiving threats. I myself had doubts about settling in Guatemala for good, because there was still so much repression. Serious violations of human rights are still part of our everyday lives. When you think how every inch of Guatemala soil has seen so many deaths! Obviously, unless things change fundamentally, the spectres of death and darkness will never leave Guatemala's towns and villages.

We remember Myrna Mack Chang, a woman of enormous professional ethics, of great intellect and courage, and an example to us all. She was the first woman to investigate the tragedy of internally displaced peoples, widows and orphans of the CPRs. She was stabbed twenty-seven times. It was clear from the investigations, from the statements of the murderers who confessed to her killing, that it was carried out on the orders of the military high command. Even now justice has not been done. We remember with sadness Dinora Pérez, and Jorge Carpio Nicolle, a politician who played a leading role in trying to create democracy in this country. His opposition was perfectly legal but even he didn't escape death. He was killed soon after his cousin Ramiro de León Carpio became President. Even that was not enough for justice to prevail.

The most terrible part of this is that people in Guatemala know who the murderers are. The only ones who seem not to know are the judges. There is always some legal reason for finding the guilty innocent or saying the case is not proven. Yet everyone knows who is responsible. Myths are created and the fight for justice continues.

I have enormous respect for the people who are fighting to change this situation. I am sure things are changing in small ways by the day but it's a long and complicated business. I should like to pay tribute to the judges and magistrates who honour their professional code of ethics and risk their lives daily to bring about change.

Some people still see me as that illiterate indigenous woman, that subversive born in squalor. I'm still the domestic servant, as some mestizos in Guatemala City refer to me. There is so much resentment against an indigenous woman being a national leader. I have to watch my back the whole time. I continue to suffer much harassment. That is why I waited so long before returning to Guatemala. Every time I came back, I received threatening letters. They tried to intimidate me, but I'm pretty used to that by now.

What has been hard to accept is the way some of the media use their power to try to undermine my role. Not only do I have to fear being killed, I also have to worry about political harassment from those who cannot tolerate the presence of an indigenous woman in politics. It's hard for them to share a platform with me.

Yet that is not my problem. I'm not going to step aside. I won't leave the field free for them. New generations will be born, new generations with a different mentality. They will allow indigenous and non-indigenous people alike to make their mark on history and work for the benefit of our society as a whole. On the few occasions that I have received an invitation to an official government function, it always specifies that I should wear a dark-coloured dress. Either they have sent the invitation to the wrong address or they have forgotten that I and my clothes are multicoloured – and proud of it.

Journalists and generous admirers have often asked me whether the Nobel Peace Prize has changed my life. On one occasion, I said, 'Of course it has changed my life, it has opened a great door and I have been lucky enough to pass through it.' It really did change my life, yet it was never going to change it that much. Quite simply, I have always had the same face, the face of a poor indigenous woman, and there is no way in which I can change that. The Nobel Prize is for life, but so too are my beliefs and my origins.

Once, we were on our way back to the United States from Geneva, after a meeting of the United Nations. At Amsterdam airport, the officials treated us as if we were dangerous characters. Before we boarded the plane, they interrogated us, they asked if we were carrying knives, or weapons, or a bomb. We answered all their questions patiently, even the stupid ones.

When we finally arrived in Minneapolis, to attend a conference of the Nobel Peace Institute, we were met by airline representatives. At passport control, the woman immigration officer just stared at us. I don't know whether she didn't recognise us, or whether she'd got out of bed the wrong side, or whether quite simply my indigenous face startled her. She wanted to let my North American assistant through, but my assistant refused to go without me.

Soon the immigration woman was cursing and swearing. I said, 'Is it up to you to decide who you let in?' She examined my passport closely, and examined the visa that had been issued in Mexico. Just to be annoying, she checked again on the computer. She wanted to question me, but I said I had already filled out the form. The woman was very overbearing, as if she represented the entire United States government. She took me to another official, handing him my papers as if I was a suspicious individual who had committed some crime.

As soon as the second official saw my indigenous dress, he didn't even trouble to look at my passport. He started trying to intimidate me. Sometimes I can pretend to be intimidated, though quite honestly I've never let it bother me. I've had to confront so many frontier authorities – the American, the Swiss, the Italian and the Mexican – that I have no problem sticking up for myself. I always say I have nothing to hide, and that if I had done anything wrong I would always admit it.

I like to observe things, because you learn a lot, and I noticed that this particular gentleman was being extremely rude. I told him, 'Excuse me, sir, I shall only answer questions I believe should be answered. I shall not answer any others.' That made him even worse. He seemed to think I was undermining his authority. He threatened to withdraw my visa altogether.

I told him not to worry, I could get on a plane and go somewhere else. I told him that if I had to choose somewhere in the world to live, it would not be the United States. He went on asking me questions. Why was I living in Mexico? What did I eat? Who were my friends? Had I ever been a member of an opposition party? It was a real interrogation. I told him if he was going to subject me to this kind of interrogation, and to treat me like a criminal, I had the right to have a lawyer present.

He flew into a rage and handed me over to another official, his superior. The airline officials looking after us were really embarrassed. They didn't know what to do. They tried to reason with the man. But this rude, overbearing bully wouldn't listen.

His supervisor asked me, 'What is your name?' 'What's yours?' I replied. He said, 'You realise that you are speaking to a United States government official and the authorities can do whatever they like with you.'

I told him he could do what he liked with me, but I would only speak to him through a lawyer. He said I had no right to see a lawyer.

That's when my Mayan spirit flared up, just as my female spirit often does. I said, 'Look, first I don't have to answer your questions. I will answer nothing but the usual questions one is asked at immigration control. I shall only answer your other questions in the presence of a lawyer. Second, I want to know why you have kept me here for over an hour.'

I told him I loved coming up against people who abuse their authority, and that's exactly what he was doing. I am totally against the abuse of authority. If he wanted to show me how it was done, I had all the time in the world. I might learn something to add to my experience. He told me that sometimes people entered the United States on false visas. 'Fine,' I said, 'are you saying my visa is false?' He said that there was a lot of corruption about, and some American embassies might issue a false visa for a consideration.

'If your government officials are corrupt,' I said, 'it's your problem, not mine. If you have doubts about your embassy in Mexico or anywhere else, it's nothing to do with me.' I told him I respected the law and my documents were legal.

In an attempt to justify himself, he added, 'The computer shows that you have a record prior to 1992. Be careful, unless you want to add to your record.'

I told him that if he had things on file about me that was fine, I could use them in my book. His whole tone was very intimidating, and I put an end to the conversation. 'Put me wherever you like on the computer,' I said, 'but let me out of here because I'm tired of listening to you. I won't put up with bullying and racism from the likes of you. It's not my fault that you were brought up that way.'

I had to put up with the man for an hour and a half. When I finally got away, I thought how wonderful it was to receive the Nobel Prize. It meant respect, red carpets, tributes, all sorts of things.

Then, as we left the airport, I thought to myself, 'The Nobel Prize may have changed my life, but this has been a test, my first since I received the Prize. I'm glad I can't get rid of my indigenous woman's face or my Mayan ancestry.'

Yet at the same time, I felt rather sad. If this sort of thing could happen to me, someone who had won the Nobel Prize, who had sent messages to the US President that were published all around the world, what might not happen to the 185,000 illegal Guatemalan immigrants living in the United States? They have been denied the right to work, denied protection under the law.

There are millions of people who have emigrated to the US, who, in the situation I was in, would have been deported immediately, by a fifth-rate official who wouldn't have been bothered to listen to a word that was said. It would be enough to scare the life out of anybody without my experience: to be passed to three, four, or five officials who would intimidate and interrogate them, especially if they knew that no one would defend their rights and no one would listen to them.

As for me, I gave a press conference and everybody sympathised with me. It was very satisfying. I felt proud to be an ordinary citizen. Yet for people who have no help at the borders, things are very tough. It's as if, at the end of the twentieth century, it's a crime to be poor, and an international crime at that, for wherever you go in the world you always come up against obstacles and laws.

I remember so many incidents in the thirteen years I have been crossing borders. I am very privileged, I know that. At every frontier, there will be men and women who are sensitive, humane, courteous and kind, but there are plenty of the other sort as well. Yet they are not all bad. I have met many nice people at the borders I have crossed. I remember so many of them, and I should like to thank them all through this book.

11

RETURN TO LAJ CHIMEL, 1995

After I went back to live in Guatemala in 1994, I realised there was one more step to take. Without it, I would never be happy. I had to go back to Laj Chimel, the village where I was born. Just imagine, if I was afraid of going back to Guatemala, I was even more afraid of going back to Laj Chimel.

There had been so much violence, so much death, and so much disintegration within the armed struggle itself. No one ever knew who killed whom, or what had happened where. It is a place which holds many mysteries, secret graves, people eaten by animals . . .

Everyone took justice into their own hands. Some people used it to act against their neighbours, because of land, or women, or for jealousy, and for all kinds of problems. Three or four communities had title to the same piece of land. They all claimed it had been held by their ancestors, and they fought over it. Chimel was probably the place where the first seeds of revolutionary consciousness were sown, the seeds of struggle, of democracy.

The problem of land is not just being aware of not having it, it is being aware of the need to fight for it. On top of that, there was the issue of

impunity. There was no hope that a person guilty of a crime would ever be punished or brought to justice. If the judicial system doesn't work any-where else in the country, what chance would it have in this little village?

Chimel is a very magical place. The land is rich in so many varieties of trees, animals, birds, flowers, lianas and fungi. The rainforest is 'misty and mysterious', one of the few left on earth, one of those places they call 'the lungs of the planet'. It has become even thicker since the repression. These gigantic mountains and forests sheltered thousands of internal refugees and displaced people.

I was very afraid. I didn't know what had happened to the murderers, to the *judiciales* who were paid to bump off catechists or to wipe out other groups. Many landowners' sons became assassins, killing in broad daylight. Their parents taught them to hate poor people, humble people, especially in the municipality of Uspantán. Fear of them sowed terror in the streets, you did not know whom to trust.

Fear of so many memories is tragic too. However much we say we never had a childhood, there must be some trace, some remains of it left, not only in Laj Chimel and in Chimel, but also in the town of Uspantán. 'The only thing to do is to steel myself and go back incognito,' I said to myself. My husband always encourages me, and he pushed me into taking the step. He is a positive man, he finds a generous answer to everything.

So we went, and a few days before leaving, I dreamed of my mother, and of the house where I grew up. They hadn't changed. I was overcome by sad-ness. I kept getting a big lump in my throat and crying. I didn't feel hatred for those who had destroyed my community, my home and my family. I just wanted to cry. I missed the past, when I was a girl, and the home that I can never have again. The heart always feels great pain. We talked a lot about my mother and my father during that time, and of the many sorrows I had thought time had erased. When something irreversible and irreparable hap-pens, our strength as human beings is put to the test.

My first surprise was that the journey wasn't the nine hours it was when I left Laj Chimel. In those days, we walked for hours and hours, up and down the hills, those interminable bends! I remember each drop of sweat. But people had worked tirelessly to open the road from Uspantán to Laj Chimel, so we only had to walk for four kilometres. We didn't get to Chimel, it was a few hours further on.

We must have arrived at about ten in the morning. I was surprised at how small the place was. It was a miniature Chimel. It seemed like a different place. Most of the rivers had dried up. The marshes, the swamps and the quicksands we had been so afraid of – the places where we hid for fear of snakes and mountain animals – these had all shrunk. Small, too, were the mysterious rocks. When we were children, we thought snakes might be asleep on them or other frightening things, or, worse still, *nawaals*.

Now we were there with my sister Anita, my brother Nicolás, my sister-in-law Juana and others who had lived in Chimel before. My husband was with us too. All of us had been born there and we were all surprised at how tiny Laj Chimel had become. That's where the name comes from. In K'iche', *laj* means little, something precious in a very small space, something small that is full of surprises.

'This isn't the land I left,' I said as we walked along. 'Where are our mountains?' The land now belonged to landowners, and they had cut down our precious trees. Part of the hillside was bare. We remembered having played as children in the great ancient forests, and many of them had now been cut down. The rivers, too, had dried up.

A small community of twenty-four families was living on my father's land. My brother Víctor's house was still there, so was Nicolás's house and Marta's house and my father's house. The people there were so neglected and hungry that I felt sad for life itself.

'This is the birthplace of a winner of the Nobel Peace Prize,' I said, 'who is much loved and respected. But didn't I grow up among worms and poverty too? How can people love me but not these children, these women, these sick undernourished people? It's as if what happened to me belongs in the past, and today it is different.'

I felt so sad. The people were like skeletons. They had a sad, hard life. Yet even so, they went to find a chicken, and we ate it. We were sorry we hadn't brought anything with us. We came from a city of consumption and waste. It's not just in the developed world that food is wasted, but in ours as well. The families who lived there were very poor. Fifteen years after I left, they were even poorer than before. At least we used to have straw houses with wooden planks. It was something, not a lot. It certainly wasn't this type of misery. We had more to eat then.

The fact is that when the repression started, the majority of the inhabitants of Chimel were killed. Many were killed in Laj Chimel itself. The army, the corrupt mayors and the regional office of the state land agency (INTA) acted fraudulently with respect to the land left by people who died in Chimel. The way corruption and injustice worked in this area was to pretend that the former owners had sold their land. Since the majority of them were dead, the title deeds were falsified and the signatures faked. According to the deed, my grandfather Nicolás Tum had arrived, at the age of 130, with a group of thirty peasants from Chimel, to sell the land in Laj Chimel to a certain Reginaldo Gamarra. In those days Laj Chimel was the centre of the community of Chimel.

The contract of sale was recorded, as was the fact that Don Nicolás Tum could not read or write. He left his fingerprints mixed up with those of everyone else. I couldn't figure out which was my grandfather's. The officials said that they had sold their land voluntarily.

When I finished reading the contract, supposedly drawn up legally by a notary, I said, 'This is an injustice.' And I went to investigate the names that were there. I found the families of several of these people, and they swore that their relatives had died before the contract of sale. The only way to prove that an injustice had been done was to go to the registry office, to find the death certificates of my grandfather and the others who had supposedly sold the lands at Laj Chimel. We soon discovered that all these documents had disappeared, All trace had gone of anything that could prove that my grandfather was already dead when he apparently sold the land. Yet how could he have lived to be 130? My grandfather did live to be 117. I don't think he ever reached 130!

When we eventually came to Laj Chimel, the people were fearful. The new landowner was a bad man. He didn't let anyone work, or cut firewood, or walk through his land. He didn't even let them cross his road, so they had to live from what was available in the village. They were afraid of him, not just because he was a *ladino* and a landowner, but because of his contacts with gangs of murderers and *judiciales*. He was well known for having stolen land.

Some of the former mayors of these areas had gone to prison, thank God, and when we arrived, we swore on the memory of our parents that we would fight for the return of that land. My brother Nicolás had been fighting all along, but he could not win against people with so much power. I never thought that the deep spirit of struggle my father taught us would well up again in me, but it did. I said, 'We must fight for it, whatever the cost. We must get our land back.' Everybody was very happy and we spent several good hours together.

We had arrived at ten o'clock. By eleven, they had prepared us a meal, and by twelve we were starting to relive our old memories of this little patch of earth. We wondered why the rivers had dried up, why the marshes were smaller. Was it only our perception? Was our land really bigger in those days? Or did our sense of belonging with our community, with our people, make it seem bigger? Who knows what had happened?

We went to find one particular tree, a *cuxín*, which we had all dreamed about (not only me). My sister Lucía once told me that she always dreamed of that *cuxín*. So did my other sister Anita. It was big and beautiful, and bore a lot of fruit. We used to eat its fruit. I remember, from my dreams over the years, sitting under the *cuxín*, or walking beside it.

We found no trace of it. I asked my brother Nicolás what had happened to it. He replied sadly, 'It died a long time ago.' 'Why did it die?' I asked. It was a huge tree, and very old. It was there when we were born.

Why did it die so soon? Other trees had been cut when we were children,

201

and their trunks are still there. Nicolás said that many of the inhabitants of Chimel had been hanged there and shot. Their blood had splattered on the *cuxín*. It lived for only a few weeks after that. It died by itself. It withered and fell, and its roots came out. It quickly decayed. Not a trace remained, nothing. We were amazed. The tree we had dreamed about so often was no longer there.

There was another tree near the house where we were born. They say a neighbour called Don Gerónimo Poli, a *compadre* of my father, was hanged on it. Another man was hanged there too. The same thing happened. It was a sturdy tree, an evergreen oak. Mountain people say that when these trees are splattered with human blood they die straight away.

We found many bones in the fields and under rocks on the hillsides. Nicolás said, 'So many things happened here and so few people are alive to tell the tale.' During the repression, most people were not buried. Bands of dogs formed, and, when people died, the dogs tore off their flesh and took the bones away to gnaw. There was a plague of dogs hunting for the bodies of the dead. They say there was a time when people were afraid to pass the village for the dogs had become so used to eating people. The army was continually laying ambushes; people seeking refuge with their families died, and so too did many guerrillas. That is why there are so many bones strewn over the land.

After that, Laj Chimel was settled by the new landowners. They brought their cattle to graze, but they didn't stay long. The cattle started dying in droves. They would go to sleep and not wake up. Many seemed alive but they were dead. The dogs became increasingly ravenous for meat. They tore the flesh off the cattle as well, and ate them. So human bones are now confused with animal bones.

My brother looked at the sky in silence, as if asking the Creator for permission, then he said with due respect, 'I had a dog that was pregnant. She joined a band of man-eating dogs. When her puppies were born, they had the eyes of humans, the expression of humans. They looked at me as a person would. I had to kill them one by one. I hope I haven't committed a crime before our Creator.' Only the Heart of the Sky knows. For how can we distinguish between a human bone and a cow bone?

When we saw all this, we remembered the six or seven groups of people who had passed through this blessed land. Nothing of them remains. They left quickly because they were afraid. The spirits in the village are very active. People believe that all those who were murdered there actually now inhabit Laj Chimel and Chimel, and are the real owners of the village and the lands. They guard it.

In the circumstances, very few people could bear to live there. They quarrelled among themselves and left. The new landowners again began selling off pieces of Laj Chimel, and dreamed of becoming rich from the vastness of its natural resources. Many of the more ambitious ones dreamed of logging and selling the fine wood of the ancient trees. What a wealth of flora and fauna is hidden in that great misty rain forest. For more than ten years so many people have wanted to exploit that land.

Our visit was not all sad and tearful. Once again we were able to breathe the unforgettable smell of Chimel. We remembered the times when we had been happy there. We remembered our games as children, the places where we took our sheep to graze, and the things that scared us. We imagined wonderful things for Chimel again, as well as for Laj Chimel. But first we have to recover it, and to get tenure of our land again.

I think we must have left Laj Chimel at about three in the afternoon. We walked the four kilometres to where we had left the vehicles. The walk was very hard, very tricky. It was very muddy. I was ill for three days when we got back. 'What could have caused it?' I wondered. 'Maybe the psychological impact?'

I have such unforgettable memories of that place. Our little community had started the revolutionary struggle there. We had broken down the barriers imposed by the landowners. We had taken pieces of land from different parts of Laj Chimel and begun distributing them. How could I escape from such memories?

A month later, a government organisation came to offer assistance, as though they had been shamed into it because the village had suddenly become news. The press reported that I had gone back to my village. How sad it was, they said, that a Nobel Prize winner's birthplace should be a poverty-stricken village! Laj Chimel was suddenly remembered.

The villagers were offered corrugated iron roofs if they would put their name to an organisation to develop a project and raise money. The community said no. They wanted to ask us first, because my brothers and sisters, and my husband and myself, were all members of that community, and they would do nothing without us.

That is how the feeling of being part of the community began to grow again in Anita, Lucía, Angel and I. We couldn't do anything about it until the end of the year, when we planned to spend a week with our people in Laj Chimel. On 23 December 1995, I did my daughter-in-law's duty and I went to my parents-in-law's house in San Pedro Jocopilas. We spent 23 and 24 December there, and on the 25th we set out for Laj Chimel.

We arrived at eight at night, in torrential rain. It was a truly impressive downpour. We stayed there, and we delved patiently into all the corners of Laj Chimel, spending time with the twenty families that lived there. We helped to create a co-operative, held an assembly, had a party, let off fireworks, burned some *pom* and brought a *marimba*. We had never forgotten either, during all our years of absence, to burn *pom* for this land.

Of course, we did not yet have a house there. But the people built us an amazing hut. We drank loads of *cuxa* to ward off the intense cold. We spent New Year there with them, and we rescued our land, again. We knew that it had been registered in the name of Reginaldo Gamarra. We knew he had got it under false pretences. We knew he was mega-corrupt. He had stolen a lot of land in these parts by threats, intimidation and force. Yet he would need a lot of dignity and moral strength to force us off our father's land again. That is where our memories are, our navel, our umbilical cord, as my brother Nicolás calls it.

Chimel and Laj Chimel is an enchanted place in the life of each of my brothers and sisters. The spirit there that shelters and protects us constantly calls to us. We gathered there again just after the family tragedy of Kalito's kidnapping. We had to purify the family again in Chimel. Barely six weeks had passed since the little boy disappeared. For us, the family unit is worth more than each individual, and that is why we went together to Paraxchaj when the kidnapping happened. We discovered the culprit because we were united by the same feelings. That's why we all had to come back to the village of our birth.

There is no graveyard or health centre in Laj Chimel. There is no school. Our embryo co-operative sprouted at the end of the year, and we gave it the name of Tikh'al Utziil, which means 'Sowing Peace'. It is 'the Sowing Peace Co-operative'. The new Chimel will grow out of the *Tikh'al Utziil*. At the moment, people can't take their maize out because the road is so bad. Lorries don't come that far, there is no transport. You can get vehicles down the road but no one wants to risk carrying people. No one in Chimel even dreams of owning a vehicle that people might ride in. They still use horses and their own backs to take things to Uspantán.

People's lives are hard, they suffer from malnutrition. When I left the first time, I knew a little girl. She now has three children. The first time I went back, she had just had a baby. When we returned in December, four months later, I asked about the baby. 'She died,' she said. 'She's dead?' I said. 'Yes, dead,' she said, as if death was normal.

I do not agree. I believe people should live. Our people are innocent, wonderful, with such a will to work and struggle. I am sure that in a few years they will prove this place to be a paradise. It will give life, happiness and food to many people. They can show that this place is beautiful and that the people here are beautiful. Laj Chimel was not the place I remembered, but I hope that one day there will be a stable community there, one that fights to maintain the ecosystem and practises sustainable development.

We will try to make sure Chimel regains its dignity, with rivers flowing again and roads that respect nature. Trees will grow once more, and people will live with nature as we were once taught to live. We want to make a decent life for our people, even though neither myself nor my sisters will live there exclusively again. I want my brother to have the right to live there, even if the grandchildren and orphans in our family do not return.

Yet for Chimel to regain its dignity, and for all of Guatemala to regain its dignity, we have to work like ants all over the country. We began the National Voter Registration Campaign before the elections in 1995. This was the Menchú Foundation's first big nation-wide activity since my return. In the old days, nobody cared if indigenous people voted in Guatemala. The political parties certainly didn't care. It was less trouble if people had no one to represent them, for the parties only had to fight over the votes of a minority. All the talk about the rights and value of indigenous peoples was nonsense. It would never happen, they weren't interested in civic awareness. They just wanted to fill the town hall with their friends, their *compadres*.

They weren't interested in the people, and much less in public meetings that might make people start believing in their own vote. Soldiers or the henchmen of the landowners would usually arrive with guns to tell people, 'Vote this way, or I'll kill you.' They did this to keep themselves in power locally.

In some areas, 30 per cent of the voters were like an audience watching a game, they would always vote for the most amusing candidate. Seventy per cent of the registered voters did not vote at all. They would always abstain. There are eleven million Guatemalans, and of these, four or five million are adults. Yet there are only 3.7 million registered voters, and not more than 1.5 million of those actually vote. A good many votes belong to people who have no identity papers. They are registered at birth, but have never gone to the local council to collect the citizen's ID card that would allow them to vote.

The day this relationship with the electorate changes, we will certainly see change in Guatemala. Yet people must also speak out. At the moment, we are too often stuck in the role of victim. We have little sense of our own worth. We find it hard to have confidence in ourselves. In many places,

Mayans prefer not to speak their own language when there is a Spanish-speaking person present, or a mestizo or a *ladino*. They prefer to speak Spanish. Even though they speak it badly, they want to show they speak a second language. We never expect a *ladino* brother who does not speak K'iche' to make the slightest effort to understand it. Yet if he doesn't understand it, at least let him respect it. He shouldn't impose his own language. Confidence in our culture and our identity is a potential tool of unity.

During the voter-registration campaign, I met a lot of really professional indigenous people who spoke two, three, four languages – from different linguistic groups. The key to success in our kind of campaign is to use these local people to explain our ideas. I have never liked speaking through a translator because I can't understand what they are saying. Why should I bring a translator with me from outside when local people understand, not just the words but also the concepts. If we give local experts and technicians more opportunity, maybe things will change nationally. It's one thing to translate literally; adapting the message to another group's way of thinking is quite another.

Politicians have never had enough confidence in us, not just to use local interpreters, but also to explain their ideas in a way our people can understand, and to discuss with us ways of building a better future. Yet it is not easy to fuse Western thought with that of an ancient culture, one with its own very special characteristics, its own symbolism, its own community-based structure.

How are we to sow the foundations for an intercultural relationship among our different peoples? Our languages are very rich, they are the total universe of a culture. Almost all their signs, symbols and references are to objective rather than to subjective things. The references in our minds and in our language are to mountains, rivers and other material things. Spanish, too, is rich, but it is very abstract. In K'iche', a single word has five or six meanings. I have to use another word to explain why I am using it. So people understand why I am saying something.

You don't have that experience in Spanish. When I have to translate thoughts from Spanish to K'iche', I find the syntax very different. Our languages express our culture, and speaking and understanding them mean learning about a new world, and thinking about things in a new way. We must both protect and develop our languages.

Often we would arrive at a town without knowing either its language or its community structure. We would give its professionals, its leaders, the chance to explain our message in their own way. If they couldn't explain the message, we would probably do it more formally, but this wouldn't be so special. We would soon be as boring as other politicians. This experience reaffirmed our belief in the need to respect local identity, and not to impose outside ways of thinking – though it was only right to propagate the logic of reasoning.

The people were happy and moved because they agreed with our message: the need to build a democratic country together. Our people essentially see elections and voting as a *ladino* custom. It is '*kaxlan*', they say. Yet it was not hard to convince them that the rules had changed, and that our people could now decide.

I have always learned that without teamwork, and without responsibility shared by creative intelligent people, it is impossible to think we can make a difference here. Change is always the result of collaboration. That is what the Menchú Foundation believes. If I go to San Sebastián Huehuetenango, which is in the Mam area, I don't understand the people there. If I arrive out of the blue, even though my intentions are good, it won't work. We usually try to arrive after our local *compañeros* there have prepared the ground, and have talked to people. They will then know who we are, and there will be mutual understanding. We arrive knowing we are among friends. There is an almost common view of the problems. Which are the most urgent? How far do our problems go? Arriving like any old politician would not make for a close or serious relationship.

So creating a team is crucial to understanding the concept of community we have here. I would not dream of talking to indigenous people in terms of political parties. Everything has to be community-based. The ideal thing would be a political community of the Mayan people, working communally with others for a political purpose. This would not be a political party. The framework would be different.

This does not apply just to Mayans, but to the whole Guatemalan nation. I get indignant when someone talks of giving indigenous people this or that, as if indigenous people were just waiting for whatever handouts the *ladinos* choose to give them. To me this notion is out of date.

The campaign is called the National Campaign for Citizen Participation. 'What is indigenous about it?' some people may ask. I reply that my concept of citizenship is an inclusive one. It is broader than that understood by some others. We are targeting women, but it would be silly to say, 'Things which are not for indigenous women do not belong in this campaign.' Everybody has a role to play in this great cultural diversity.

The voter-registration drive of the Menchú Foundation surprised people by claiming to be independent. I said I was not going to support any political party. I wanted the campaign to be neutral and autonomous, and I was not going to allow it to be used by any one body. Nobody believed me. If you say you're acting for the general good, everyone thinks you have some personal hidden agenda. I didn't want the campaign to have its credibility compromised by links with any one group. It was ridiculous that twenty-four political parties were fighting for barely a million votes. Siding with one party, however much I shared its beliefs, and even if we had fought common battles, was always going to be a sad role for a Nobel Prize winner. Supporters of all excluded candidates would be offended.

Besides, I couldn't promise that things in Guatemala would actually change. Could any candidate guarantee respect for indigenous peoples and respect for women? Could anyone guarantee that human rights would not be violated, that the civil war would end and the peace agreements be complied with, that a real peace process would be started, that the historical memory of Guatemala would be treated with respect? Was there really a candidate who would make an effort to change things and listen to people?

For me the secret has always been in knowing how to listen to people, in recognising their problems and helping to solve them. It is not a question of going round like some lord inaugurating dams, to get publicity on television and your name in the papers.

I don't think I would be in a position to promise all these things. I have the same role as any ordinary citizen. Yet together with other ordinary citizens, I can make Laj Chimel the paradise I remember. I can help make all of Guatemala a treasure house for the sake of generations to come.

12

UNDERSTANDING AND ACCEPTING
DIVERSITY

Religions have sometimes been used as weapons of oppression, and at other times as weapons of conquest and colonisation. Our experience, as indigenous peoples, is that religion was used as a powerful shotgun, a powerful machine-gun, a powerful arrow, to try to dismantle our cultures. When the celebrations for the Columbus Quincentenary started, we indigenous people made our feelings about the Catholic religion felt in no uncertain terms. Until that time I had not fully realised the role that religions have played in history.

I want to distinguish, however, between religion as a doctrine and as the beliefs of a people. Our faith means having something to hold on to, somewhere to deposit our sorrows – and to feel humble towards life and suffering, towards nature, and towards past generations and history itself. It means being strong enough not to falter, believing in the hereafter, adopting religion in practice and not just as a concept. All that is faith. Mayan faith is believing in the greatness of life. The gift of prayer is a humble sign of respect to the hereafter; a tribute to the world beyond.

My mother prayed to nature. She went out at midnight whenever something special happened in the family or in the community, and whenever nature was angry. When hurricanes destroyed the harvest, my mother went straight out to burn *pom*, to pray to nature, to render homage to the essence of life, to *Rajaaw juyub'*, the Master of the Universe. She also prayed to give thanks for food, for life, for new things, for good and evil. Ever present in all aspects of my mother's life was a love of life, the sun, the moon and the earth.

You had to greet the sun very reverently, very respectfully, every time it appeared. Each time, as my mother used to put it, 'the eyes of the sun begin to peep over the hill in the morning', you had to greet it, take your hat off, bow deeply, because it was the Father Sun, the Grandfather Sun.

The Moon, on the other hand, was like the loving and serene grandmother, always mysterious, and wise enough to give harmony to life. The light, the fire and the burning heat of Father Sun needed the coldness and serenity of Grandmother Moon to complement it. They represent the duality of life. In February and March, we would go out into our yard with my mother, or maybe the night would surprise us when walking home, and my mother would stop to look at the moon, huge, round and luminous. 'How lovely our Grandmother is tonight,' she would say. 'It is a good time to sow. There will be a good harvest.'

Life is duality. We need a mother and a father. My mother taught us that Mother Earth is governed by Grandmother Moon and Father Sun (both are *uh'ux'kaj*). Mother Earth is fertility. When we ask Father Sun to let rain fall, it is because we think Mother Earth is fertile, she is the receiver of the seed. The seed is then fertilised and grows. The moment of contact of the rain and the earth is as if they have made love to beget a son.

Our elders are not only synonymous with wisdom, hope and culture, they also transmit tradition and possess experience. A son begat by the rain and earth begins a pilgrimage of experiences. The elders respect each stage of a person's life, and the rectitude of their character. They recognise the size and significance of someone's mistakes and behaviour, and the thread of their destiny, until they too grow old and become elders themselves. Our elders are science and wisdom; they are our history books; the library that we consult and, in the last instance, we trust. Old people are strong in wisdom and guarantee respect.

Our elders tell us all this from the time when we are very young. They explain that a star fell because Grandmother Moon sent a messenger. Our parents always tell us not to stare at the sun, as the sun is so fierce, yet his fierceness is tempered by the tenderness and love of Grandmother Moon. They also explain that both good and evil are necessary, for they complement each other. This thinking is part of our spirituality and part of the way we live our lives. It is a beautiful religion when it is natural and authentic, and not manipulated or ridiculed. It is beautiful when its integrity is respected, for it is the faith of a people.

My father didn't believe this. He was a fervent Catholic. He grew up being a *chajal* – an altar boy. He put candles on the saints and dressed them. He put out flowers for them and sometimes burned incense. He devoutly attended Mass. He venerated the church as the great temple of God. He became a catechist, preaching God's word. He understood that life and death are inseparable. He told us Bible stories when we were little, and he taught us what a good Christian must do in the community. He saw the Bible as the shining light of hope, as the source of experience and of faith.

As children, there was never an imbalance in what we chose to believe from Mama or Papa. Both of them were the bedrock of our community. They taught us that either way of praying is deep and sincere, and that the Creator will know in which way to receive them. Mama learned a lot from Papa's faith, and he learnt from her and from us, his children. They both asked God for his blessing. Papa taught us to be catechists, to preach the word of God, to respect religious symbols and to pray devoutly.

When I left Chimel, I didn't realise I was professing the Mayan religion. My parents never told me that it came from thousands of years ago. They simply said it was passed down from our ancestors. Only when I left my village did I realise there were divisions between the religions. The Catholic

Church always claimed that our *ajq'iij*, the elders who know the movements of time and the sun, were sorcerers or clairvoyants. That was unacceptable to the God that the Catholics worshipped. I did not really understand, for I had no problem praying in the way that I had learned in the hut where I was born.

Conflicts between religions have always frightened me. Over the years, I have had the privilege of going into churches of many dominations, and being invited to meetings of different religious groups. In the United States, I was lucky enough to meet the Navajos, the Hopis and the Lakotas. I also went to Big Mountain, Arizona, where the Navajos believe there are seven generations of their people. These seven generations are the source and guarantee of life for their people. I also went to Sweat Lodge, a sacred place of prayer for the Navajos and the Dakotas, and for all the first nations that lived in North America. After seeing all these things, I became convinced that the problem of our peoples does not lie in their faith, and still less is that faith a reason for despising someone.

Belief can be something else too. In the Committee for Peasant Unity (CUC), we used to say, 'Clear head, caring heart and fighting fist of rural workers,' and the words were said with great conviction. We wanted justice, and we wanted human dignity to be respected. We wanted the equal distribution of land to be a basic right. Each time we wanted something good for our people, it became a conviction. These in turn became part of a deep belief, that of aspiring to a better world. We believed that it was necessary and possible to change society.

The problem with religion only occurs when, in its institutional form, it introduces political projects and counter-insurgency plans, or prevents the just demands of the people from being recognised. We have seen this happen in many countries in the world, and it has been our own experience too.

The first time I went to Rome I thought that Rome was part of heaven, not part of earth. I thought we only went there at the end of our lives, not while we were still alive wearing a multicoloured *huipil*. When I was told we were going to Rome – and I knew the Pope lived there – I felt very strange. I had the same feeling when I went to Israel, to the areas where the Western religion was born. We learned all those names in the Bible, so they didn't seem real. They seemed more like a region of heaven, beyond the clouds. Going to Rome moves you, and makes you reflect. Yet Rome is not part of heaven. It's just a city, as ordinary as any other city in the world. It has its own man-made history.

I went to the place where they used to sacrifice Christians. I have always wondered why the Aztecs, who loved life, sacrificed human beings. I never found the right answer, nor could I find a way of defending myself when the question was put by reactionary racist people who tried to make me answer for Aztec wrongdoing. They used the Aztecs as a way of provoking me, or to invalidate the cause of indigenous peoples. Then, when I went to Rome, I said, 'But the Romans sacrificed human beings too!' I found clear traces of human sacrifice and came to understand it much better. That made a big impression on me. It was a lesson I will never forget.

I used to have an almost magical image of the Pope. He seemed to be someone very distant and unobtainable, impossible to see or know. Seeing photographs of him, a saint yet human, gave me a strange inexplicable feeling. Maybe he performed miracles. I didn't think that he could fly, I knew he was flesh and blood. Yet I continued to think of him as extraordinary and mysterious. When my mother told me about the moon, the sun and Mother Nature, I knew I would never see them close to. I felt the same about the Pope. As a child I had learned not to judge what I don't know, or what I cannot touch.

Rome was a great revelation for me, especially when I discovered that God's House is built with treasures from our countries, the so-called Third World – with precious stones from America and the Caribbean and Africa. Accompanying us was a historian who explained, piece by piece, the various precious stones that the Vatican is built of. I would have loved my father to see what I was seeing. I would have given anything for him to see Rome and the Vatican before he died. I had imagined it would be very different, not full of material things – luxury, bureaucracy, tourism. I know this is a controversial issue, but I just want to stress that religions can be tools of empire. It is up to their congregations to see that this does not happen.

I am deeply religious, yet I also believe in nature. I believe in life and peoples. I believe in people's faith and their communion. I believe in the life experiences and faith of the early Christians, above all because they believed in sharing things. I believe we human beings must fight for creation; and by this I mean all of the planet's living things.

I also believe firmly that people need to believe. I have always maintained that the faith of a person or a people is sacred and private. It cannot be bought or sold. It has no price. A people's religion and their religious sensibility must be respected. We Mayans have retained the essence of our faith. It must be allowed to flourish, and we must have the right to proclaim it. If the religions of the Mayans, and the Incas and the Aztecs lack full recognition and a measure of institutionalisation, then we must fight for these things too.

A people's religious sensibility is based on daily practice and a humble attitude to life. If religion is not understood in this sense, it becomes a commodity or an obstacle to peaceful coexistence. It risks becoming a weapon of colonialism, of discord and racism, of dictatorship and war. Religious sensibility is ingrained in a people, throughout their history and down the generations. It lies behind the laws that have governed the daily life of our civilisations for thousands of years.

The first thing the colonisers did when they arrived was to make new laws; laws that excluded the previous ones, including religious laws. Yet the harmony inherent in the religions of the Mayans, the Aztecs, the Incas, the Araucanians, the Aymara and the Lakota was an important legacy. It should have been recognised as such, and been respected and adopted by all humanity.

The challenge for the future lies in understanding and accepting diversity. We must prevent religious conflicts from concealing fundamental economic problems. The rich and powerful can always use religion to cover up injustices and, worse still, religion can be used as one of the main planks of impunity. 'He who knows no sin, does not need God's forgiveness,' they say. People can hate and oppress and kill, and then they seek God's forgiveness. This is often the religious message that the victims are given, to make them forget their tormentors. God is so great he forgives every sin. I hear this kind of message almost every day, and I find it very worrying.

In Chiapas, for instance, many people have been expelled from their communities in the name of religion 'X'. Yet the problem there is not really a religious one. It is derived from *caciquismo*, corruption, plunder, the take-over of traditional indigenous lands. It arises out of racism, social injustice and oppression. When peace negotiations are under way, a religious problem may suddenly appear. The big mistake that governments and some religious institutions have made is to say that people rebel because they have been taught the Bible, or because a priest or a nun has told them they are poor and hungry. They blame the Bible or the priests instead of doing away with the real sources of discontent: hunger, poverty and oppression.

We still have to find a way of preventing instruments of religion becoming instruments of war. Whenever the indigenous peoples of the continent reaffirm their own religion, governments often say that they are attacking national unity. Yet what the people really want is to make governments understand that both diversity and national unity must be based on mutual respect. Our contradictions do not stem from religion, but from a lack of mutual respect and of intercultural coexistence.

For some people, science has become an alternative to religion. I believe that science and technology belongs to us all. It is our greatest achievement. With each passing day, I marvel at these great advances more and more. I am especially impressed by technological advances in medicine. Yet the fact that I admire science and technology does not mean that I am not aware of its negative repercussions. The mistake has been to concentrate scientific knowledge in the hands of only a few people. The world's great powers have monopolised the most destructive inventions in order to control the rest of humanity. I refer especially to weapons of war, to the arms race that may lead to the destruction of life on our planet.

A few years ago, at the United Nations and on my speaking tours, I saw a lot of protests against nuclear weapons and chemical weapons. People's memories are short. They forget about problems until another disaster comes along. Hiroshima, Nagasaki and Chernobyl left great shadows of suffering and destruction over the human race. Yet today, they risk turning into historical myths that become gradually forgotten. The sad thing is that people are often not aware of the terrible consequences of these weapons until they actually experience them.

We do not know what kind of experiments are being carried out today on plants, trees, rivers and seas. Nor do we hear much about the experiments carried out on people, sometimes using street children for organ transplants, for instance. The thirst for knowledge has sometimes meant altering a human being's natural development. Science has also been used to control individuals. To a large extent, science and technology have helped to change the direction of our natural world. Solidarity, trust and communication, the feeling of being part of the same species, are all slowly disappearing.

I have also seen how the various economic co-operation projects between the nations of the world now work. In Guatemala, and in other Latin American countries, these so-called 'development projects' are often designed behind desks by technocrats. These are 'experts' who supposedly know all about everything, even about what the indigenous people feel, yet they are actually imposing their own world-view.

These 'experts' may spend years in a region, 'educating indigenous people, studying indigenous people, teaching them, teaching poor people, teaching everybody'. Yet humanity does not need 'experts' to rectify the profound social inequalities and the contempt for life that still exists today. These 'experts' live well on a guaranteed income. They finish their term of duty and leave the country. Yet the people remain in the same state of poverty as before, or worse.

This occurs when the purpose of scientific and technological advance has been forgotten. It no longer belongs to everybody, it merely serves petty interests. It ignores ethical considerations and is often used to eliminate the wisdom and creativity of indigenous peoples. That creativity taught us to play with a lamb or a bird, it taught us to play with the flowers of the field, it taught us to use Mother Nature without harming her.

Sometimes I get the impression that science and technology have lost contact with people's needs. They have ceased to reflect or serve them. In many cases, science has become an end in itself. If science and the great mass of the people worked together, humanity might find ways of discovering new things without abusing life, or using life as a guinea pig.

We indigenous people admire science, of course. Yet we also have a right to it ourselves. I always travel with my little computer under my arm. I am Mayan, I belong to the Mayan culture, and I need a computer because it serves my work, but I do not serve it. The moment people start serving their inventions, they ride roughshod over morality, ethics and dignity. They move away from their own species.

One thing that shocked me in the houses of the so-called 'First World' was seeing children of barely three spending hours in front of the television. They watched films of shooting, murder and crime, or soap operas about family break-ups, about lies, greed, lust, power and adultery. What they watched often affected me, and I am an adult. How could it possibly not affect them? That child may one day be the bureaucrat who pushes a button to decide important world issues. Adults should be aware of the damage we do when we fail to instil ethics and civil values in children.

At first I thought this problem only existed in the developed world. Now I understand that it affects children everywhere. Anything injected into the eyes of childhood is a way of interfering with a child's own natural development, a way of taking away the great gift of being a child. All this violence and intrigue is insidious, it acts like chemicals. The same thing happens to plants in our natural world. If you use chemicals on a cucumber or a *güisquil*, they will certainly grow quickly, but the natural process will have been interfered with.

Television does not have to be used like that. It would be wonderful if our humble people had access to these means of communication: television, radio, the written word and all kinds of verbal material. I am sure they would use them differently. They would create new generations that are sensitive to life. Instead of a grandfather passing on wisdom solely to his grandson, he could teach society as well. Television might be able to spread knowledge of our traditions without having them ridiculed and belittled by tourist folklore. Indigenous people would love to have a computerised network of information. We would love to reach mestizos, *ladinos*, and our non-indigenous brothers and sisters, and tell them how we live, and share our knowledge, equally and respectfully.

So I am not hostile to science and technology as such. I'm just against the way in which it has been used. Correcting the mistakes of science and technology will not be done by good intentions alone. A real revolution is needed, in which indigenous peoples can control their own destiny. Let them be the protagonists of their own experiences and share in science and technology. This implies change at the highest levels of decision-making. If ancient cultures have contributed definitively to scientific advance, then they should also be involved in applying these advances. Their contribution would be in social terms: the value of the collective, the community, as a mechanism of social organisation, and as a way of living. This would change the focus of science and technology and the way it is disseminated and applied. The norms and values would be different.

Many of the new rules of science and technology tend to undermine people's identity. Many men and women do not serve humanity, they serve technology. It would be disastrous if we did not realise the social conflict inherent in this contradiction. Indigenous peoples believe in their past, in their history and their knowledge. They also believe that they are a fundamental part of the present. This is where the problem of identity comes in.

The last few years have seen much debate about autonomy and the self-determination of peoples. Governments have often reacted by saying that this separatist tendency implies an attack on 'national unity', ignoring the fact that, so far, there has been no single experience of autonomous development. Real 'national unity' does not exist in most countries. Even in the best of cases, what exists is unity around national or sectional interests.

National unity must be defined in the context of the right of the whole society to diversity, protected by and reflected in a democratic state. Eventually governments will have to tackle the issue of the self-determination of diverse peoples within national boundaries. This applies particularly to indigenous peoples. Understanding our own people will help create new relationships throughout the globe: pluralistic, diverse, multi-ethnic and multi-cultural. We must accept that humanity is a beautiful multi-coloured garden.

The modern world is often fragmented – divisive, destructive and discordant. Indigenous peoples are always on the periphery. They are never the ones who make decisions. It is our responsibility to see that one day these people become the central protagonists in their own destiny and culture. The power we feel crushing us is the power to buy, to sell and to earn: the power of intolerance, arrogance, silence, indifference and insensitivity. I believe that there are important values, and beautiful things, that can never be bought or sold. They include the memory of indigenous peoples. They include life itself. Awareness cannot be forced on people, it is a process of understanding, identification and commitment. It is something we cultivate. There is a time to sow, a time to grow, and a time to reap.

This natural process, unfortunately, is often interfered with. Some people want to be constantly reaping, so that everything is accelerated. In an onion patch, we see the juicy onion heads and say, 'This probably took two months to grow,' when in fact it took five or six months to grow. Most consumers do not even ask what they are consuming, let alone how long it took to grow.

Although indigenous peoples have none of the political power or economic resources of the present world order, I believe humanity will finally come to recognise the wealth of values our peoples possess. I am certain of this. There are new times ahead. Just as problems arise through a complex and difficult process, so this same process can bring about a re-evaluation of our cultures, and an appreciation of what has been lost.

During my long years of crossing borders, I worked at the United Nations. I always had to produce dozens of elegant credentials to explain my indigenous face. An indigenous face, a poor face, creates suspicion. It often means we will be badly treated. When we come up against authority, we expect trouble. Indigenous people are recognised by their faces. It does not matter what they wear, their faces are indelible. People see my face and immediately think I am an immigrant, legal or otherwise. I always dress in the multicoloured fabrics of my native Guatemala, but that wasn't the problem. It was my face that counted. I could change everything, except my face. In Guatemala, the military detect people by their ethnic group, and by their clothes. At one time, being Ixil or K'iche' in a Mam area was very dangerous. We had to take off our K'iche' or Ixil clothes and disguise ourselves. Our languages and clothes became a risk. They played a dual role. Sometimes we used them to save our lives; sometimes we used them to hide ourselves.

Our identity is based on tradition, on ancient culture and history. We have a cosmovision, a philosophy all of our own. Watching a bird on television is different from watching a bird in the immensity of nature – knowing where its nest is, seeing how it feeds its young with natural wisdom, distinguishing between the times when it is crying and when it is singing. Many people are preoccupied by their own small world. They do not know about the conflicts that exist between indigenous cultures and other cultures. No one culture is greater than another. Each culture is simply impregnated with its own greatness, and the greatness of the peoples whose culture it is.

In this respect the situation in Guatemala is very sad. Now that our typical jumpers are the fashion in Paris and our multicoloured costumes are considered elegant, the *ladinos* in Guatemala wear them too, although they do not appreciate them in the same way. This shows how insecure *ladinos* are. They need to copy and follow stereotypes because they have no values of their own. They are not taught to value what they have. *Ladinos* are often foreigners in their own country.

The same is true of the majority of intellectuals. They are not secure in their volcanoes or their rivers, or even with the peoples of this beautiful pluri-cultural continent. They are always looking for another point of reference. Many of them go to live elsewhere, to try and find inspiration. They often have one foot in the Americas and the other in Paris, a fact that has helped slow down the cultural development of our peoples.

What was it, by contrast, that kept the Guatemalan refugees in the south of Mexico alive? The solid indigenous culture they received from their parents. The sacred value of their community, the ancient system of electing leaders, the roots which bore them, the wisdom of their ancestors. You have to have been fortunate enough to be born into this culture to truly appreciate it. It was this that helped them to adapt in Mexico, and to form their own system of community organisation.

I believe in the community as an alternative way forward, and not simply as a memory of the past. It is not just a myth, it is not something sterile. It is something dynamic. Identity is not just nostalgia for eating *tamales*. It is holistic, and comprises all the integral aspects of a culture. Understanding indigenous peoples today, at the end of the twentieth century, will surely help us to understand the world we live in. Yet it is important that those who study us be humble and modest.

I know people who think they know everything about indigenous people. People make careers out of us, people who think they can live by studying other human beings yet do not make the slightest effort to help them define themselves in society and history. We create defences against these parasites. Getting to know another culture is wonderful, but it is ignoble when certain irresponsible individuals try to put human dignity in a bottle and make a profit from selling it.

The world of Chimel, of Guatemala, has something to teach everyone. Our Mayan elders, our *ajq'iij*, are the trustees of time, the trustees of much of our people's spiritual wealth. The *ajq'iij*, man or woman, are of the sun. They are holders of our intellectual patrimony, which, although it has been usurped at different times, is still with us. It is present in the old people, in the *K'amal b'e*, in the community, in the essence of a child who knows the world.

There are laws governing harmony, and the *ajq'iij* are central to the ritual offerings that are so important to our concept of harmony. They play an important role in maintaining consensus and resolving conflict. Many people think we are passive, that we don't know what we want, that we are rebellious and mistrustful. They do not realise that we are following our own rhythm.

We indigenous Guatemalans think of ourselves as maize, as a cob of corn. If a grain is missing from the cob we notice that there is an empty space, that single grain occupies a particular place. We are all both individuals and a part of society. An individual cannot confuse the importance and status which qualifications give him with his humble role in society as a whole. When there is a wound in this beautiful K'iche' land of ours, I feel it as a pain in the heart of humanity, because El Quiché is like a grain in the cob of humanity.

The world has lost this sensitivity and that is why it has allowed so many crimes to go unpunished, and why it has allowed life in the heart of El Quiché to be so despised. The world does not feel its suffering as its own. It does not feel the suffering of the Kurds. The same is true with Brazil or El Salvador or with many other countries. Humanity must recover this sensitivity if it is to avoid wars and conflicts, and the indigenous cosmovision can contribute to this.

I am not a romantic myself, and I know that there is no ideal society. I understand culture as the evolution of knowledge and the continual discovery of the richness of life. Our aim must always be to enrich the life of our planet, our animals, our waters, our rivers and seas. And also the life of men and women of future generations, the life of our children.

Our people have our own technology and our own idea of development. We know the rhythms of the seasons and of the earth and of the weather. We know the perfection or imperfection of seeds, and what should be done with them. We know that when our Grandmother bathes, it is time to sow, just as a mother knows her child's intimate signs and gestures.

A river's rhythm cannot obey man's wishes. If it does, it is truly polluted and is no longer transparent, or it has dried up never to return. The rhythms of indigenous peoples are natural rhythms. Peasants are patient and honest. Their struggle has been eternal, continual. They aspire to progress, their hopes have been dreams, distant but longed for. Yet no one can live only with utopias. No one can live only with dreams.

On the roads from Sololá to Xela, the road that joins Cuatro Caminos and Los Encuentros, you see sacks of corn by the roadside, and maize and potatoes. Beside them is a machete. They might have been there for five nights, twenty nights, a month, just waiting for a lorry to collect them. The people's patience is boundless, and so is their honesty, their transparency, their respect. Five or seven days later, the machete has not disappeared and the sacks of maize or beans are still there. The people may be hungry but they are also honest. May things stay that way!

People also have a deep sense of the value of their word. Their word means dignity. It means trust. This sense of trust transcends the community, and transcends the ways society behaves. As we get nearer to the town, on the other hand, we find our sheep have disappeared, our goats have been stolen, someone has been killed for their earrings. People become increasingly rotten.

Sometimes I get shivers down my spine when I talk about society's parasites, though nature too has destructive bugs. There are men and women who contaminate society. This contamination is the source of conflict, war and confrontation.

The solution may lie in educating people differently, or in strengthening the judicial system – giving heavy sentences so that people who commit crimes do not get away with them. It may lie in creating a culture of peace, a lasting peace that stems from a system of values, not one that is simply the aftermath of war. It is here too that our ancient civilisation, with its ebbs and flows, has a concrete contribution to make.

The burden of the past five hundred years has almost destroyed our culture. We have had to defend it. If our civilisation had been allowed to continue at its peak, to fly freely like the *quetzal*, I think it would have reached a new era of coexistence with the world's other cultures. I am certain that the Mayan culture, the Aztec culture, the Inca culture, the Aymara culture, all the ancient cultures of the Americas, are deeply embedded in every community, every village, every child, every corner. I often wonder why people criticise the Aztecs for offering human sacrifices to their gods when they never mention how many sons of this America, *Abia Yala*, have been sacrificed over five hundred years to the god Capital.

The great gulf between rich and poor probably began thousands of years ago, but it is undeniable that it was accentuated in Guatemala five hundred years ago when our culture was subjugated. The pluri-ethnic culture is young. It has to merge with the ancient culture so that American man and woman can feel a common birth. No one can live without a mother or father. The ancient cultures are our mothers and fathers. Time and experience make us grow. However small and insignificant, we are born of something.

I am not a woman who idealises my identity. I am simply proud of having been born a Mayan. The Mayans are much greater than one generation. We are merely bridges from one generation to another. Examples and experiences pass through us. Others will follow. They will know how to assimilate what we have left and, through their own experiences, add continuity to the development of our culture.

Identity passes through the community, it passes along pavements, it passes down veins, and it exists in thoughts. Identity is the pride I have in my roots and in creating something new. Each day it provides the chance to be reborn, to flower again, to be rejuvenated. Identity is not studied in a dark room. It is like the *nawaal*, the shadow that accompanies you. It is the other, the one beside you.

Identity is also protection. It is invisible to the human eye, because the visible is incarnate, but the invisible is what is visibly incarnate. This might seem like a play on words, but that shadow is the *nawaal*. It can be an animal, a sheep, a deer or a coyote. It can also be a hill or a tree. Or it can be a mere shadow transported on the wind or scurrying along paths.

It is important to understand that a hill and a tree live longer than a person. So your identity lives longer than you do. That other part is almost the same as the identity. It is what cannot be seen and touched but is lived and experienced. You cannot think of your identity as something solitary. We are all born of a mother, of a womb. That womb can be those ancient civilisations which we have slowly forgotten, or, out of ignorance, have failed to value, or that the modern world considers backward, perceiving merely simple myths and legends that are considered worthless and can be discarded. I do not consider them worthless, and I do not discard them.

GLOSSARY

achiote	a red-coloured vegetable flavouring.
caballería	a measurement of land, equivalent to 64 *manzanas*, 45 hectares, or 2,471 acres.
cacique	a local strongman, often a big landowner.
chafas	the slang name for the military, uttered with considerable disdain.
Chapín(es)	the colloquial, slang name Guatemalans use for themselves.
chiclera	a fly found in regions where there are rubber (*chicle*) planta-tions; the bites of the *chiclera* fly produce serious lacerations of the skin.
cofradía	literally, a guild or union; in the Guatemalan context, these are more like clubs where Mayan rituals are practised.
CUC	Comité de Unidad Campesina; literally, the Committee of Peasant Unity, also known as the United Peasant Organisation.
compadre	usually a close friend, relative, or godparent; the feminine is *comadre*.

compañero   a term widely used in Latin America to mean friend, companion, or colleague; more specifically, in political terms, it means comrade.

CONAI   Confederación de Nacionalidades Indígenas de Ecuador, the Ecuadorean Confederation of Indigenous Nationalities.

corte   multicoloured material used as a skirt, the bottom half of traditional costume.

cuxa   a local eau de vie in Guatemala, usually made illegally.

despedida   literally, a farewell party; in the Mayan sense, it is a ritual ceremony performed for the couple before marriage.

filóchofo   distortion of *filósofo* (philosopher); *filo* also means blade and indicates a sharp, cutting humour.

finca   an estate or plantation, usually growing coffee or sugar.

güisquil   a root vegetable similar to a potato.

huipil   also *guipil*, from the Nahuatl word *huipilli*, this is a blouse with a low neck and short sleeves used by indigenous women; it is the top half of the traditional costume, and the multi-coloured embroidery changes according to ethnic region.

INTA   Instituto Nacional de Transformación Agraria, or the National Institute of Agrarian Transformation; this is the state land agency.

Ixim Uleew   the land of maize; the affectionate name for Guatemala.

judiciales   or *Policía judicial*, the judicial police; this is a much feared paramilitary organisation, with soldiers doing police work, often in plain clothes.

kaxlan   literally, 'what *ladinos* do'.

K'ox   a mythical figure, a dwarf, associated with horses.

ladino   someone of European stock or mixed blood, and, by extension, an indigenous person who rejects indigenous values.

los compas   short for *compañeros*; the phrase *Compa Nica* is short for *compañero nicaraguense*, i.e. a *compañero* from Nicaragua.

marimba   a percussion instrument usually made of thirty slats of wood, with sound boxes of gourds or wood; the instrument is hit with sticks with rubber balls on the end, and works on the same principle as a xylophone.

nawaal   also spelled *nahual*, this refers to the shadow, the double or the alter ego, be it an animal or any other living thing, that Mayans believe all humans to possess; there is a relationship between the *nawaal* and a person's personality; it is a parallel existence.

ONIC   Organización Nacional Indígena de Colombia, the National Indigenous Organisation of Colombia.

panela   unrefined sugar, or brown sugar, obtained from sugar cane.

PAC   Patrulla de Autodefensa Civil, the Civil Defence Patrol, a paramilitary police force known by its Spanish acronym.

pelón(es)   slang for indigenous person; comes from *pelo* (hair), and the fact that indigenous men do not have beards.

perraje   from the K'iche' word *peraaj*, a coloured cotton shawl.

pintos   derogatory slang for soldiers.

pom   an incense widely used in Guatemala, made from aromatic resin.

pul-ik   also called *pulique*, this is a kind of fricassée or stew made with meat or chicken and vegetables, and a lot of highly flavoured gravy containing tomatoes, onion, garlic, pepper, sesame seeds, pumpkin seeds, coriander, cumin and, naturally, chili (the suffix *-ik* means chili).

puulik   this means 'soft like bread, pie or earth'.

quetzal   the name of the monetary unit in Guatemala, as well as being the national symbol; one hundred *centavos* is one *quetzal*; the amount mentioned was about US$100.

RUOG   Representación Unitaria de Opposición Guatemalteca, the Unitary Representation of the Guatemalan Opposition, or the United Guatemalan Opposition Front.

tamales   maize paste wrapped in maize or banana leaf and cooked.

Tatic   a word that means Sir, or, more familiarly, 'father'.

temascal   a steam bath made with hot stones.

URNG   Unidad Revolucionaria Nacional Guatemalteca, Guatemalan National Revolutionary Unity; this was the political arm of the Guatemalan People's Army.

Xela   the old Mayan name for the city of Quelzaltenango.

xe'xew   usually, 'a cure for evil eye'; in this context it is more likely to mean 'sore eyes'.

zaraguate   a typical bird of the rainforest.

LIST OF FAMILY MEMBERS

Vicente Menchú Pérez (father)	burned alive in the occupation of the Spanish Embassy in Guatemala City on 1 January 1980
Juana Tum K'otoja' (mother)	kidnapped on 19 April 1980; raped, tortured and killed
Nicolás Menchú Tum (brother)	died as a child of malnutrition on a coffee plantation
Marta Menchú Tum (sister) and Matias Chitop Damián (husband)	survived
Nicolás Menchú Tum (brother) and Juana Zapeta (wife)	survived
Víctor Menchú Tum (brother) and María Tomás (wife)	shot on 7 March 1983 kidnapped and killed in early 1980
Rigoberta Menchú Tum and Angel Francisco Canil (husband)	survived

Lucía Santos Menchú Tum (sister)   survived

Patrocinio Menchú Tum (brother)   kidnapped on 9 September 1979; tortured and burned alive

Anita Menchú Tum (sister)   survived

Felipe Menchú Tum (brother)   died as a child, asphyxiated by pesticide fumes on a coffee plantation

INDEX